William Godwin and Thomas Robert Malthus

David Reisman

William Godwin and Thomas Robert Malthus

Economics, Justice, Population and the Poor

palgrave
macmillan

David Reisman
School of Economics
University of Surrey
Guildford, UK

ISBN 978-3-031-62112-3 ISBN 978-3-031-62113-0 (eBook)
https://doi.org/10.1007/978-3-031-62113-0

This Palgrave Macmillan imprint is published by the registered company Springer Nature Switzerland AG.
The registered company address is: Gewerbestrasse 11, 6330 Cham, Switzerland

Paper in this product is recyclable.

By David Reisman

Adam Smith's Sociological Economics
Alfred Marshall: Progress and Politics
Alfred Marshall's Mission
Anthony Crosland: The Mixed Economy
Aristotle's Economics: Ethics and Exchange
Conservative Capitalism: The Social Economy
Crosland's Future: Opportunity and Outcome
Democracy and Exchange: Schumpeter, Galbraith, T.H. Marshall, Titmuss and Adam Smith
The Economics of Alfred Marshall
Galbraith and Market Capitalism
Global Political Economy: Beyond the Nation State
Health Care and Public Policy
Health Policy: Choice, Equality and Cost
Health Tourism: Social Welfare Through International Trade
Ideology: Conservatives, Liberals and Socialists
The Institutional Economy: Demand and Supply
James Buchanan
James Edward Meade
Market and Health
Plato's Economics: Republic and Control
The Political Economy of Health Care
The Political Economy of James Buchanan
Richard Titmuss: Welfare and Society
Schumpeter's Market: Enterprise and Evolution

Sidney and Beatrice Webb: An Academic Biography
The Social Economics of Thorstein Veblen
Thomas Robert Malthus
Social Policy in an Ageing Society: Age and Health in Singapore
State and Trade: Authority and Exchange in the Global Age
State and Welfare: Tawney, Galbraith and Adam Smith
Theories of Collective Action: Downs, Olson and Hirsch
Trade in Health: Ethics, Economics and Public Policy

Contents

CHAPTER 1

Introduction

Godwin's *An Enquiry Concerning Political Justice and its Influence on Morals and Happiness* in 1793 had a profound effect on the British intelligentsia. The French Revolution in July 1789 was followed by the execution of Louis XIV in January 1791. The *Declaration of the Rights of Man*, the commitment to liberty, equality, fraternity and property, was a major watershed in world history.

On 4 November 1789 at the Dissenting House in Old Jewry Dr. Price addressed the London Revolution Society (its mission was to perpetuate the spirit of 1688) on the liberation of all men from tyranny and superstition. William Godwin was there to hear him. Calling his speech a *Discourse on the Love of our Country*, Price said that all of us have an absolute right to 'chuse' and 'cashier' our own rulers and to 'frame' our own constitution (Price, 1790: 24). A king who is 'a fool and a bigot' (Price, 1790: 33) has no claim to the throne. 1789 had sent the message loud and clear. 'Tremble all ye oppressors of the world' (Price, 1790: 50). It was, purely by coincidence, the day before Guy Fawkes Day.

In 1790 there was Burke's reply to Price in his *Reflections on the Revolution in France*: 'Few harangues...have ever breathed less of the spirit of moderation' (Burke, 1790 [1968]: 94). In 1791 and 1792 there were the two parts of the *Rights of Man* in which Tom Paine collectivised the state: 'Government is nothing more than a national association acting on the principles of society' (Paine, 1792 [2000]: 178). Banned in 1792,

D. Reisman, *William Godwin and Thomas Robert Malthus*,
https://doi.org/10.1007/978-3-031-62113-0_1

its author was tried for treason in absentia. In 1793 there was the Aliens Act. In 1794 Habeas Corpus was suspended. In 1795 the Sedition Acts were enacted. Dissidents were transported to Australia.

Yet 1789 was not the end. Following on from 1789, there was mob rule in Paris, widespread violence and, from 1793, Robespierre's Reign of Terror. War with France broke out in 1793, only days before Godwin's *Justice* was published on 14 February. It was, purely by coincidence, Valentine's Day and Malthus's birthday. Continuing until 1815, accompanied by the 'Continental System' of disruption to trade, war was the background to the ideas of Godwin and Malthus. France had, within a decade, become a military dictatorship. Napoleon made himself First Consul in 1799 and Emperor in 1804. By 1798 when Malthus entered the debate about progress, English Jacobins, republicans and free thinkers like Godwin were increasingly abused and marginalised. They were the Fifth Column within. They were closet Catholics, unEnglish outsiders, corrupters of the youth. Reds under the bed were a serious concern. Even moderate Whigs were not exempt from criticism.

Optimism and perfectibility were under threat. The clergy were preaching original sin and the revealed moral code. British public opinion was returning to the devil it knew. Readers would have reacted differently if Malthus, responding to Godwin, had broken into print only ten years earlier. The American revolution in 1776 and the American constitution in 1787 had said that even wise Socrates had to be bound by the rules. George III was experiencing bouts of insanity. The aristocracy was riding roughshod over the peasantry.

Britain had staged its own 1789 with the execution of Charles I in 1649. There had been Cromwell's puritans, the Diggers, the Glorious Revolution in 1688, the halting steps to electoral reform. The London Revolution Society, the London Corresponding Society and the Friends of the People had been interfacing with a more receptive British public than was the case when the navy mutinies at Spithead and Nore in 1797, the French landings in Wales in 1797, the suspension of convertibility in 1797, the Irish rebellion in 1798, the food riots in 1799 and the Luddite riots in 1811 were reminding the British people that it might be inadvisable to undermine a going concern. Self-made Napoleon invaded Switzerland in 1798. It was not just the kings and the lords that could sacrifice lives and livelihoods for *la gloire* and *Lebensraum*.

Talk is cheap. Riots are not. At least 285 people had lost their lives in the Gordon Riots in 1780. 'Orator Hunt' and his dissatisfied leftists were demonstrating in Spa Fields, Islington, in the post-war recession and deflation that was the ugly face of Malthus's fifth *Essay*. It could happen again if Jack Cade were allowed to create chaos under the banner of Tom Paine.

Challenged by republicanism at home and war on the Continent, Britain by the mid-1790s was turning from Wordsworth's 'Bliss was it in that dawn to be alive' (Wordsworth, 1791, 1851 [1994]: 40) to Burke's 'revolution harpies of France, sprung from night and hell' (1796 [1826]: 21). Regeneration was no longer being taken for granted. Godwin went out of fashion. Malthus's *Essay on Population* in 1798 reminded a public that did not need much reminding that utopias always devour their children. It became part of an ongoing debate on sudden change versus tried-and-tested continuity. The French way was frightening the horses.

Qu'ils mangent de la brioche was being superseded by *il faut cultiver son jardin*. The cotton industry, Malthus said, had grown 'wonderfully' (SE II 33). An 'admirable machinery' had been raising productivity (SE II 33) in the new manufactures that had been turned loose by Hargreaves's spinning jenny in 1764, Watt's steam engine in 1769, scientists like Joseph Priestley and entrepreneurs like Jedediah Strutt. An industrial revolution was announcing a new dawn of commerce and prosperity.

That, however, was in Lancashire and Yorkshire. Malthus near Hartford, Godwin in London, neither had much first-hand experience of the new technology. Their image of manufacturing was more likely to have been small-scale craftsmanship on the model of the silk weavers in Spitalfields or the Wedgewood workshops in Staffordshire than of child labour in the Manchester mill towns or the long production-runs in the fixed-capital-intensive Carron Steelworks at Falkirk. Their imaginative reconstruction of working-class attitudes to population, mobility, subsistence and stratification was, Francis Place says, little short of 'puerile' (Place, 1822: 156). What they knew better than capitalism was unimproved agriculture, the landowning aristocracy, inherited influence in House of Lords, restricted suffrage, and the 'rotten boroughs' in the House of Commons. Politics was the liberal-leaning Whigs and the reactionary Tories. The fringe was fringy. Overheated dreamers, utopian visionaries and unwashed conspirators dismissive of the mainstream would have to be won over if they were to play a useful role in reform.

William Godwin (1756–1836) had been, like his Calvinist father, grandfather and uncle, a dissenting minister up to 1783. Unable to sign the Thirty-Nine Articles of the Faith, he had had no university education.

Apart from the Hoxton Academy in London, he was largely self-taught. Godwin was a voracious reader. He was drawn to the high ideals of Greece and Rome, to Voltaire and the French Age of Reason, to British individualists like Milton, Locke and Swift who, he believed, had seen correctly that 'teaching virtue through the instrumentality of regulation and government' (PJ 486) would not long survive. *Pilgrim's Progress* (1678) which he first read at the age of five must have appealed to a bookish ascetic, never averse to being self-righteous and over-critical.

Godwin when he left the church made plans for a small school in Epsom. After that he became an independent writer and journalist. He lived in London, as frugally as one would expect from a lapsed Calvinist, on his pamphlets and (unsigned) articles in the *Morning Chronicle* under pseudonyms such as 'Mucius' or 'A Lover of Order'. In *Cursory Strictures* in 1794, he objected that the treason trials were stifling free speech and assembly. In *Considerations on Lord Grenville's and Mr. Pitt's Bill* in 1795 he attacked 'the enemies of science', comparing their barbarism in the 'gagging Acts' to that of the Goths and Vandals, 'drenched and disfigured with human gore' (UW 212).

Godwin, dependent on his earnings, was extremely prolific. He knew that the mercenary and the mediocre will necessarily fall short of excellence. It was the price that a jobbing freelancer had to pay. There were works of history such as the *Life of Chatham* (1783) and, about Cromwell and, obliquely, the Levellers, the Diggers and Winstanley, the four-volume *History of the Commonwealth* (1824, 1826, 1827, 1828). There were Drury Lane plays. There were long novels and word-intensive thrillers with a message. Whether *St. Leon* (1799), *Mandeville* (1817) or *Cloudsley* (1830), the message was always the same. The weak do not stand a chance against the 'gore-dripping robes of authority', the 'cold-blooded prudence of monopolists and kings' (CW 219).

In *Caleb Williams* (1794), published at the time of the treason trials, an innocent peasant on the run from 'a man of rank and fortune' (CW 178), is pursued by the Javert-like bulldog Gines. A paid agent of the aristocratic murderer Falkland, the lawman Gines never grasps the true cause of crime. Caleb does: 'Oh poverty! Thou art indeed omnipotent!...Thou fillest us to the very brim with malice and revenge' (CW 121). Only the powerless cast out from society know what iniquitous persecution means: 'We, who are thieves without a license, are at open war with another set of men who are thieves according to law' (CW 224).

There were also the big books on the big ideas: *Thoughts on Man* (1831), the *Enquirer: Reflections on Education, Manners and Literature* (1797) and, most of all, the *Political Justice* (1793). Despite its length, it was completed in 16 months (PJ 4) at the rate of three or four hours a day. It sold 4000 copies and made Godwin famous. Brown calls it 'one of the strangest and most influential books of the century' (Brown, 1926: 45). Godwin's *Political Justice* became for anarchy what Locke's *Second Treatise* had been for liberalism and Marx's *Capital* was to be for communism. At the zenith of his popularity, Hazlitt recalled, Godwin 'blazed as a sun in the firmament of reputation; no one was more talked of, more looked up to, more sought after; and wherever liberty, truth, justice was the theme, his name was not far off' (Hazlitt, 1825 [1971]: 31).

Godwin's was the first philosophic treatise to argue for stateless spontaneity. It had an especial appeal to the young and idealistic. Wordsworth told a fellow student: 'Throw aside your books of chemistry and read Godwin on Necessity' (in Hazlitt, 1825 [1971]: 33). Southey 'read, and all but worshipped' the *Political Justice* (Brown, 1926: 62) to which his *Wat Tyler* in 1794 paid tribute. Coleridge even before he had finished reading Godwin's book wrote a 'Sonnet on Godwin' to say how much the ancient mariner had changed his life: 'Thy steady eye has shot its glances keen....Thy voice, in Passion's stormy day/Bade the bright form of Justice meet my way' (Coleridge, 1795 [1880]: I 141). Only one year later Coleridge decided that proto-Jacobinism was not after all to his taste: 'I do consider Mr. Godwin's policies as vicious, and his book as a pander to sensuality' (in Brown, 1926: 153). Coleridge decided that Godwin on Helvétius to the exclusion of Holbach had had missed the point. Mind is not superior to matter. A field cannot plough itself by a gigantic act of will. Death cannot be cheated because a sovereign thinker is not in the mood. Godwin, Coleridge suggested, should get out more.

Political Justice was revised in 1796 and 1798. The changes were not so extensive as to affect its underlying message. As George Woodcock says: 'The later editions of *Political Justice* contained no single alteration in the basic principles, and no deletion of any importance in the social conclusions to be drawn from them....The principal social criticisms remained, uncompromising and unanswerable' (Woodcock, 1946: 150–1).

Godwin confirms the integrity of the core. Such alterations as he made, he recalls, were 'not of a fundamental nature' (PJ 10). His assessment is supported by F.E.L. Priestley's detailed comparison of the three versions (Priestley, 1946) and by Mark Philp who regards the differences as marginal: 'Godwin did not renege on the central beliefs of the first edition—they remain central' (Philp, 1986: 218). Peter Marshall says of Godwin that 'the spirit and outline of his system remained intact' (Marshall, 1984: 4). The present book takes the 1798 *Political Justice* as Godwin's considered judgement save where there is an indication that he changed his mind on a matter of substance.

After 1798 there was a gap of two decades before Godwin returned to social and political thought. In the Preface to his *Essay on Sepulchres* in 1800, he describes himself as 'a man of no fortune or consequence in my country; I am the adherent of no party; I have pursued the greater part of my life in solitude....There are numbers of men who overflow with gall and prejudice against me' (Sepulchres, vi). He was more sensitive to the status of hate figure than he was to the lack of income.

Political Justice, costing £1.16.0 in 1793, was never banned. Paine's *Rights of Man*, at five shillings (the same price as Burke's *Reflections* and one shilling less than Malthus's first *Essay*), was cheap enough for the common man. *Political Justice* was more of a stretch for an average labourer on £25 a year.

Pirated (in Dublin) and shortened versions conveyed the message more widely. The 1796 edition sold for only 14 shillings. There were the reading clubs and circulating libraries. On balance, however, the censor was confident that the lower classes would find Godwin's long book difficult, confusing, repetitive and often leaden. A total of 895 pages bound in two heavy folios would test the understanding of the less educated. The workers would be alienated by the atheism and the rejection of marriage. The censor knew that the author, a self-avowed gradualist, had never been a member of the revolutionary societies. He had never been active in anything that could be called treason. Godwin was not Paine. His book was unlikely to do any harm.

Fame turned into infamy within only five years. It was followed by obscurity and neglect. Hazlitt in 1825 described the author of the *Political Justice* as a once-was one-hit wonder: 'Now he has sunk below the horizon, and enjoys the serene twilight of a doubtful immortality....He is to all ordinary intents and purposes dead and buried' (Hazlitt, 1825 [1971]: 31, 32). With Catholic Emancipation in 1829, the Reform Act in 1832, the suppression of the Test and Corporation Acts in 1828, a more liberal Britain had lost interest in a discredited firebrand. The French Revolution was fading into history. Malthus, despite what Hazlitt calls the factual inaccuracy of his philosophically 'poisonous' double ratio, was doing better: 'His name undoubtedly stands very high in the present age, and will in all probability go down to posterity' (Hazlitt, 1825 [1971]: 253, 272).

Largely ignored, the ageing Godwin was running a children's bookshop. The Juvenile Library in Hanway Street could risk the name M.J. Godwin when the business moved to Skinner Street. Godwin was also operating a small publishing house: Charles and Mary Lamb's *Tales from Shakespeare* which he commissioned is still in print. Not a natural businessman, he eventually went bankrupt. Acolytes such as Shelley, Francis Place and (Thomas) Wedgwood gave him money. Shelley's early death in 1821 meant financial embarrassment. Loyal friends launched a subscription for their fallen star. They secured him a sinecure in Parliament as Yeoman Usher. He always denied that there was a parallel between private assistance to a deep thinker and alms to the poor: 'I ought to receive your superfluity as my due, while I am employed in affairs more important than that of earning a subsistence' (PJ 545).

The young and idealistic continued to view Godwin as their prophet. Shelley, aged 19, wrote to the dazzling 'luminary' (then 56) in 1812. Proclaiming his 'reverence and admiration', he declared himself both surprised and delighted that 'you still live' and are 'still planning the welfare of humankind' (Shelley, 1964: I 220). Soon he was telling Godwin how much *Political Justice* had 'opened to my mind to fresh and more extensive views': it had 'materially influenced my character' (Shelley, 1964: I 227).

Shelley was dissuaded by Godwin from establishing an ideal community to demonstrate the viability of social anarchism. Godwin told his young disciple that a better way to political justice would be quiet discussion and a rule of reason rather than a self-extinguishing chimera like the French 1789 that did not last. Mind could do to state, property and religion what matter could not. It gave Shelley a cause. The poet, Shelley declared, was de facto a visionary who 'beholds the future in the present': 'Poets… are the institutors of laws, and the founders of civil society, and the inventors of the arts of life' (Shelley, 1821 [1891]: 5, 6). In poem after poem in the decade after 1812, Shelley did his part to change men's minds as if a great legislator in touch with the facts.

In 1812 and 1813 there was *Queen Mab* on 'the drones of the community' who 'feed on the mechanic's labour': 'Kings, priests and statesmen blast the human flower/Even in its tender bud….Nature rejects the monarch, not the man; the subject, not the citizen' (Shelley, 1972: I 250, 252, 256). In 1817 there was *Laon and Cythna* (*The Revolt of Islam*) on murders that 'pale' and gold that 'grows vile': while 'Want, and Plague, and Fear from slavery flow', while 'the Tyrant peoples his dungeons with his prey', nonetheless 'the seeds are sleeping in the soil' that will one day flower into social justice (Shelley, 1972: II 158, 227, 250). Shelley lists Malthus among the sophists behind the Tyrant's throne. Looking up, however, he sees a mighty eagle soaring high who will in the end liberate mankind from forced servitude to the few.

In 1820 there was *Prometheus Unbound*. In 1822 there was *Hellas*. There were also the letters on Godwin, 'greater none than he', in which Shelley praised the wise leader who had opened his eyes: 'Added years only add to my admiration of his intellectual powers, and even the moral resources of his character' (Shelley, 1964: II 202–3). By then, still married to Harriet, Shelley had eloped with Godwin's daughter.

Godwin's first wife was Mary Wollstonecraft. Her *Vindication of the Rights of Man* (a reply to Burke) was published in 1791, her feminist *Vindication of the Rights of Woman* in defence of equal reason and thus of equal education in 1792. They were married in 1797 when he, probably celibate (Marshall, 1984: 89), was 41 and she was 38. They maintained separate premises before setting up home together at The Polygon, in Chalton Street, Somers Town. The site, now Oakshott House, bears a plaque to Mary. There is no mention of William.

Philosophically, William regarded both cohabitation and marriage as unfreedom: 'Nothing can be so ridiculous…as to require the overflowing of the soul to wait upon a ceremony' (MEM 154) So did Mary, who once wrote to him that 'a husband is a convenient part of the furniture of a house….I wish you, from my soul, to be rivetted in my heart, but I do not desire to have you always at my side' (in KP I 251). She died in childbirth in the year they were married. Her portrait by John Opie, now in the National Portrait Gallery, hung in Godwin's study until his own death 40 years later. His own portrait, by James Northcote, is less frequently on display. Godwin's *Memoir* of Mary's life, deeply felt as it is, reveals privileged information about her friendships with Fuseli and Imlay, her attempted suicide at Putney and the birth out of wedlock of her daughter Fanny. A more sensitive widower would have kept personal confidences to himself.

Their only child, their daughter Mary (Shelley), was the author of *Frankenstein* (1818). Showing the influence of her father (to whom it is dedicated), it warns that artificial intelligence is no substitute for the human spirit. A second marriage followed in 1801, to Mary Jane

Clairmont. Francis Place called her 'the Infernal devil'. Mary Shelley complained that 'she plagues my father out of his life' (in Brown, 1926: 298, 299). Jealous, possessive, deceitful, bad-tempered, unkind, Godwin was less happy with her. There was one son, educated at Charterhouse. Despite talk of a separation, the marriage did last for almost four decades. Godwin was a lonely man, in need of a companion, a housekeeper, a book-keeper and a mother to what would become a blended family of, at its peak, five children. Godwin is buried with the two Marys (together with Shelley's heart) at St. Peter's Church in Bournemouth. Mary Jane is not.

Don Locke calls Malthus's *Essay* 'the book which would prove the most enduring of all replies to Godwin, a work whose reputation would soon obliterate that of its original inspiration....Godwin himself regarded it as the best, perhaps the only reasoned critique of his theories, and he went out of his way to make Malthus's acquaintance, and invite him to breakfast' (Locke, 1980: 161). Following an exchange of letters in early 1798 the meeting took place on 15 August, and there were at least three others (Letters II: 54). The contact may have been made through Malthus's publisher, Joseph Johnson, a unitarian and a friend of Paine (Winch, 1996: 255). Johnson will have known Godwin's own publisher, George Robinson.

In 1801 Godwin answered Malthus in his *Thoughts Occasioned by the Perusal of Dr. Parr's Spital Sermon, Being a Reply to the Attacks of Dr. Parr, Mr. Mackintosh, the Author of An Essay on Population, and Others.* Malthus wrote to Godwin that they had much in common but that the ratios were keeping them apart: 'You think that the present structure of society might be radically changed. I wish I could think so too' (in KP I 322). In the 1803 edition of the *Essay* Malthus replied to the *Perusal.* The sections were deleted in 1817.

Godwin, who had once captured the spirit of the age, was sinking into history. Caleb Williams in 1794 had glimpsed the future: 'Henceforth I will be contented with tranquil obscurity, with the cultivation of sentiment and wisdom, and the exercise of benevolence within a narrow circle' (CW 200). It was Godwin at his peak talking to Godwin at his nadir. Malthus fared better. Like Marx and Keynes, the name of Malthus, noun or adjective, was becoming a cultural artefact in itself. Malthus was the toast of the town. Godwin was just toast. By the end of the decade Godwin's *Justice* was not being read and the dinner parties had moved on to Malthus.

Smith's *Wealth of Nations* in 1776 had presented a different alternative to late feudalism. In contrast to Godwin, it was a vision of competition, markets, growth, affluence, acquisition, interest, aspiration, property, frugality, productivity, moderate statism and rising real incomes across the board. It was about wealth. Bentham's *Fragment on Government* in 1776 and his *Introduction to the Principles of Morals and Population* in 1789, both of them about morality without God and progress without anarchy, had opened the door to philosophic radicalism that followed the tramlines of the going concern. Malthus in the 1817 *Essay* was devoting his attention to a new target, Robert Owen and Owen's just-published *New View of Society*. The smiling Enlightenment was gone. Winch believes that Malthus was 'seeking a middle way between Burke and Godwin' (Winch, 1996: 253). A middle way between no-change and all-change proved hard to find.

In 1820 Godwin published *Of Population: An Enquiry Concerning the Power of Increase in the Numbers of Mankind: Being an Answer to Mr. Malthus's Essay on That Subject*. He repeated his view that population does not increase precipitately. Even if it did, the earth's surface is largely uninhabited. It could without difficulty feed its own. Malthus reviewed *Of Population* in the *Edinburgh Review* in 1821. He added a few words on Godwin in a postscript to the 1826 (sixth) *Essay*. He made clear that Godwin no longer had anything to offer.

Thomas Robert Malthus (1766–1834) was a country clergyman. A Jesus College, Cambridge, graduate, chiefly in mathematics, he took holy orders and from 1788 was a curate at Okewood, in Surrey. After 1803 he was the rector of Walesby, in Lincolnshire. From 1809 until his death in 1834 he was Professor of History and Political Economy—'he was born before the age of specialisation' (James, 1979: 51)—at the East India College, Haileybury. He had had no previous experience of teaching.

The monopoly status of the company that owned the college appears not significantly to have offended his (qualified) free trade sympathies. At 18 miles, Haileybury was near enough to London for him to keep up his professional contacts but distant enough to insulate him from urban even if not from rural poverty. Malthus married in 1804 at age of 38. True to his principles, he had only three children.

His father, Daniel Malthus was a small landowner and political radical. Daniel Malthus was in tune with the Enlightenment idea of improvement. He had met Hume and Rousseau. Thomas Robert Malthus was more cautious. Perfectibility did not make sense so long as the lower classes, uneducated and impulsive, were magnifying the poverty that the 1601 Poor Law and its accompanying Laws of Settlement had been put in place to relieve.

The full title of the first *Essay* was *An Essay on the Principle of Population as it Affects the Future Improvement of Society with Remarks on the Speculations of Mr. Godwin, M. Condorcet, and Other Writers.* It drew on the 1793 and 1798 editions of Godwin's *Justice.* The declared subject was advance and improvement. The hidden subject was Paris. Paris had shown that Hobbes had not been civilised away and that anarchy could destroy an ongoing way of life. Population was a case study. It had as little intrinsic interest to Malthus as it had to Godwin when he wrote the *Enquiry.* Its importance lay in its close proximity to the overriding topic of the free individual become a part of an orderly whole. Jacobinism was an impossible goal. Evolution was more in line with the natural law.

The *Essay* went through six editions. The subtitle was revised in 1803 to read *A View of its Past and Present Effects on Human Happiness; with an Enquiry into our Prospects Respecting the Future Removal or Mitigation of the Evils Which it Occasions.* Godwin and Condorcet lost their star billing. The first *Essay* in 1798, published anonymously, clearly the work of a new man attacking a celebrity, was the one that seemed most succinctly to refute the French *philosophes* and the English troublemakers. The first Census in 1801 confirmed that the English population was indeed growing. The second *Essay* in 1803 added further statistics that shifted the test still further from deduction to induction. Social science was emerging. Philosophy was on its trial. Malthus regarded his new *Essay* in 1803 (no longer anonymous) as effectively a new work. It had grown from 55,000 words to 200,000 words in length.

There were changes and some excisions. Data was added. There were revisions in 1806 (with an important new Appendix) and 1807. In the fifth edition of 1817, there were new sections on checks in Britain and France, poverty, the Poor Laws, and another new Appendix. There was a sixth edition, only slightly altered, in 1826.

Malthus's other major work, his *Principles of Political Economy*, was published in 1820. It, together with Ricardo's *Principles* in 1817, consolidated the template of the classical economics. A second (posthumous) edition appeared in 1836. The *Principles* dealt with population but also with social stratification and economic policy. It reinforced Malthus's defence of the Corn Laws. Rich landowners were creating aggregate demand that in turn was keeping the poor in work.

The masses recur in the entry on *Population* that Malthus contributed to the 1824 *Supplement to the Encyclopedia Britannica.* It was reprinted in 1830 as *A Summary View of the Principle of Population.* Malthus's ratios, simplified and even caricatured, influenced the views of the Royal Commission on the Poor Laws that sat between 1832 and 1834 and led to the strict and judgmental New Poor Law of 1834. By then the grand old man had given evidence to the Select Committees on Artizans and Machinery (1824) and on Emigration (1827). The Establishment did not give an equivalent platform to Godwin. Even the 'Peterloo' demonstrations and the mass unemployment caused by demobilisation after 1815 did not return Godwin to the forefront of debate.

This book is about Godwin and Malthus. They carried on a proxy debate on population and poverty in order to conduct a much fuller debate on economics and justice. Market capitalism was gaining ground. The poor were still with us. State and nature were in competition for the commanding heights.

French ideas of liberty, equality and fraternity were in the 1790s already ensconced in Calais. It was only 26 miles from Dover. The London Revolution Society believed that the English *ancien régime* would be the next domino to fall. Grenville, Pitt and George III put a different gloss on the good society. The nation was divided. The intellectual community was divided. This book shows how two great thinkers, both committed to universal wellbeing that transcended the beefsteaks and the cinemas, sought to make ideas into weapons in order to make swords into ploughshares.

This book shows that Godwin and Malthus, writing in the shadow of 1789, were united in their search for balanced betterment. Their world is not our own. Or is it? Godwin and Malthus were united in their cross-disciplinary quest for an ethical consensus that would transcend the lonely crowd. Their journey remains as relevant in our own times as it was in theirs. The nation is divided. The intellectual community is divided. Ideas are not just history. Ideas are survival. This book demonstrates just how important it is for all of us, in the tradition of Godwin and Malthus, to listen and learn.

Ideas are survival. This book is about ideas. Returning to the bedrock classics themselves, it visits the building-blocks and reassembles the structures. It compares and contrasts. It does not keep score. An author's vision is uniquely his own. Clark says: 'Godwin never offers a proof of the power of reason' (Clark, 1977: 38). That is just the point. There is no proof. Great thinkers string together the frequencies and estimate the probabilities. At the end of the day their numbers will not be the equal of their questions. Without ideas there would be nothing but the hemlock to think them out of the cave.

Chapters 2, 3, 4, 5 and 6 explain how Godwin made his way to population through a broad and full vision of economy, society and the state. Chapter 7 shows how he extended that worldview of equality and equity in the *Enquirer*. Chapter 8 deals with Malthus's first *Essay* that was his first confrontation with Godwin. Chapter 9 examines Godwin's reply to Malthus, together with Parr and Mackintosh, in his 1801 Spital essay. Chapter 10 considers Godwin's last word on Malthus and the ratios in his *Of Population* (1820). Chapter 11 analyses Malthus's last word on subsistence in the *Edinburgh Review* and the *Principles of Political Economy*, Godwin's last word on social philosophy in the *Thoughts on Man*. The concluding chapter says that it was the commitment to fair play and the satisfaction of ingrained need that brought the two authors together. They wrote about population and poverty because their real interest was a just economy in which the differences between rich and poor would be less striking than the shared participation in a going concern.

References

By W. Godwin

Godwin, W. (1794 [1988]). *Things as They Are, or the Adventures of Caleb Williams* (abbreviated as CW). Penguin Books.

Godwin, W. (1795 [1968]). In J. W. Marken & B. R. Pollin (Eds.), *Considerations on Grenville*, reprinted *in William Godwin Uncollected Writings 1783–1822* (pp. 281–374). Scholars Facsimiles and Reprints.

Godwin, W. (1798a). *Memoirs of the Author of A Vindication of the Rights of Woman* (abbreviated as MEM). J. Johnson.

Godwin, W. (1798b [1976]). *Enquiry Concerning Political Justice* (abbreviated as PJ). Penguin Books.

Godwin, W. (1800). *Essay on Sepulchres* (abbreviated as Sepulchres). W. Miller.

Godwin, W. (2011). *The Letters of William Goodwin* (abbreviated as *Letters*) (Vol. I). Oxford University Press.

By T.R. Malthus

Malthus, T. R. (1803 et seq. [1989]). *An Essay on the Principle of Population: Or A View of its past and present Effects on Human Happiness, with an Inquiry into our Prospects respecting the Removal of the Evils which it occasions* (2nd ed., 1803; further editions in 1806, 1807, 1817, 1826) (abbreviated as SE I and SE II) (2 Vols.). Cambridge University Press.

By Other Authors

Brown, F. K. (1926). *The Life of William Godwin*. J.M. Dent and Sons.
Burke, E. (1790 [1968]). *Reflections on the Revolution in France*. Penguin Books.
Burke, E. (1796 [1826]). Letter to a Noble Lord. In *The Works of the Right Honourable Edmund Burke* (Vol. 8, pp. 1–73). Rivington.
Clark, J. P. (1977). *The Philosophical Anarchism of William Godwin*. Princeton University Press.
Coleridge, S. T. (1795 [1880]). *Sonnets on Eminent Characters*, in *The Poetical and Dramatic Works of Samuel Taylor Coleridge* (4 Vols., Vol. I, pp. 133–145). Macmillan.
Hazlitt, W. (1825 [1971]). *The Spirit of the Age*. Scolar Press.
James, P. (1979). *Population Malthus: His Life and Times*. Routledge.
Kegan Paul, C. (1876). *William Godwin: His Friends and Contemporaries* (abbreviated as KP) (2 Vols.). Henry S. King.
Locke, D. (1980). *A Fantasy of Reason: The Life and Thought of William Godwin*. Routledge.
Marshall, P. H. (1984). *William Godwin*. Yale University Press.
Paine, T. (1792 [2000)]). The Rights of Man. In T. Benn (Ed.), *Common Sense and The Rights of Man* (pp. 53–278). Phoenix Press.
Philp, M. (1986). *Godwin's Political Justice*. Duckworth.
Place, F. (1822). *Illustrations and Proofs of the Principle of Population*. Longman, Hunt, Rees, Orme, and Brown.
Price, R. (1790). *Discourse on the Love of our Country*. T. Cadell.
Priestley, F. E. L. (1946). *Critical Introduction and Notes to Enquiry Concerning Political Justice* (3 Vols.). University of Toronto Press.
Shelley, P. B. (1821 [1891]). *A Defense of Poetry*. Ginn.
Shelley, P. B. (1964). *The Letters of Percy Bysshe Shelley* (2 Vols.). Clarendon Press.
Shelley, P. B. (1972). *The Complete Poetical Works of Percy Bysshe Shelley* (4 Vols.). Clarendon Press.
Winch, D. (1996). *Riches and Poverty: An Intellectual History of Political Economy in Britain, 1750–1834*. Cambridge University Press.
Woodcock, G. (1946). *William Godwin: A Biographical Study*. The Porcupine Press.
Wordsworth, W. (1791, 1851 [1994]). The Prelude. In *Selected Poems* (pp. 307–429). Penguin Books.

CHAPTER 2

Justice: The Part and the Whole

The science of society is a dialogue between the part and the whole. Godwin is an individual-ist who factors down. Only I know where the shoe pinches and by how much. He is also a social-ist who scales up. Godwin believes that the good society is one that goes straight to the horse's mouth. He also believes that the good society is one in which the social organism morally and methodologically comes first. Godwin's worldview is a synthesis of the part and the whole.

There is more. Alongside the part and the whole there is the truth. The individual and his society may be in perfect agreement that shoplifting and murder, like commerce and charity, are in conformity with the normative benchmark. Philosophically speaking, however, they are not the same. *De gustibus* is debasing and divisive. No one has a right to a gold-plated mousetrap when his fellow citizens are sleeping rough on the street: 'Godwin's conception of pleasure is firmly rooted in his conception of man's *telos* as an ever-expanding rational consciousness' (Philp, 1986: 137). The objective trumps the subjective. The truth to Godwin must always have the final say.

2.1 Factoring Down

The irreducible building block is the discrete social actor: 'The universe is no more than a collection of individuals' (PJ 156). Nations are fictions that hide the tool that is doing the work: 'Usefulness and public spirit, in

D. Reisman, *William Godwin and Thomas Robert Malthus*,
https://doi.org/10.1007/978-3-031-62113-0_2

relation to them, chiefly belong to the transactions of their members among themselves' (PJ 435). The decisions that sum up to the polity are the choice-calculus of thee and me. Nothing is beneficial to a nation 'that is not beneficial to the great mass of individuals of which the nation consists' (PJ 445). Godwin says 'great mass'. What he means is 'all because each'. Democracy makes the particular into the general. It is a blunt instrument. Only I know where the shoe pinches and by how much.

It is misplaced concreteness run wild to say that a nation can experience pleasure or pain: 'Happiness, in order to be real, must necessarily be individual' (PJ 432). The totality is the sum: 'Society is an ideal existence, and not, on its own account, entitled to the smallest regard. The wealth, prosperity and glory of the whole are unintelligible chimeras. Set no value on anything but in proportion as you are convinced of its tendency to make individual men happy and virtuous' (PJ 431).

The aggregate consists of its atoms: 'Individuals are everything, and society, abstracted from the individuals of which it is composed, nothing' (PJ 452). The whole abstracted from each sequential part is nothing. Autonomous, self-willed, self-determined, it is the element and not the compound that makes things what they are: 'All the great steps of human improvement' have been 'the work of individuals' (PJ 482). Scientific advance, economic innovation, war and peace, all is ultimately the value added of the unique one-off: 'Individuality is of the very essence of intellectual excellence', of 'mental strength and accuracy' (PJ 677). 'The proper method for hastening the decline of error' is 'by exciting every man to think for himself' (PJ 678). *Every man. Each man.* Conformity is a dead end. The social actor who lives by the script that his community has drafted 'lives forgetting and forgot' (PJ 678).

It is both a statement of fact and a *desideratum* in itself: 'The universal exercise of private judgment' is 'unspeakably beautiful' (PJ 141). It must be treated with respect: 'Every man should stand by himself....No man must encroach upon my province, nor I upon his' (PJ 132). John Stuart Mill was a classical liberal who believed in the hegemony of the unique one-off: 'Over himself, over his own body and mind, the individual is sovereign' (Mill, 1859 [1974]: 68). So was Milton Friedman, who saw in the economic market an affirmation of 'the free man's belief in his own responsibility for his own destiny' (Friedman, 1962: 1). William Godwin was an anarchist. He shared with the great libertarians the conviction that I am I. Take away your n + 1 and your *sui generis.* We live by Wicksell's unanimity of consensus around here: 'When it comes to benefits which are so hard to express numerically, each person can ultimately speak only for himself' (Wicksell, 1896 [1958]: 90). You have no mandate to meddle in my province.

We think differently. We feel differently: 'The opinions of men must be expected to be as various as their education and their temper' (PJ 498). The discipline of the barracks stifles all that is one-of-a-kind in the non-standard self. 'We cannot be reduced to a clockwork uniformity' (PJ 679). We may not be squeezed into 'a common mould' (PJ 681). It is clearly in everyone's interest that each distinctive isolate should enjoy maximal freedom from outside constraint. Without that tolerance of diversity the chance of personal and collective betterment would disappear into stagnation and knee-jerk repetition: 'Man is a species of being whose excellence depends upon his individuality; and who can be neither great nor wise but in proportion as he is independent' (PJ 480). The state is a threat. Other people are a threat. Emile, Robinson Crusoe, Godwin himself, it is laissez-faire and 'enlightened self-interest' (PJ 59) wherever you look.

Godwin had grown up a dissenter. Malthus himself, always Church, had been exposed to unitarian ideas at school and university. Extreme Protestants like Robert Sandeman and Jonathan Edwards had taught that each man has a duty to think for himself. Godwin in the Norfolk meeting houses of his youth had been socialised into the Calvinist creed of self-reliance and in the limit predestination. It was not just the captains of industry but the natural romantics who had imbibed Weber's ethic of know thyself because other people cannot be known or trusted. Godwin's lifelong individualism extended to a condemnation of communistic jointness in suspect team-sports like business organisations, theatres and cooperatives (PJ 678). As much as he enjoyed the company of actors such as John Kemble and Mrs. Siddons, he knew that they were practicing concealment rather than sincerity when they colluded to reveal the preferences of a character other than their own.

Independence makes sense if man is Robinson Crusoe. Self-sufficiency, intellectual and economic, is what makes autarchic Crusoe most authentically himself: 'We ought to be able to do without one another. He is the most perfect man to whom society is not a necessary of life, but a luxury' (PJ 681). Fraternity is pleasurable but still every man is his own Crusoe. No one should be asked to sacrifice his authentic identity in order to fit in with a regimented herd that leaves him one-dimensional and unfulfilled: 'This is neither desirable, nor even possible' (PJ 314).

Separation is fulfilment. It is rarely if ever encountered. Independence can be a cause of disagreement and conflict once the egos interact. Self-love can be Hobbes and the *bellum*. The stranger can be seen as an instrument that passively satisfies the wants of the cut-off: 'The good of our neighbour, like the possession of money, is originally pursued for the sake of its advantages to ourselves' (PJ 307). Even philanthropy might be regarded as the exchange of kindliness for gratitude, prestige and 'the joys of self-applause' (PJ 310). There can be generosity 'without one atom of true sympathy' (PJ 308). Pleasure will 'result to ourselves from our neighbour's well-being' (PJ 310). Feel-good costs two pounds. It is cost-effective at the price.

A minus is a plus. Altruism is just a word. Sacrifice cannot be termed 'purely disinterested' precisely because it embodies 'the love of agreeable sensation' (PJ 310). A gift pays a dividend. Words play tricks. Self-interest is the bottom line: 'When we perform the most benevolent action, it is with a view only to our own advantage, and with the most sovereign and unreserved neglect of that of others' (PJ 313).

Self-love is ubiquitous, 'universally confessed' (PJ 390). There is Mandeville's *Fable of the Bees* (which he references [PJ 671n]) and Smith's *Wealth of Nations* (which he does not). Godwin writes that private vices can unintendedly be public virtues, as if guided by an invisible hand. The butcher, the brewer and the baker serve us not from benevolence but because of the financial reward or the non-pecuniary approbation that will be their private quid pro quo: 'It is, generally speaking, the interest of each individual that all should form their plan of personal pleasure with a spirit of deference and accommodation to the pleasure of each other' (PJ 318).

Each complements the other: 'All men are his fellow labourers; but he is the rival of no man' (PJ 315). The anarchy of self-determined interdependence leaves each of them, all of them, better off in their own estimation. Words are weasels. Other-regarding deontology is not the sine qua non so long as the consequences raise the felt well-being of the pool: 'In this sense, we may admire the system of the universe, where public utility results from each man's contempt of that utility' (PJ 313). Individual interest boomerangs to the advantage of the whole. To say that 'individual interest, accurately understood', coincides with the public interest 'is for the most part certainly true' (PJ 390). It is I and I. We comes later. We is an unintended outcome that can safely be left to the footnotes that no one ever reads.

2.2 A *Tabula Rasa*

Locke had argued that the mind at birth is a *tabula rasa* on which a lifetime of experience writes its runes. It is a piece of 'white Paper, void of all Characters, without any Ideas' (Locke, 1690 [1975]: 104). Helvétius had maintained that each child is born without an innate essence that would forever distance him from his natural equals: 'All the operations of the Mind consist in the powers we have of perceiving the resemblance and difference, the agreement and disagreement, of various objects among themselves....Every thing is reducible to feeling' (Helvétius, 1758 [1807]: 7). Knowledge is observation: we 'cannot pass these bounds' (Helvétius, 1758 [1807]: 8). Thought is impression: 'Every judgment is nothing more than a sensation' (Helvétius, 1758 [1807]: 10). Peer Gynt is the layers of an onion. At the core there is nothing to distinguish the true Peer from the authentic Boyg.

Godwin had clearly been influenced by his distinguished forebears when in the *Political Justice* he declared the human mind at birth to be all but virgin wax upon which an unfolding journey stamps its mark: 'We have no instincts....The only things which can be said to compose the nature or constitution of man are our external structure, which itself is capable of being modified with indefinite variety' (PJ 72). Peer or Boyg, each brain is all but an empty box: 'The human mind is of so ductile a character that it "believeth all things and endureth all things" ' (Neocromancers, xii).

It was never 100 per cent. Godwin acknowledged that there are ingrained propensities analogous to Malthus's indolence, hunger and sex, Veblen's instinct of workmanship and Durkheim's external validation. There are person-specific proclivities like Jack's anal retentiveness, Jill's boredom threshold, which 'we cannot wholly destroy' (PJ 72). An essence there has always been and always will be. Leaning towards Locke and Helvétius and away from the biological determinists' 'original bias' (PJ 52), what Godwin believed is that situation and not bedrock is by far the greater influence.

Godwin never denied the existence of an irreducible hard core. The raw makes a contribution alongside the cooked: 'Though education is a most powerful instrument, yet there exist differences of the highest importance between human beings from the period of their birth' (in KP I 294–5). Every man is 'influenced by motives peculiar to him as an individual' (in KP I 295). White paper or natural endowment, the human potential is not the same: 'It would be ridiculous to question the real differences that exist between children at the period of their birth' (PJ 43). What Godwin is asserting is that the differences are small. They are '*almost* nothing' (PJ 45, emphasis added). Most or *almost*, it would be unscientific to pretend that they are not there.

For all that, Godwin's assessment may be termed a 93 per cent theory of life-course nurture relative to lifetime nature: 'It is impression that makes the man' (PJ 44). The mind is moulded cumulatively by the succession of events to which the self is exposed. The chapter heading reads 'The Characters of Men Originate in their External Circumstances' (PJ 34). The text makes clear that none of us really is his own man: 'The actions and dispositions of mankind are the offspring of circumstances and events, and not of any original determination that they bring into the world' (PJ 35).

External reality is doing the heavy lifting. History is the parent. The atom is the child. Small as it is, the variance between one infant and another does suggest that the individual is something more than a clone to be duped and doped. It makes the chicken before the egg before the chicken into a two-way street: 'The link which binds together the inward and the outward man is indissoluble' (PJ 246). Man is shaped but also shapes. Public opinion is tempered by ego's idiosyncratic perceptions and preferences.

Godwin never says that the essence at birth is quintessentially other-regarding: 'Innocence is not virtue' (PJ 86). The noble savage can be more savage than noble: 'The spring of motion within him will certainly not be a sentiment of general utility' (in KP I 295). What Godwin is contending is that man's essence and his existence must reach a mutually acceptable accommodation that is fully in line with the superordinate standard of absolute truth: 'Do I desire to raise him to the energy of which he is capable? I must teach him to feel himself, to bow to no authority, to examine the principles he entertains, and render to his mind the reason of his conduct' (PJ 613). Outsiders must come on board. They must teach the individual to reconcile the stuff of which he is made with the eternal virtues which reason has laid down.

Man is not born all that he can and will become. Formal schooling, learning through interaction, learning through personal discovery, 'the characters of men are determined in all their most essential circumstances by education' (PJ 47). An individual's tastes and preferences are 'nothing more than the result of his education, and of the circumstances in which he happens to have been placed' (PJ 318). Socialisation 'for the most part determines the character of the future man' (PJ 348). It is the *for the most part* and not the *tabula rasa* that inputs the bulk of what the libertarians call I. The conditioned lightly salted with the innate makes the man the social individual that he is. A Scotsman wears a kilt. A king wears a crown. They have been carefully taught. Individual choice is bunk: 'No man stands alone' (PJ 318).

That is why the stimuli to which the individual is exposed must be made the most favourable to benevolence, the least tainted with grab. Behaviour is malleable. The monster, a man-made Caleb Williams, says it in Mary's *Frankenstein*: 'If I have no ties and no affections, hatred and vice must be my portion; the love of another will destroy the course of my crimes....My virtues will necessarily arise when I live in common with an equal' (M. Shelley, 1818 [2007]: 186). Percy Bysshe repeats it in his essay 'On Frankenstein': 'Treat a person ill, and he will become wicked....Too often in society, those who are best qualified to be its benefactors and its ornaments, are branded by some accident with scorn, and changed, by neglect and solitude of heart, into a scourge and a curse' (P.B. Shelley, 1832: 730). Godwin makes it his guiding light in his novel *Mandeville*: 'Man is but a machine....He is just what his nature and his circumstances have made him; he obeys the necessities which he cannot resist. If he is corrupt, it is because he has been corrupted....Give him a different education, place him under other circumstances, treat him with as much gentleness and generosity, as he has experienced of happiness, and he would be altogether a different character' (Godwin, 1817 [1992]: 153).

Right or wrong is a conditioned response: 'In a vast majority of cases circumstances make the man good or ill' (Essays, 66). Life in society must be made such as to free fallen Adam from false consciousness. Circumstances must be reformed in order to generate an upgraded narrative. It can be done: 'Every child, not particularly defective in his make, is susceptible of the communication of wisdom' (EQ. 25). Wisdom is absolute. Godwin, rejecting the charge of brainwashing, indicates that he is doing no more than doctoring to a state of preexistent ill health. The truth is always true. It cannot be wrong to free a slave from the unhealthy temptations that divert him from the single right way: 'There is one thing, or series of things, that constitutes the true perfection of man' (PJ 318). *One* thing. Science is not ideology. It has been said many times before and since. U-turn if you want to turn. The truth is not for turning.

2.3 Scaling Up

Godwin was an individual-ist: I am I. Godwin was also a social-ist: I am We. The social environment shapes the malleable individual. No one is alone: 'It will be idle and erroneous to consider each man separately, and leave each to find his source of pleasure suitable to his particular humour. We have a common nature, and that common nature ought to be consulted' (PJ 318).

Individual freedom is not unlimited. Mill had introduced the caveat 'to prevent harm to others' (Mill, 1859 [1974]: 68). He will have seen that spillovers and externalities do not stop short at the smoking chimney or the effluent that poisons the fish. Pigou's 'uncompensated services and uncharged disservices' (Pigou, 1920 [1932]: 191) must be extended to collective customs and shared conventions. Godwin as an individual-ist made the wider constraint explicit. Excessive autonomy is a rudderless craft. Man's liberty must be boxed in by 'the wholesome temperament of society' (PJ 674). Man's 'love of society' is if anything more essential to his wellbeing than is his 'love of solitude': 'Society is our proper sphere' (Essays, 219). A means, an end, we are social beings: 'Nature is love. See how the bending branches kiss the stream! Each portion of nature nourishes its neighbour portion; and hence delivers health and vigour and harmony to all' (Mandeville, 158).

Freedom is unfreedom. Individual-ism is social-ism. Praise and censure in the High Street are valued fixed points on the compass: 'What could be more beneficial than for each man to derive assistance for correcting and moulding his conduct from the perspicacity of his neighbours?' (PJ 674–5). Neighbourly advice cannot reasonably be resented or resisted. It is 'incumbent' on each 'member of society' to act in a 'particular manner' and in the 'general welfare' (PJ 675). 'Brute regulations' are for brutes and not for men: 'Govern them through no medium but that of inclination and conviction' (PJ 675). But govern them nonetheless.

Robinson Crusoe has given way to man in society. Other people are constants and variables in our system: 'To be virtuous, it is requisite that we should consider men, and their relation to each other' (PJ 599). Bystander assessment is our judge and jury. The outcome of the feedback corrective is the standard size: 'Mind will rise to the level of its situation' (PJ 613). Hard-line libertarians, consumer-led economists, self-sufficient eccentrics and opt-out backwoodsmen will say it is more likely to sink. Their views should be disregarded. The truth is always true.

Paradise and prison are one and the same. The end justifies the means: 'Human beings are formed for society. Without society, we shall probably be deprived of the most eminent enjoyments of which our nature is susceptible' (PJ 675). In society, and in an 'insensible and gradual way', we grow from the disparate into the symbiotic: 'Our opinions, our tempers and our habits are modified by those of each other' (PJ 677). Robinson Crusoe has no Other to guide him along. For the rest of us, social pressures are likely to promote a harmonious way of life in concert with our fellows.

Society places our citizens 'under the happier and more rational restraint of public inspection' (PJ 586). Individual choice is a topic in collective choice: 'No longer contented to stand alone in the world', Crusoe when he dwells among us must smooth down the rough edges in his personality (PJ 248). He is obliged to do this in order to avoid 'hatred', to win 'confidence', to be 'truly friends' with the rest of us (PJ 248). 'Unpopularity', 'disgrace' and 'odium' will be the unwanted sanction for a social outlier deemed by the representative insider to be 'absurd or atrocious' (PJ 613). Peter Grimes never stands a chance.

We live in each other's pocket. Robinson Crusoe, free-standing and self-defining, has made himself the willing member of a 'public or political society', of a 'social state' in which 'the general improvement and happiness' (PJ 17) is only possible if all the participants have a critical mass of norms and values in common. Life in society is total immersion in political justice: 'Nearly all our impressions of right and wrong flow from our intercourse with each other' (PJ 386). Public opinion is 'the sense of the people at large', 'the sense of the whole' (PJ 388), the 'sympathy of the public' (PJ 389). Man in society has no choice but to conform: 'It surely cannot conduce to the benefit of mankind that each man should have a different standard of moral judgment, and preference' (PJ 107).

Aristotle was right. No one wants to bowl alone: 'Man is a social animal....The soul longs, with inextricable longings, for the society of its like' (PJ 598). Man in society longs for 'the good will of his neighbours' (PJ 61). He is willing to fine-tune his conduct and character in order to win their approbation. Their acceptance makes him feel good about himself.

Our standards are filtered and confirmed 'by the suffrage of our neighbours' (PJ 244). The done thing is the sounding board and the benchmark for what we do and do not do in time and space: 'It is impossible that I should have...any precise perceptions of virtue and vice, unless assisted by the concurrence of my fellows' (PJ 245). My fellows buy lace curtains in order to monitor my conduct. They say that Mr. Gallileo and Mr. Picasso should make more of an effort to fit in.

Other people see everywhere I litter. Aristotle took his 'good society' to be a polis so small that every man would be his brother's keeper (Aristotle, 1981: para. 1326b). Plato assigned it a numerical value: 5040 (Plato, 1970: para. 740d). Other-directedness was perpetually on duty in ancient Athens. Godwin was in the bloodline of Aristotle and Plato who had resisted pan-Hellenic unification when they eulogised the small district or reference group: 'Every individual would then live under the public eye; and the disapprobation of his neighbours...would inevitably oblige him either to reform or to emigrate' (PJ 568).

Esprit de corps (PJ 390) and normative convergence are pleasure. 'The general discountenance, and sober condemnation of every spectator' (PJ 582) are pain. The 'public eye', as Munro stresses, makes a strong case for decentralisation and devolution: 'Godwin approves of the small self-governing community. If a man is to be judged, let him be judged by his friends and neighbours, who know him intimately' (Munro, 1953: 33). Local government will inevitably be superior to central government. So long as government of any kind survives, Our Town will have its finger on Our Pulse. Our Nation will not.

The 'public eye' scores and ranks. Challenged by a murderer, a fraudster or a thief, 'every enlightened spectator exclaims with horror' (PJ 578). The peers and the consensus place our citizens 'under the happier and more rational restraint of public inspection' (PJ 586). The done thing provides a reliable guarantee of 'reciprocal forbearance' (PJ 586). We resist the low-hanging fruit of antinomian lawlessness because smiling faces all around are something that most of us desire even more.

Living in society, 'we find by observation that we are surrounded by beings of the same nature with ourselves' (PJ 308). We come to see ourselves as others see us. We learn to ascertain the 'intrinsic and absolute value' (PJ 308) of our conduct through the metric of their non-random reactions. Sensitive social man derives pleasure, 'an uncommonly exquisite source of happiness' (PJ 309), from whichever patterns his neighbours, acting with an 'honest and enlightened mind' (PJ 247), expect him to emulate. Error correction closes the loop. Proportion becomes self-reinforcing. Virtue becomes an 'irresistible object of imitation' (PJ 261).

Other people see everywhere he litters. Even when they do not, he himself, as a continuing member of a community with which he is 'indissolubly connected' (Essays, 218), knows when he has done right: 'When he looks back, he applauds the state of his own affections' (PJ 309). Applauding it, he duplicates it. Thus do the patterns, internalised over time, become an integral part of his community's social capital. The individual is a *social* individual. I think I am I. It is at once a truism and an exaggeration. Society wears a cloak of invisibility. Well and good, but it is always there.

Impulse or emotion cannot be allowed to seize the moment. Deviance must be kept in check by 'the general inspection that is exercised by the members of a limited circle', 'the gravity and good sense that would characterize the censures of men' (PJ 467). No one would 'defy the general consent of sober judgment that would surround him' (PJ 467). No one would risk the 'unequivocal disapprobation, and observant eye, of public judgment' (PJ 475). Everyone wants a good reputation (PJ 519). No one wants to be shunned or excluded. The 'public eye' (PJ 520) measures, enhances, protects or destroys our self-image. We do not need Saruman and Sauron to keep us off the gin. The generalised Other is always there.

The 'public eye' ensures the conformity that is the standard size. It is our duty as members of the community to act as barefoot schoolmasters. It is 'the duty of every man to contribute to the intellectual health of his neighbour' (PJ 597). Precisely because socialised citizens 'feel no sentiments but those of kindness and compassion' (PJ 601), they are obliged to assist their fellow citizens to rise to a higher plane of happiness: 'The genuine propensity of man is to venerate mind in his fellow man' (PJ 595). Because we venerate it, therefore we improve it. 'New situations make new minds' (PJ 602). The man in the street smooths our adaptation to moving constraint.

It is the common value system but also a trimming-down of the self-perceived self. A thinking animal reacts badly to repression from outside: 'Man is an intellectual being. There is no way to make him virtuous but in calling forth his intellectual powers' (PJ 599). Godwin as an individualist accepts that even heretical Gallileo and *avant garde* Piccasso are experiencing a strong desire to be heard. Society, showing us 'our true advantage as consisting in independence and integrity' (PJ 583), is not unsympathetic to their claims. Even so, an even stronger claim is being exercised 'by the general consent of our fellow citizens' when they bind us 'to the dictates of reason' (PJ 583). Cohesion is the active ingredient. Without our fellow citizens it would be the luck of the draw. Because of public opinion there is an agreed-upon true north and not a licentious *fays ce que voudras.*

The real spectator sanctions our conduct. So too does Adam Smith's 'impartial spectator' (MS 192). Well-informed, firmly embedded in the psyche, the all-seeing St. Peter knows that men desire 'not only praise, but praise-worthiness; or to be that thing which, though it should be praised by nobody, is, however, the natural and proper object of praise' (MS 166). Social harmony is upheld by the man within. It is conditioning by consent. It is enough.

Godwin put his faith in the power of the 'impartial observer' (PJ 259) to ensure convergence on a common code. Socialised man can be expected to divest himself of his self-centred impulses and predilections in order to listen to the voice of his conscience that knows best: 'We are able in imagination to go out of ourselves, and become impartial spectators of the system of which we are a part' (PJ 308). The enforcer state, its policemen and its law courts are as nothing compared with the determination of the cell embedded in the collectivity to fit in: 'The soundest criterion of virtue is to put ourselves in the place of an impartial spectator, of an angelic nature...beholding us from an elevated station, and uninfluenced by our prejudices' (PJ 107).

2.4 Community and Association

Social evolution is often said to proceed from status to contract in the sense of Maine, from the open to the closed in the sense of Weber, from the mechanical to the organic in the sense of Durkheim, from the militant to the industrial in the sense of Spencer, from *Genossenschaft* to *Herrschaft* in the sense of Gierke, from *Gemeinschaft* to *Gesellschaft* in the sense of Tönnies. Once there was community: bound together by affect, the members of the social family 'stay together in spite of everything that separates them' (Tönnies, 1887 [2001]: 52). Later there was association: shuttered ships in the night 'remain separate in spite of everything that unites them' (Tönnies, 1887 [2001]: 52). The centripetal tendencies, Tönnies warned in Bismarck's Germany, were going too far: 'The entire culture has been overturned by a civilisation dominated by market and civil Society, and in this transformation civilisation itself is coming to an end' (Tönnies, 1887 [2001]: 257).

Child psychology demonstrates that the new-born infant evolves from the egocentric detachment of *me* and *mine* to the seamless web of felt integration that Maslow saw as the true fulfilment of the part within the matrix of the whole: 'Duty became pleasure, and pleasure merged with duty....How could selfish hedonism be opposed to altruism, when altruism became selfishly pleasurable?' (Maslow, 1962: 149). Maslow saw that association in the sense of Tönnies was putting at risk all that was best in the home away from home of man in society.

Homo economicus, Tönnies and Maslow warned, must not become the master when sociopathic self-seeking ought at best to remain the servant. Godwin was in their camp. Godwin was an individual-ist: 'Individuals are everything' (PJ 452). Godwin was a social-ist: 'No man so truly promotes his own interest as he that forgets it. No man reaps so copious a harvest of pleasure as he who thinks only of the pleasures of other men' (PJ 321). Liberals will call Godwin's appeal to both the accelerator *and* the brakes a clear case of stunted development that reveals a profound fear of freedom. Tönnies and Maslow will see in it a compromise and a mix in the tradition of Marshall's pair of scissors that requires both blades to cut its cloth.

Individualism without collectivism, like association without community, is a horse divided against itself that cannot stand. Gain-seeking, emulation-maximising market economists pare away all but 'frigid prudence and mercenary self-interest' (PJ 314). Abstract, reified, one-dimensional, their interpretation of external reality is incomplete so long as their isolated I is not rooted in the *terra firma* of the surrounding We that gives the lost soul a home. Whether playing tennis or swapping apples for nuts, the precondition for the ritual is a shared book of rules. External sanctions, internal sanctions, consensus comes first.

Individualism is only legitimate to the extent that it conforms to the conventions and customs of the scaled-up collectivity. Radical atomism is forever being blocked from the descent into *anomie* by the 'generous and magnanimous sentiment' (PJ 314) of a common mind. The psyche shared deploys approbation and preference in such a way as to enhance the common 'utility', the 'general good' (PJ 282).

It is not a Manichean either/or but rather both pillars of Marshall's arch that ensure a fruitful combination, like supply *and* demand, of association *and* community. *De gustibus* must be washed through the sense of the meeting. Each lump of clay must sacrifice a portion of his free will to his fellows. He must make an investment in the smooth functioning of the social machine.

Godwin anticipates that each factored-down will spot the superior *ought to be* in the supermarket of codes. He recognises that in the imperfect present day there is many a slip. Because of the evolution from ascribed to achieved status, the greased pole to success will inevitably enflame the fissiparous passions: 'Ambition is common to all men; and those who are unable to rise to distinction are at least willing to reduce others to their own standard' (PJ 241).

Envy and *Schadenfreude* divide the polity. No one in the open society is safe: 'The wisest, the brightest, the most generous and bold will often be most exposed' (PJ 586). The hard-working, the energetic, the wealthy, the egg-headed, all of them can fall victim to the tyranny of the conspicuously might-have-been. In the invidious society, and in deference to the axial principle of equality, the state will not be able to remain protective alone. It will be forced by the substandard majority to introduce crowd-pleasing legislation that levels down the high-flyers who make the low-flyers feel small.

Pretence, props and self-presentation are non-rational signifiers that conceal the truth about good men and bad. 'The basest hypocrite passes through life with applause' (PJ 245). 'The purest character is loaded with unmerited aspersions' (PJ 245). The 'benefactors of mankind are frequently the objects of their bitterest hatred and most unrelenting ingratitude' (PJ 245). Distinction is bought with 'external splendour, and unmeaning luxury' rather than with 'moral attainments' (PJ 245) that promote the common good. Moral rectitude is all too often not praised and not honoured at all.

Liberal democracy together with market economics might not be building up the moral muscles on which the good society depends. In the imperfect present day, the good all too often die young. Short-term setbacks should not, however, be confused with the underlying trend. Existence comes and existence goes. Morality has time on its side. A dog is not a cat. Truth is not untruth. Virtue in the long run must inevitably come top in the continuing competition for best-attainable consequences.

Malfunction exists. The antidote, as Plato and Aristotle had taught, lies the discovery and dissemination of truth. Judgement is 'feeble' where men are 'not accustomed to hear the truth' (PJ 246). It is strong when lasting truth slowly but surely makes its way through the fog: 'If a just and impartial character were awarded to all human actions, vice would be universally deserted, and virtue everywhere practised' (PJ 245–6).

Truth, pushing out falsehood, promotes the 'true interests of society' (PJ 247). 'Consolations of sympathy and frankness' (PJ 248) draw men together. 'Disinterested sympathy' (PJ 247) reinforces their ties. Men less and less expect 'a higher consideration than they deserve' (PJ 314). 'True sincerity will be attended with that equality which is the only sure foundation of love' (PJ 251).

The real world is not ideal. Informed judgement is nonetheless taking its course. Evolution is already divesting men of 'selfish and personal considerations' (PJ 314). Hobbes is even now withering on the vine. Looking to the future, men will more and more be 'influenced by other and better motives' (PJ 314), less and less by duplicity, concealment and beggar-thy-neighbour. Neither money nor approbation will be the principal driver: 'The perfection of mind consists in disinterestedness' (PJ 314).

It is not a random taste but a lasting absolute. The sun rises. The sun sets. Reason shows that disinterednesss is the only name on the ballot. Conviction libertarians will reply that what Godwin is asserting is not a structural necessity at all but merely his own wish-fulfilment false-advertised as fact. Neither side presents any hard evidence or theoretical schemata to prove that its conjectures are the better ones.

Today men are governed by interest. Tomorrow they will put the authentic needs of the whole above the selfish wants of the part: 'The man who shall have attained to this improvement will be actuated neither by interest nor ambition, the love of honour, nor the love of fame. He has a duty indeed obliging him to seek the good of the whole; but that good is his only objective' (PJ 315).

Life in the veil of tears will be superseded by enlightened mind sponsoring upgraded matter. Knowledge-driven, base self-interest will mutate into sympathy, spontaneity and sociability. The role models will be those front-runners who 'lose the feeling of their personal existence, in the pursuit of general advantage' (PJ 314). I see it as my duty to do 'all the good in my power' (PJ 107) for you. You see it as your duty to do all that you can for me. In economics, justice, population and the poor, it is in the last analysis of Plato's, Pareto's, Marshall's 'The One in the Many, the Many in the One'. The truth is irresistible. Science is unstoppable. Rational anarchy is knitting the kingdom into a skein. There is no other way.

References

By W. Godwin

Godwin, W. (1798 [1976]). *Enquiry Concerning Political Justice* (abbreviated as PJ). Penguin Books.

Godwin, W. (1817 [1992]). *Mandeville: A Tale of the Seventeenth Century in England* (abbreviated as Mandeville), in *Collected Novels and Memoirs of William Godwin* (Vol. 6). William Pickering.

Godwin, W. (1834). *The Lives of the Necromancers* (abbreviated as Necromancers). F.J. Mason.

Godwin, W. (1873). *Essays: Never Before Published* (abbreviated as Essays). Henry S. King.

By Other Authors

Aristotle. (1981). *The Politics* (T. A. Sinclair, Trans.). Penguin Books.

Friedman, M. (1962). *Capitalism and Freedom*. University of Chicago Press.

Helvétius, C. A. (1758 [1807]). *Essays on the Mind (De l'Esprit)*. M. Jones.

Kegan Paul, C. (1876). *William Godwin: His Friends and Contemporaries* (abbreviated as KP) (2 Vols.). Henry S. King.

Locke, J. (1690 [1975]). *An Essay Concerning Human Understanding*. Clarendon Press.

Maslow, A. H. (1962). *Toward a Psychology of Being* (2nd ed.). Harper and Row.

Mill, J. S. (1859 [1974]). *On Liberty*. Penguin Books.

Munro, D. H. (1953). *Godwin's Moral Philosophy: An Interpretation of William Godwin*. Oxford University Press.

Philp, M. (1986). *Godwin's Political Justice*. Duckworth.

Pigou, A. C. (1920 [1932]). *The Economics of Welfare* (4th ed.). Macmillan.

Plato. (1970). *The Laws* (T. J. Saunders, Trans.). Penguin.

Shelley, M. (1818 [2007]). *Frankenstein: A Modern Prometheus*. Penguin Books.

Shelley, P. B. (1832). On Frankenstein. *The Athenaeum*, 10 November (p. 730).

Smith, A. (1759 [1966]). *The Theory of Moral Sentiments* (abbreviated as MS). Augustus M. Kelley.

Tönnies, F. (1887 [2001]). *Community and Civil Society* (J. Harris & M. Hollis, Trans.). Cambridge University Press.

Wicksell, K. (1896 [1958]). 'A new principle of just taxation', selection from *Finanztheoretische Untersuchungen* (J. M. Buchanan, Trans.). In R. A. Musgrave & A. T. Peacock (Eds.), *Classics in the Theory of Public Finance* (pp. 72–118). Macmillan.

CHAPTER 3

Justice: The Truth

The truth is not relative but absolute. It 'must always be victorious over error' (PJ 73). It is 'irresistible' (PJ 76, 707). It is 'omnipotent' (PJ 73, 415, 568). It is 'the rudder of our undertakings' (PJ 707). Ill-informed assertions, free-floating assumptions and 'implicit faith' (PJ 514) are as nothing compared with the truth: 'The laws of reason…are equally obligatory wherever man is to be found' (PJ 562). In the age of reason each of us is compelled by the logic of the human condition to be an Athenian: 'Understanding is essential to the improvement of man' (PJ 631).

There had long been the hard sciences. Godwin saw interpersonal interaction as a fruitful new area into which non-prescriptive investigation could usefully expand: 'Politics is a science. The general features of the nature of man are capable of being understood' (PJ 207). Economics, sociology, psychology, statecraft, the philosopher has a duty to his society to uncover the hidden repetitions that make up the seamless web.

3.1 Sense Perception

The truth exists. The complete blueprint of this table, this chair, is stored in God's filing cabinet. God's filing cabinet is not, however, open to public inspection. The best-attainable picture that inquiring mankind can obtain of external reality is the stock of images that is built up by the five senses: 'Man is an animal purely sensual' (PJ 67). We are profoundly in the dark. Even the five senses cannot access the verified coordinates of the essence

D. Reisman, *William Godwin and Thomas Robert Malthus*,
https://doi.org/10.1007/978-3-031-62113-0_3

out there: 'We know nothing of the substance or substratum of matter' (PJ 35n). All that we can sense is 'our own thoughts, ideas, perceptions or sentiments' (PJ 35n).

Solipsism is all we know. There are no innate ideas such as Socrates believed he had uncovered in the *Meno*. There is no sixth or moral sense such as Shaftesbury had posited in the iron dome of speculation. Epistemological sceptics like Locke, Berkeley and Hume, predating Godwin and influencing him, had expressed their frustration that mind is an imperfect mirror. Godwin shared their disappointment: 'We cannot penetrate into the essences of things....We have no sound and satisfactory knowledge of things external to ourselves, but merely of our own sensations' (PJ 78). The hard core will forever be unknown and unknowable. It is a leap in the dark even to contend that the essence exists. Nature is niggardly. She keeps the full truth to herself.

In the 1793 edition of *Political Justice* Godwin had been more confident about the 'necessary connexion' that can be established in the world of things (PJ 1793, 292). He had argued, with reservations, that circumstances circumscribe choice. Within the cage, no rational being could in 'any moment of his existence have acted otherwise' (PJ 1793, 285). In the mid-1790s, under the influence of the immaterialism that he encountered in Berkeley's *Principles of Human Knowledge* (1710), Godwin became more sceptical about man's contact with external reality. Likelihood is all we have. Essence is hid in night. *Esse est percipi*.

In the 1793 edition Godwin had said that objectivity not only exists but can be documented value-free through 'number, weight, and measure'. By the 1796 and 1798 editions (Priestley, 1946: I 118), he had downgraded his epistemology from knowledge that inheres 'in the objects themselves' (PJ 1793 303) to 'regularity' and 'certainty of conjunctions' (PJ 266) that are no more than fleeting observations taken to be a non-random frequency distribution. Necessity yields to perception and thence to inference that gives man the confidence to think he has lifted the veil on natural law. Ignorance is the human condition. Exposed to impression, at least the mind is able to proceed on the basis of what it believes to be fixed points. As P.H. Marshall says: 'Where Godwin had originally placed the emphasis on the lack of choice in human behaviour, he now stresses its predictability' (Marshall, 1984: 199).

The empirical method collects up the sequences. In the spirit of Bacon, Petty, Condillac and Hartley, patterning is a second-best make-do that only skates on the surface. Recognising that induction from experience is no match for God's filing cabinet, it nonetheless derives tentative inferences from the association of ideas and the conjunction of concurrences. Similar phenomena are correlated with similar outturns. Our knowledge is effectively downgraded, in Hartley's words, to 'the usual order and proportion', 'the perpetual recurrency of the same impressions' (Hartley, 1749 [1810]: 387). What we see is what we get. Appearances veer from the deceptive to the spurious. They may be enough to get us through the day.

Hume knew that recollection and sequence did not answer the big questions: ' 'Tis still certain we cannot go beyond experience; and any hypothesis, that pretends to the ultimate original qualities of human nature, ought at first to be rejected as presumptuous and chimerical' (Hume, 1739–40 [1969]: 44). Sense perception is the shadow on the wall. It is, as Locke observes, better than no knowledge at all: ' 'Tis of great use to the sailor to know the length of his Line, though he cannot fathom with it all the depths of the Ocean' (Locke, 1690 [1975]: 15). Even the experiments of a Newton or a Boyle only scratch the surface. An apple falls due to the law of gravity. Behind the law of gravity, however, there stands yet another law that makes the law of gravity do what it does. Infinite regress answers every question with a question.

Half a slice is better than no cake. Malthus said it. The only option, circumventing the 'mental intoxication' of grey-bearded classics that might be wrong, is to go directly to 'patient investigation' from 'the book of nature' for our 'well-authenticated proofs' (FE 126, 131). Godwin said it too. Past sequences must be relied upon for conjectures and inferences that putatively foreshadow 'future probable consequences' (PJ 268). 'If we would acquire knowledge, we must open our eyes, and contemplate the universe' (PJ 340).

Authority is no substitute for making oneself 'an actor in the scene' (PJ 342): 'We cannot understand books till we have seen the subjects of which they treat' (PJ 340). We learn by living. The Enlightenment was right about the unbiased and questing mind: 'God said *Let Newton be!* and all was light' (Pope, 1730 [1966]: 651, emphasis in original). Pope was right about Newton. Inspection is the only proof. The fire is hot. Touch it and you will see.

3.2 Past and Future

Association is not causation: 'We cannot discover the causes of things' (PJ 78). What we see is contiguity, uniformity, co-relation and co-incidence. What we do not see and cannot know is the causative relationship between push and shove. Either or neither, any or none of our observations could have been the independent shock that initiated the big bang.

Causality is context: 'Many single actions, if carefully analysed and traced to their remotest source, would be found to be the complex result of different motives, to the amount perhaps of some hundreds' (PJ 62). Action or reaction, it is all a skein: 'We inhabit a world where sensations do not come detached, but where everything is linked and connected together' (PJ 317).

There is no *other things remaining equal* in a spiral of feedback. Nor does time freeze over long enough to permit a subset of the data to be collected. Heraclitus's river knows nothing about equilibrium states or comparative statics. Today's kaleidoscope is only the latest knock-on in an ongoing sequence. It is the billiard break. 'Man is in no case, strictly speaking, the beginner of any event or series of events that takes place in the universe, but only the vehicle through which certain antecedents operate' (PJ 280–1). Antecedents, consequents, all we can know is the flow.

The 'true state of man' (PJ 527) is eternal negation: 'Continual flux appears to take place in every part of the universe' (PJ 298). It is the nature of the human condition to move on. Creative destruction and not 'eternal quietism' (PJ 527) is essential both to thinking and to doing: 'We should never stand still' (PJ 490). New observations result from new experiences. Everything changes. Social actors must be flexible and open-minded in the construction and deconstruction of never-settled contingency.

There is neither first cause nor final outcome in an uninterrupted transition. Time, as Alfred Marshall says, is 'absolutely continuous' (Marshall, 1920 [1949]; vii). No one steps into the same perpetual motion more than once. Godwin was in no doubt that history is forever on the horizontal axis: 'All things past, present, and to come' must be viewed as 'links of an indissoluble chain' (PJ 287). Mind and matter, the *was*, the *is* and the *will be* are all inns and stopping places on a common mystery tour (PJ 60). We learn from the past in order to make sense of the present. As for the future, we gamble that existing empiricisms will be adequate to interpret a process that is inexorably if also marginally changing its mind.

World-historical mould-breakers attempt to impose their will on loose extrapolation. Every free being 'has an option to exercise or not to exercise that capacity' (PJ 282). Most people prefer to let non-ego reality continue its journey: 'The most uninstructed peasant or artisan is practically a necessitarian' (PJ 273). Development is gradual. The probability is high that the future will incorporate salient characteristics from past and present.

Yet being is becoming and evolution is surprise. Trapped in the 'uncertainty of history' (PJ 579), we are continuously error-correcting the misapprehensions that hobble our past and present. We are doing so in order to enjoy 'a nobler and more honourable character in the future' (Necromancers, vi). Change is inevitable. Unknowledge is the consequence. We do our best to keep our reactions up to date. We do not always succeed.

Look and see is hit and miss. We lack knowledge about the present: 'Everything under the sun is uncertain' (in KP II 331). We lack knowledge about the future: 'A man cannot tell what shall be' (in KP II 331). We are 'precluded from comprehending the whole of what claims our attention' (PJ 254). Desperate like a Weberian Calvinist to obtain early reassurance about actions and their consequences, we are forced into 'adopting the greater probability' (PJ 260). Our obsession with meaning is perpetually under assault from restless history-to-come that keeps its frequency distribution to itself. No oracle is fail-safe against uncertainty. The best possible is not the best. There is no alternative. Godwin rejects the poisoned chalice of epistemological nihilism. He believes that an avowal of radical know-nothingness would be infinitely worse.

Decision-making in the present requires a working knowledge of a future that has yet to be made. It is Heisenberg's rippling indeterminacy. It is Shackle's black box: 'Valuation is expectation and expectation is imagination….What is the future but the void?' (Shackle, 1972: 8, 122). Godwin was more confident about internal shocks. While an unanticipated asteroid could shut down the casinos, still the record of past recurrences provides workable protection for new ships navigating an existing stream: 'Hence the necessity of resting-places for the mind, of deductions, already stored in the memory' (PJ 253).

Burkean conservatism, Burke's 'solid test of long experience', makes hesitant prediction possible: 'When antient opinions and rules of life are taken away, the loss cannot possibly be estimated. From that moment we have no compass to govern us; nor can we know distinctly to what port we steer' (Burke, 1790 [1968]: 148, 172–3). Theory and practice confirm that summer follows spring. 'The decisions of our ancestors' (PJ 186) live on. The advantage of the remembered heuristic, of Herbert Simon's 'bounded rationality' (Simon, 1965: xxiv), is that it keeps impetuosity and guesstimate within the limits set by stereotype, prejudice and preconception. The disadvantage is that learned responses 'suspend the elasticity and progress of mind' (PJ 187). Routine goes on autopilot. It is safety first.

Social actors get into a well-worn rut. Ideas and events sink into grooves: 'Thus the drunkard and the lecher continue to pursue the same course of action long after the pains have outweighed the pleasures' (PJ 307). The miser clings to his hoard even after current utility no longer equals the bliss gone by (PJ 311). Time moves on. Perception is trapped in the past.

The individual is 'the creature of habit' even as he is rational and problem-solving (PJ 482). The time-stamped blinkers he acquires through a life in society necessarily impede an ab initio response. His understanding 'is no longer a novice' (PJ 60). His sense perception is no longer a *tabula rasa*. Pre-judgement, like a snow-plough, will already have cleared the road.

The social actor making sense of sense will already have internalised a classificatory schema that colours his interpretations and perpetuates his associations. New observations will have to be 'modified and refined through certain intellectual strainers and alembics' (PJ 66). Scientist or layman, he will see what tradition and 'prepossession' (PJ 61) have taught him to see. The handed-on lesson has been that all swans are white. A black swan can only be a white swan that an ill-intentioned rival has mischievously painted black. The senses play tricks. There are mirages and illusions out there. It is best to refract new associations through a familiar lens, a handed-on filter that we did not invent. We buy insurance against the madness of infinite impression. Rule-utility bounds our freedom but gives us peace of mind.

Godwin is able to be a political anarchist because he is also an epistemological conservative. We perceive and act in response to present-day stimuli that were conditioned in us by past-tense structures. Sunk bygones have not gone away. Some hand on an ethical uplift. Feudal paternalism foreshadows present-day philanthropy. The chivalry of the epics becomes the model for courtesy and after-you. Even where there is no content-specific payoff, the very fact that human beings are so easily seduced into habitual correlation suggests that rational expectation is only more of the same.

External phenomena in the here-and-now are perceived through the gauze curtain of the historical once-was. The ancients preestimated 'the greater probability' upon which the moderns must depend. Trialled crutches, familiar images and handed-down schemata are inns and resting places that fix our thoughts and choices in a time and space other than our own: 'It is impossible to believe that the same moral train would not make nearly the same man' (PJ 44). No investigation, however scrupulous, is ever completely fresh. No action, however voluntary, is able to escape from the antiquity of its context. Try as we might, each of us is, some more, some less, 'the dupe either of prejudice or superstition' (PJ 229).

Veblen knew that antecedents have consequences. The *once was* is the family tree for the *about to become*: 'The growth of culture is a cumulative sequence of habituation' (Veblen, 1919 [1994]: 241). Commons was equally convinced that reality begins in the 'Institutionalized Mind' of an intertemporal cohort that was here before its current intake and 'will live after them' (Commons, 1934: 73, 74). We are creatures of culture and custom on which we neither can nor ought to turn our back. Godwin was part of a long tradition in evolutionary thinking which made much of social biology and warned against precipitate table-turning. *Natura non facit saltum*. Neither should we.

Godwin was anchored and cautious. Sudden change must be eschewed in favour of gradual transition that keeps a firm hand on its baggage and does not lose sight of its roots: 'The true friend of equality will do nothing unthinkingly, will cherish no wild schemes of uproar and confusion' (PJ 192). Excessive change is a threat not just to political stability but to mental tranquillity and the ability to predict. Yet inadequate change is also a threat: 'Better were a portion of turbulence and fluctuation than that unwholesome calm in which all the best faculties of the human mind are turned to putrescence and poison' (PJ 414). Extremes are extreme. *Festina lente*. Always advancing, still it is better to mimic the continuity of a biological organism and to make haste slowly. Darwinism was not made in a day.

3.3 The Discovery Process

The truth exists. It is hidden but intact. It is there to be found: 'Truth does not lie upon the surface. It is a laborious enquiry' (PJ 216). There is observed association. There is understanding. There is discussion. There is agreement. There is quantification. There is bedrock knowledge. God's filing cabinet contains an eternal stock that 'discovery will never undermine, and wisdom never refute' (PJ 229). We do our best to approach ever closer to the gold standard in the files.

Impressions are individual. Probability is selective. Rubrics are shared. Error contains in itself 'the principle of its own mortality' (PJ 75).

Experiment establishes a 'frequent recurrence' (PJ 74). Fellow scientists retest and confirm. The 'intercourse of mind with mind' (PJ 681) echo-chambers the imperatives. The scientist is a modern missionary. Triumphing over 'blind reverence for established systems' (PJ 74), he peels away the veil to reveal the truth that no amount of prejudgement can permanently obscure.

The methodology is rational. The motive is not. Plato said that the thinker is 'wholly intent on knowing what the truth is' exclusively 'because of the way he is' (Plato, 2012: paras. 485e, 581b). Adam Smith said that the scientist is driven by 'Wonder' and not 'any expectation of advantage' to find out 'what sort of thing can that be?' (Smith, 1795 [1980]: 39, 51). Godwin was building on acknowledged authority when he concluded that it is idle curiosity and not unsentimental utility that is the true 'spring of action' (CW 6).

Caleb in the Old Testament is a spy sent by Moses to reconnoître the land of Canaan. Caleb in Godwin's *Caleb Williams* discloses that it was his intellectual interest in causes and their effects that made him 'a sort of natural philosopher' (CW 6). Cognition is an end in itself. It is, as Philp says, the small contribution made by each restless mind to the process of 'deification': 'The highest pleasure does not result from wisdom; rather, true wisdom is true feliciy' (Philp, 1986: 87).

The advancement of knowledge drives falsehood into a corner. Mankind will never penetrate to the Greeks' pure and absolute truth. A penumbrum of ignorance, gut-reaction and working hypothesis 'will always remain' (PJ 64). What evidence-based investigation will nonetheless do is to reduce the realm over which mistaken associations and fallible suppositions hold sway. The economics of frivolity versus fellowship, the poverty that is the consequence either of feckless overbreeding or capitalistic injustice, the statistics and the theories will shine a light.

Brute ignorance holds us back: 'The perturbations of sense frequently seduce the judgment' (PJ 63). Fresh-faced reality sets us free: 'No individual can resist the force of truth' (PJ 75). The outcome is inevitable. The opinion that is 'intrinsically the best founded' (PJ 64) will capture the intellectual high ground. The man in the street will be convinced: 'Nothing is necessary but to show us that a thing is truly good and worthy to be desired, in order to excite in us a passion for its attainment' (PJ 70–1).

The truth 'conduces to the happiness and virtue of the individual, as well as to the improvement of our social institutions' (PJ 230). The truth will turn us loose: 'The legitimate instrument of effecting political reformation is knowledge' (PJ 487). Enlightened people are happy people: 'No one is ignorant of the pleasures of knowledge' (PJ 230). Happiest of all are the fact-gatherers who, with 'ardour' (PJ 229), are pushing back the frontiers. Aristotle had made contemplation the 'the highest form of activity' and truth the supreme source of pleasure (Aristotle, 2004: para. 1177a). Godwin built on Aristotle (PJ 230). All of humanity should do so as well.

It is the task of the republic of letters to unearth the facts that will put myth and fallacy in their place. 'Men of study and reflection' (PJ 6), 'men of genius' (EQ 11), have a duty, precisely because they are 'enlightened and wise' (PJ 704), to lead their less educated, less intellectual brethren to a better place. Godwin situated himself 'among the enlightened' (in Kegan Paul II 195). He knew that he had a duty to get the message out.

Broadminded individualists say *de gustibus*. They believe that sense perception is by definition as factored down as there are people on earth. Godwin in contrast argued that the facts are *non est disputandum*. Writing as an essentialist, Godwin refused to conflate truth with taste or to make a core *agendum* into an Evanescent preference. Truth is not a brand of ice-cream. There is one truth. We can approach it even if we cannot open wide God's file. It stands uncompromising against the biases and temptations that twist the observations into a sequence that is not their own.

The shortest distance from Larissa to Piraeus is not a matter of opinion. The good life presupposes the discovery and deployment of the intelligence upon which smooth passage to Piraeus depends. Each member of the community has a vested interest in knowing when and how to put up his umbrella in the rain. We are all scientists nowadays.

Some of us nonetheless are better scientists than others. The intellectual vanguard has an absolute advantage in assembling the pieces of the puzzle that will conduct the masses and the classes to the highest-attainable level of contentment. It would be an infringement of their mandate for right thinkers to seek a conciliation with wrong thinkers who mistakenly state that George III is superior to Paine. No traveller will ever reach Piraeus if he fails to reject a guide such as that.

Intellectuals investigate and debate: 'From the collision of disagreeing accounts, justice and reason will be produced' (PJ 521). Artifice, inconsistency and misapprehension will be defeated by evidence backed up by explanation. No revolution in matter can equal the transformation in mind: 'Writing and speech are the proper and becoming methods of operating changes in human society' (PJ 518).

Thinkers make use of their platform in society 'not only to maintain in its members those virtues with which they are already imbued, but to extirpate their errors, and render them benevolent and just to each other' (PJ 583). Contact purifies opinion. Facts have consequences. Delusion 'in a calm and tranquil season' is 'destitute of power' (PJ 425). 'Erroneousness and insufficiency' (PJ 421) will be scrapped for want of proof.

Thinkers gone by are paving the way for thinkers yet to come: 'The next generation will not have so many prejudices to subdue' (PJ 87). Mind in motion is clearing the blur. Yet matter too is in motion: 'Nothing is stable and permanent' (PJ 41). Godwin concedes that where phenomena are in flux, images and shadows will also be 'in a state of perpetual mutation' (PJ 187). Blur then, blur now, Godwin's critics will object that there can be no lasting ratchet but simply 'opinion contending with opinion' (PJ 64) in an everlasting seminar and marketplace for perspectives. A new set of circumstances will be associated with a new set of ideas. One man's George III will be another man's Paine.

It will be anything goes. It will be a new filing cabinet. Godwin refuses to regard permissive fashion as a serious challenge to lasting truth. There is only one right answer. Dynamics on the surface does not disturb the statics underneath. Even Newton was not strong enough to refute the law of gravity. Persuasion and propaganda are as nothing compared with 'reason and good sense' (PJ 502), 'the greatest practicable advantage' (PJ 231), 'the most solid and permanent happiness' (PJ 231). Unthinking reflex falls away. Discovery is living up to its promise. Knowledge is converging on a single standard. Wisdom is identifying a common road up.

3.4 Perfectibility

'Perpetual progress' (PJ 78) is in the air: 'Man is perfectible', 'susceptible of perpetual improvement' (PJ 73). Life can only get better: 'There are no obstacles to our improvement' (PJ 46). The apocryphal Fall is being reversed: 'The vices and moral weakness of man are not invincible' (PJ 73). Falsehood is being bred out. The truth is conquering new ground.

The ascent into full disclosure is irreversible: 'Not one step has been made in retrogression' (PJ 214). The human body passes through a life cycle of birth, youth, golden age, decay and death. The body politick is a superior organism. A one-way bet, it traces out an 'irresistible advance' (PJ 214) that is at once linear and plus-sum. Knowledge is cumulative. The old is not lost. The new is added on. The size of the encyclopaedia is increasing over time.

Present-day thinkers are making the 'clearness and amplitude of evidence' (PJ 487) the precondition for 'the rousing of the mind' (PJ 568). They are turning to new technology such as the printing press (PJ 213) to universalise access to their new departures. Science is testing the links: 'We must bring everything to the standard of reason' (PJ 72). Superstition is being challenged by hard evidence: 'Nothing must be sustained because it is ancient' (PJ 73). Persons of 'narrow views' who regard 'everything as natural and right that happens' (PJ 72) are being forced by the facts to relax their grip.

Compare the past with the present. Our eyes have been opened. We have more knowledge and therefore more happiness than our ancestors did: 'The pleasures of a savage, or, which is much the same thing, of a brute, are feeble indeed compared with those of the man of civilization and refinement' (PJ 67). An Englishman has a better life than a caveman or an aboriginal. In the know and not pitiably benighted, he is less and less at the mercy of blind fate to shape his destiny.

Godwin, like the French *philosophes*, was turning to nature to show him the way. The facts make a cast-iron case for themselves: 'Truth is adequate to excite the mind....If I apprehend the value of any pursuit, shall I not engage in it?' (PJ 570). Everyone knows that it is so: 'Who ever saw an instance in which error, unallied to power, was victorious over truth?' (PJ 486).

The truth is leading us ever upward into grace. Always assuming, of course, that the 'highest wisdom' (PJ 499) will have a 'clear stage' (PJ 486) and an open road. If discovery is definitively to set the people free, then the testimonials must be 'fairly presented' (PJ 486). Education, formal and informal, combined with the 'freedom of social communication' (PJ 221) must be putting new breakthroughs in the public domain. Last but not least, disinterested curiosity will only be able to produce constant and 'unlimited improvement' (PJ 424) if never-ending investigation is free from the 'fatal interference of government' (PJ 487). Liberal individualism and the invisible hand are enough. Meddling politicians should trust to nature and shut down their shop.

Grenville, Pitt and George III were seeing the freedom to search as a vote for the tumbrils. Conservatives were regarding Godwin's rejection of Freud's anal retentiveness as the slippery slope to de Maistre's unthinking knee-jerk: 'Human reason is manifestly incapable of guiding men, for few can reason well, and no one can reason well on every subject' (de Maistre, 1821 [1965]: 207). Reactionaries were demanding that scholars venerate the constitution instead of testing it for truth (PJ 539). Godwin saw the new censorship as a step backward into coercion and obscurantism. The Church was perpetuating exploded fabrications in order 'to form all minds upon one model' (PJ 539). The universities were sinking into 'formal dullness' (PJ 538) because their facts and figures were being spring-cleaned by *raison d'état*. Thought was becoming unthought: 'He that is often imposed on will be no judge of the fair and the genuine' (PJ 424).

It was the *ancien régime* and the darkness before dawn. It would not last. Tyranny had in the short run braked the rate of advance. History shows that in the long run it had never 'stifled the voice of truth' (PJ 539). The truth is eternal. It can afford to wait.

3.5 A Science of Morals

The truth is omnipotent. It is beneficent. It makes us happy. That is the proof that the truth is in line with the moral code.

3.5.1 Utility

Morality is 'the science of human happiness' (PJ 229). Its sole end and purpose is the enhancement of utility (PJ 557): 'Whatever will make a reasonable nature happy will make us happy' (PJ 73). Good equals pleasure. Evil equals pain (PJ 317). Right and wrong are encoded not in abstract principles but in deeds and effects: 'Morality itself is but a calculation of consequences' (PJ 50). Results talk. Outcome makes the final cut.

'The criterion of morals is utility' (PJ 643). Happiness is its own justification. Things are not always as they seem. On the surface Godwn's utility is a single individual's unique and non-comparable enjoyment. Drilling down it is the pooled or 'public utility' (PJ 99) of an established reference group that sees itself as one.

Godwin's utilitarian ethics is not factored-down hedonics but instead the scaled-up payoff. Morality to Godwin is 'the production of the greatest *general* good, the greatest *public sum* of pleasurable sensation' (RP 34, emphasis added). External to the one-off, binding on the member of the group, normative constraint cannot be reduced to the supermarket choice of the unembedded monad. An action in the sense of Godwin can only be called moral if it is 'attended with a balance of *general* pleasure and happiness' (PJ 252–3, emphasis added).

Morality is the general and not the partitioned stock. A friend and not 'an enemy to humankind' (PJ 617), right and wrong capture 'the greatest utility of the *whole mass* of beings' (PJ 616, emphasis added). The greatest utility is an objective magnitude. It is not a preference or a choice but rather a constraint. Absolute and binding, keeps us together and permits us to live as one. Justice is more than an ostracised one-off bowling alone.

Morality is consequentialism. Even sincerity is practised '*only* for reasons of utility' (PJ 256, emphasis added), *only* because of its tendency to 'disarm the bitterest foe' (PJ 259). Like a designer handbag or a limited-edition print, regression to the shared *ought to be* is an investment in personal standing and even pecuniary success that strict moralists would term the means to an end rather than a *desiratum* in itself.

Morality, crucially, is deontology as well: 'The most beneficent action that ever was, if it did not spring from the intention of doing good to others, is not of the nature of virtue' (TM 212). There can be no moral conduct, Godwin states, 'except in instances where our actions flow from intention' (PJ 305). Not only must we identify the norms that are most beneficial to the *whole mass* of beings, we must will ourselves to do what is right: 'There can be no morality, however passionate the stimulus, that is independent of understanding' (PJ 176).

No one stumbles into normative constraint without grasping its role: 'Benevolent intention is essential to virtue' (PJ 311). Never random or accidental, moral conduct is rational choice. Man the thinker must use sense perception to deliberate his way to the truth. Epistemology or ethics, the mind is never switched off.

Morality to Godwin maximises the 'general happiness' (PJ 119). Simultaneously, it proceeds from 'kind and benevolent intention' (PJ 122) that is its own reward: 'Virtue is nothing else but kind and sympathetic feelings reduced into principle' (PJ 431). Virtue is feeling. Both the donor and the recipient have a share in 'the greatest quantity of happiness' (PJ 432). It is win-win.

3.5.2 *The Role of the Rules*

'Morality is nothing more than a calculation of pleasures' (EQ 104). Taken literally, Godwin's marketplace for morals, not stoic but epicurean, appears redolent with sensuality, libertinism and downright indulgence. Considered carefully, it is more nearly an austere form of utilitarianism which looks outward to group memory and mutual aid. Morality is 'the principle which binds the individual to the species' (PJ 229). It is a non-ego standard which impels us 'to model our conduct in the way most conducive to the advantage of all' (PJ 229). Even after the state is gone, society will still be all around. The role of the rules is to assure social cohesion. Utility, intention, it is the We and not the I that stands behind the function.

A thin moral code stops short at the injunction to 'inflict no injury on others' (PJ 616). It is Berlin's negative justice, pointedly hands-off. A thick moral code is one which commits the integrated team-player not merely to respect existing entitlements but proactively to enhance the 'benefit or pleasure of another' (PJ 625). Justice is what a man 'owes to the whole' (PJ 616). If he owes it, then he must deliver it. We do not value passengers and parasites around here.

Our common *ought-to-bes* are 'enjoined upon us by the dictates of enlightened reason' (PJ 99). They stream our conduct in the direction of 'the greatest general good' (PJ 99). Robinson Crusoe can pursue his own private utility as he judges best. What he cannot pursue is justice. It is only when, living in a group, that he becomes obliged to adopt the standards most consonant with 'the general welfare' (PJ 616).

Durkheim says that 'societies cannot exist if there are only individuals' (Durkheim, 1897 [1952]: 38): 'Man is a moral being only because he lives in society, since morality consists in being solidary with a group' (Durkheim, 1893 [1933] 399). It is an interlock with which Godwin is entirely in sympathy: 'No being can be either virtuous, or vicious, who has no opportunity of influencing the happiness of others....The true solitaire cannot be considered as a moral being' (PJ 557).

Morality is the property of the All. Collective conventions impose order on Veblen's, on Commons's going concern. They are 'the constant associate of all our transactions' (PJ 562). Socialised into society, we acquire 'distinct and accurate notions of the merits of every moral question' (PJ 562). There is no situation 'respecting which duty is silent' (PJ 562).

Awareness accompanied by intention is not enough: 'A good motive is of little value when it is not joined to a salutary exertion' (PJ 562). A moral man is one who follows the word with the deed. He replicates the done thing because it is the group-sanctioned means to an end which goes beyond the selfish desire to win a prize or avoid a punishment. Failing that, it loses its categorical imperative: 'If self-love be the only principle of action, there can be no such thing as virtue' (PJ 311).

Virtue is voluntary self-restraint. Treating like as like, handing forward the familiar expectations, self-government in line with the template delivers 'excellent and permanent pleasure' (PJ 322). It delivers a subjective return that is different from the objectivity of its function. Service, sacrifice, generosity make us happy as part of a group even if as individuals we have had to give something up. Unpleasant means become superpleasant ends. To sow happiness is to reap happiness. Motive, consequence, it is a closed system. Private interest and public interest coincide (PJ 386). Mandeville and market economics beware. Private *virtues* are public virtues. No one in the circumstances would choose a free ride.

Mancur Olson uses the logic of narrow self-interest and calculative rationality to deduce that in the anonymity of the crowd the common asset, available to all if available to any, will not voluntarily be supplied: 'The larger the group, the smaller the fraction of the total group benefit any person acting in the group interest receives, and the less adequate the reward for any group-oriented action' (Olson, 1965: 48). Elinor Ostrom, in contrast, concludes from the ethnographic evidence that group-thinkers keep within their traditions even when they are in a position to over-fish, to over-fell—or, Malthus-like, to over-populate—a common-pool resource: 'Given the temptations involved, the high levels of conformance to the rules in all these cases have been remarkable' (Ostrom, 1990: 59). Not everyone drops litter all of the time. Neoclassical economics only goes so far.

Godwin is on the side of Ostrom and not of Olson. Both in the present day and in the self-regulating anarchy that will succeed to the enforcer state, the moral consensus has the character of a public good, a societal contract from which few if any players will consciously deviate: 'Confidence, in the characters of our fellow men, that they will for the most part be governed by the reason of the case, that they will neither rob, nor defraud, nor deceive us, is not less essential to the existence of civilized society' (PJ 255).

It is essential and it will evolve. Some of us will default (PJ 173). Most of us will not. It is human nature to want to share. That is what we are. Rational people will not overbreed if their community is living by the rule of stop-at-two. Malthus, Godwin would say, makes the mistake of taking the individual out his broader context. Social-ism solves the population problem at a stroke.

Moral man has 'a *desire* to promote the happiness of intelligent beings' (PJ 235, emphasis added). It is a desire which goes beyond a dog-whistle to which even a non-rational animal will respond. Virtue is not the blind obedience of the slave (PJ 562) but rather a thinking man's *desire* to make an investment in the whole of which he is a part: 'Eminent virtue requires that I should have a grand view of the tendency of knowledge to produce happiness....I should perceive in what manner social intercourse may be made conducive to virtue and felicity' (PJ 236). Virtue is a 'disposition of the mind' (PJ 235). It is not a Pavlovian reflex but a dispassionate evaluation: 'The purest kind of obedience is where an action flows from the independent conviction of our private judgment' (PJ 174). The individual in society is driven to uncover the truth about his entitlements and his obligations. Inquiry sets self-regulation free from both the confusion of normlessness and the tyranny of Leviathan.

Moral people know: understanding 'never fails in some degree to generate capacity' (PJ 237). Moral people act: 'He is truly the virtuous man who produces the greatest portion of benefit his situation will admit' (PJ 175). Perfectibility is the result. The steady progress of the truth is unlocking all that is best in human potential. 'Sentiments of the purest philanthropy' (PJ 324) are being released. The warm-hearted attractions of 'society', 'social feeling', 'benevolence' and 'sympathy' (PJ 232) are crowding out the antiquated aberrations of superfluity, property, appetite and conflict. Mind is everywhere setting matter free: 'No order of mankind will for ever remain ignorant of the principles of justice, equality and public good' (PJ 386). The progressive revelation of the truth is moving us up. The truth will be kept in place by its ratchet. Agreement will stay. Ostrom will stay. Olson will have to go.

3.5.3 *The Tyranny of Consent*

The moral code has the social function of 'preventing future mischief' (PJ 559) hazardous to the security of the whole (PJ 594). A legal code is not needed if internalised norms, diffuse and unwritten, are able to produce 'an overbalance of good' (PJ 558). Society polices itself. The 'universal consent of mankind' (PJ 558) takes on the role of enforcer that Hobbes had assigned to the protective state. Anarchy takes over from Sir. 'Preventing evils subversive of general security' (PJ 596) becomes not Sir's job but your job and mine.

The moral code is the social code. It is a topic in scaling up. Man in society 'will not refuse attention to the state of opinion in the present or any preceding generation of men' (PJ 178). It is simultaneously an exercise in factoring down. It is always wrong for me to 'commit my conscience to another man's keeping' (PJ 581). Godwin is both a social-ist and an individual-ist. He is anticipating that what *I* want will be what *We* want. De Tocqueville warned that it might not be so (de Tocqueville, 1835, 1840 [1961]: II, 313, 314).

Godwin, like de Tocqueville, believed that the tyranny of the majority over the minority was 'inseparable from political government' (PJ 416). A margin of 51 per cent in a general election that legitimises a policy-mix of 51 per cent in the Assembly, first-past-the-post may command 'tacit consent' (PJ 166) but still not come with the warranty of Wicksellian unanimity or all-encompassing grassroots consultation (PJ 469). There is no inherent rationality in a show of hands that leaves the losers in the cold: 'Nothing can more directly contribute to the depravation of the human understanding and character' (PJ 469).

That is politics. Politics is bad. The action of government, 'in conferring rewards, and superintending opinion, is of pernicious effect' (PJ 555). Conformity backed up by coercion is 'wrong', 'deeply to be regretted' (PJ 198). What Godwin does not do is to extend his reservations about tyranny from politics to society. It is not just Big Brother but Big We that is cookie-cutting Little I into a manageable size. The collective mind can be supremely intolerant of the inspired lunatic who believes that the earth goes round the sun or wishes to read a banned book like *Fahrenheit 451*.

The Big We can be the new Bastille. The 'empty phantom of public opinion', de Tocqueville says, 'can be 'strong enough to chill innovation' (de Tocqueville, 1835, 1840 [1961]: II 314). de Tocqueville visited the future. He came back with serious misgivings about what he had seen: 'I know no country in which there is so little independence of mind and freedom of discussion as in America'' (de Tocqueville, 1835, 1840 [1961]: I 310).

Godwin knew that the tyranny of public opinion could destroy all that was unique and special in the self: 'The consequence is clear. I then become the most mischievous and pernicious of animals. I annihilate my individuality as a man....I put an end, as to my own share, to that happy collision of understandings upon which the hopes of human improvement depend. I can have no genuine fortitude, for fortitude is the offspring of conviction' (PJ 581). He knew that public opinion can terrify its victims into a fictive peace where no one has the fortitude to stand up for the fringe. Social tyranny is pernicious. As with political tyranny, it levels down the differentiated into an off-the-peg standard size: 'To dragoon men into the adoption of what we think right is an intolerable tyranny' (PJ 197).

Godwin knew that the median man on the Clapham omnibus can be a tyrant who inequitably condemns the discrete I to a lifetime of 'torpor and imbecility' (PJ 490). Change is anathema: 'Whatever is wholly new is sure to be pronounced by the mass of mankind to be impracticable' (Sepulchres, vii). It would be a violation of both liberty and equality for the general will to deny to each free-standing entity the opportunity 'to pursue its own ideas of propriety' (PJ 534) in its own way: 'The conviction of a man's individual understanding is the only legitimate principle imposing on him the duty of adopting any species of conduct' (PJ 141). The 'only legitimate principle' cannot legitimately be sacrificed in the interests of a bogus fraternity that forces massified man into 'the grossest and most contemptible errors' (PJ 470).

Godwin was aware that it would be an intolerable infringement of the self for the collective consciousness 'to put fetters upon the subtlety of thought': 'The attempt to punish opinion is absurd' (PJ 500). In spite of that, he refused to equate social tyranny with political tyranny. The reason was the existence of a supreme court that champions the individual against the mass.

That supreme court is the truth. A dog is a dog. There is no way that a badly informed majority can expect a well-informed minority to accept that it is a cat. Godwin was not a sociological relativist but an empiricist and an objectivist. Deception becomes impossible once science marches out to 'introduce the light of reason' (PJ 500). Fadlallah, Zemroude, Mocbel and Arzshank, together with a host of other wizards, ghouls, witches, seers, fairies and diviners, are seeking to ensnare 'the folly of imbecile minds' into their 'pestiferous clouds' (Necromancers, 465). Their make-believe will be no match for honourable men who have the facts on their side. Bad laws are made by bad men. Social tyranny is nonetheless a practical impossibility once the fact-gatherers have assayed out the truth.

It is not de Tocqueville's America but Archimedes's eureka that stamps its *ought-to-be* on a non-ego fact. The individual will refuse to give his informed consent until he has been presented with 'intrinsic evidence' (PJ 178, 458). The mystified self 'by whom that study was never undertaken' (PJ 179) will trust to unassailable experts to table information on which his rational decision will depend. He will trust to Great Prophets and Great Books. Even more will he trust to the truth: 'As truth is an endless source of tranquillity and delight, error will be a prolific fountain of new mistakes and discontent' (PJ 233). Truth is contentment. Untruth is unhappiness. Even ordinary people know that.

A dog is not a cat. Microscopes and telescopes offer convincing proof that puts the physical world into the public domain. They allow ordinary people to pass a valid judgement (PJ 178, 181). Perhaps they do, but physics is not ethics and certainly not taste. We are all different: 'Is Pope a poet? Is Boileau a poet? These are questions still vehemently contested' (EQ 285). We see the same thing differently: 'There is scarcely a question in the world, that does not admit of two plausible statements' (EQ 302). Godwin is over-confident when he puts his faith in science to protect the one-off agency from the force and violence of the neighbours and the peers. We say to them: 'Do not seek to enslave our minds' (PJ 180). They say to us that abortion is murder and luxury is waste. A dog is not a cat. To proceed beyond physics into ethics and taste is, however, to expect the empiricists to square every circle.

Godwin is confident that his court of appeal will return the right verdict: 'Mankind seldom think much of any particular subject without coming to think right at last' (PJ 521). Two sides to every question are not made to last. Convergence puts the seal of truth on free will and obedience: 'No one will maintain that we have a right to trespass upon the dictates of morality' (PJ 127). We do not have a right to 'absurdity' and 'injustice' (PJ 130). We do not have a 'right of doing wrong' (PJ 130). It is not social tyranny. It is the duty of the smaller unit to the larger unit to protect the common good.

Godwin, factoring down, is an individual-ist: 'Men should judge for themselves, unfettered by the prejudices of education, or the institutions of their country' (PJ 180). Godwin, scaling up, is a social-ist: 'Not a talent do we possess, not a moment of time, not a shilling of property, for which we are not responsible at the tribunal of the public, which we are not obliged to pay into the general bank of common advantage' (PJ 371). Looking inward is the sine qua non: 'Happiness, in order to be real, must necessarily be individual' (PJ 432). Looking outward, however, is the *nec plus ultra*: 'Each man is but a part of a great system', an element in the 'general stock' (PJ 111). Godwin does not regard the inward and the outward as radical alternatives. The reason is his unwavering confidence in the verifiable truth. Should his confidence in empiricism, science and sense perception go the way of his confidence in God and in the state, he would be reduced to the status of Camus' Mersault. Mersault killed on a whim because killing killed time and he had nothing else to do.

3.6 Science and Faith

In or about 1783 Godwin lost his faith in Christianity and in an anthropomorphic God. The shadow of the *Acts*, the *Proverbs*, the *Gospels* and the *Epistles* never left him for a single day in his life. For all that, approaching 30, he became, Kegan Paul says, a 'complete unbeliever' (KP I 26). The state had no right to impose artificial laws and conventions that go against the verdict of sensory sequence gathered in a specific context. Nor did the church.

Priests, prayers, prayer-books, revelations, rituals and catechisms were institutionalising 'blind submission and abject hypocrisy' (PJ 492). They were teaching their devotees that virtue consists in obedience rather than inquiry. Cutting off men's access to the raw data of experience, instructing the coal-face vanguard 'not to improve upon the science of their ancestors' (PJ 493), organised religion, like Pitt, Grenville and their censors, was restricting man's ability 'to think for himself' (PJ 492). It was capping the flow of new knowledge. 'Unnatural and unfortunate', it was rewarding the 'imbecile and unworthy spirit' (PJ 494) that had a vested interest in the perpetuation of exploded untruth. The church is the 'malicious enemy of mankind' (PJ 495). Its tyranny is incompatible with induction from nature that is the proper cornerstone of right and wrong.

Religion is immoral where it requires laymen to assent to what they do not believe. It is functionless where an honest plaintiff must swear an oath or where a prelate preaches a truth that everyone already knows: 'If public worship be conformable to reason, reason without doubt will prove adequate to its vindication' (PJ 496). There is also politics. Godwin knew that the Church of England was in close alliance with the landed aristocracy and the state. Its attitude to dissenters and Irish Catholics was divisive and bigoted.

The Old Man with a Beard does not exist. In his unfinished *Genius of Christianity*, Godwin called it 'the most irrational and ridiculous anthropomorphism' (in Woodcock, 1946: 169) to pretend that an intelligent shepherd is in ever charge. Nature is older than God (KP I 310). Prescientific humanity, frightened of the unknowable, found it convenient to postulate an 'intelligent Creator and Governor' in the image of man (in KP I 357). It was the fear of freedom and nothing more.

Godwin found such a reconstruction repugnant, 'irrational' and 'foolish' (in KP I 357). A formal creed is a tissue of 'incoherent and contradictory dreams', strong on 'absurdity and impossibility', weak on 'final causes', an open invitation to 'imposters and fanatics' who seek to 'enfeeble' their flock (in Woodcock, 1946: 151). In a note to himself dating from the late 1790s, Godwin said it was essential to 'sweep away the whole fiction of an intelligent former of the world, and a future state' (in Woodcock, 1946: 151). Miracles, first causes, salvation, damnation, probation, redemption, deliverance, the Trinity, the resurrection, the next life, angels with wings, devils with tails, providence, it is all Santa Claus. It is all made up.

Godwin had no time for churches in general, Christianity in particular. Describing it as 'preposterous', 'trite' unsupported by uninhibited empiricism, he called Christianity 'a mass of contradictions' which, even for professing Christians, had had 'scarcely any influence on their actions and lives': 'A sharp fit of the toothache will have a much more powerful effect than the prospects of eternity' (Essays, 21, 23, 130). Like Smith, Rousseau and Coleridge, however, what he did have was a 'reverent and soothing contemplation of all that is beautiful, great and mysterious' (in KP I 358). Nature, Godwin wrote in his diary in 1820, 'fills me with love and astonishment. My soul is bursting with the mystery of all this....This is what I call religion' (in KP II 264). Happiness is feeling. Informal sanctions are feeling. Religion is feeling. Godwin was a rationalist who repeatedly invoked non-reason to complete his circuit.

Religion, Godwin proclaims in *Mandeville*, is what distinguishes the human from the animal world: 'It is our special prerogative, that we can converse with that which we cannot see' (Mandeville, 225). The sacred fleshes out the profane. It empowers anxious mankind to tap into a parallel universe of non-rational discrimination that is supported by 'none of our senses' (Mandeville, 225). In his 20s a Christian, in his 30s an unbeliever, by his early 40s Godwin was drifting into an amorphous natural theism, a non-confessional deism, that took its sermons from the stones. Sense perception would remain man's primary point of contact with the world around him. It could nonetheless be complemented with a non-confessional spirituality that has a natural appeal to the yin as well as the yang. Mary Wollstonecraft was a believer. She showed by her example that even the scientific mind could find room for awe.

Awe and sense perception need not be mutually exclusive. Nature is wonder-full. If God exists, then it is in the world of nature that the divine plan can provisionally be glimpsed: 'We know nothing of God but from his works' (TM 414). God's works are all around (PJ 236). Mankind does right to approach the natural order 'with wonder and awe' (Essays, 12). Observation is the key to whoever or whatever imposed the natural law on people and things. An inspection of external reality confirms that the teleology is good. Happiness and purposiveness are on the increase. God is hid in night. If 'The Divine' does exist, then the evidence suggests that he is on our side.

Godwin by the time he wrote *Political Justice* was convinced that there was something approaching a world spirit 'out there': 'A man is wrong who is without religion' (in KP II 263). Religion is more than an afunctional luxury: 'A certain portion of what may be called the "religious sense" is necessary to the sound and healthy condition of the human mind' (Essays, 12). A this-worldly 'religious sense' is not in dispute. Non-empirical, non-quantifiable, it makes a supra-logical contribution to the whole truth that extends to feeling as well as analysis.

Godwin saw no need to put his faith in the Old Man with a Beard. Super-natural Janus to him was on the one hand a focus for Pareto's non-rational residues, on the other an inductivist's basepoint, a construction line that assists the scientist to put his finger on the pulse of his community. Like Smith's 'Author of Nature' (MS 235), Godwin 'intelligent Creator' (in KP I 357) was a bulwark against false consciousness precisely because he never forces through his own text but rather draws his lessons from the landscape before him.

What is is the situation. *What ought to be* is the imperative: 'Morality is nothing else but that system which teaches us to contribute upon all occasions, to the extent of our power, to the well-being and happiness of every intellectual and sensitive existence' (PJ 126). Either way, God's will is the only will. Text is context. There is no eternal steersman in the sky.

Intuitively, one would expect that Malthus, a Christian clergyman, would have distanced himself sharply from Godwin, a heathen agnostic. Malthus knew there was no substitute for the Word and the Bible. A man of his times, however, he sensed that there was more to religion than a single Book: 'It seems absolutely necessary that we should reason from nature to nature's God and not presume to reason from God to nature' (FE 201). Godwin or Malthus, nature had to be given the chance to reveal important truths that had not made their way into the Gospels.

Malthus was curious about the scope for sense perception. His interest in the real world brought him into conflict with the hard-line fundamentalists of the established Church (Reisman, 2018: 285–90). Paley's utilitarianism and Hume's empiricism, they objected, were a poor substitute for Biblical exegesis that took its social theory from the revelations of Jesus.

The Archbishop of Canterbury was prepared, like Mathus, to look downward with Aristotle rather than upward with Plato. Unwilling to accept that God had intended the earth to be a veil of tears, John Bird Sumner declared that 'the happiness of mankind was consulted by his Creator' (Sumner, 1816: II 186) when he put in play both the population multiplier and the shortage of food. Other elders and luminaries were more critical. The result was that Malthus almost immediately repudiated the controversial chapters 18 and 19 of his 1798 *Essay*. Orthodox Christians were calling his summing up 'a libel against the Almighty himself' (in James, 1979: 117).

There was always more to Malthus than evangelical piety and theological dogma. Even so, God's will was paramount. The gap between Godwin and Malthus would have been smaller if Malthus had not been led by his faith to him to make 'the Almighty himself' a third partner in the debate. As a clergyman, Mathus was committed by his theodicy to impute an eternal link between evil and indolence on the one hand, utility and inclusion on the other. The secular had to remain the sacred. As a professor of history and political economy, he recognised nonetheless that he had to incorporate the great lessons of Paley and Hume into his account of misery transcended and vice driven out.

Godwin had the easier task. He was able to inspect the evidence and codify the ethics without having to reconcile his institutional betterment with the Scriptures. Inflexible religion drew them apart. The 'mistaken guardianship' of 'inauspicious' government (PJ 491) brought them together. Malthus, Waterman states, 'wrote with *Political Justice* at his elbow' (Waterman, 1991: 100). *Political Justice* had said that we should 'trust to the direct and fair verdict of our own understandings' (PJ 491). It had said that we should make friends with the world around us. Internalised in the 'group mind', disseminated through the 'public voice' (PJ 488), in the end our 'own understandings' will set us free.

3.7 Two Steps Backward?

They might. They might not. 'Our understandings' are in the mind: 'Man…is governed by the apprehensions of his understanding' (PJ 278). Progress is assured: 'Nothing further is requisite but the improvement of his reasoning faculty to make him virtuous and happy' (PJ 278).

Not every reader will be convinced. Living through the most brutalising phase of the British industrial revolution, Godwin looked primarily to mind, only secondarily to matter, to rescue suffering humanity from the unemployment, the alienation and the exploitation. Godwin's critics will say that it is Hamlet without Karl Marx. It is Hegelian idealism without the economics that might have seized the contradictions and the conflicts by the scruff of their neck.

Godwin anticipates that it will be the wise and thinking who will put sunrise knowledge at the service of the transition. He concedes that their track record has not always been inspiring: 'The whole history of the human species…appears a vast abortion' (PJ 327). The facts do not suggest that humanity has of necessity been making unbounded progress. 'The creed of optimism…has done much harm in the world' (PJ 328).

The past has been scarred by 'vice, disorder and misery' (PJ 323), 'folly and mistake' (PJ 324), 'pain and calamity' (PJ 326), 'ignorance and superstition' (PJ 327), 'distress, distemper and crisis' (PJ 330). The poor have been 'oppressed, hungry, naked' (PJ 326). They have been the innocent victims of war, injustice, low cunning and narrow selfishness. 'Misery and vice' (PJ 589) have defeated even the best-willed of the philanthropists. Hobbes has not gone away. Perfectibility has been playing the tortoise to capitalism's hare. There must have been some doubt about its capacity to overtake.

That, however, is the past. Ideas have consequences. The mind is teasing out the truth. Given time, 'every benefit may ultimately be expected, untarnished with violence, and unstained with blood' (PJ 589). The path of evolution is on the side of betterment 'from the savage stage to the highest degree of civilization' (PJ 589). It 'gives us reason to expect that, as men collectively advance in science and useful institution, they will proceed more and more to consolidate their private judgement, and their individual will, with abstract justice, and the unmixed approbation of general happiness' (PJ 314).

There are bound to be reverses along the trend. Public opinion in the short run might mistake its birthright for a mess of shopping. Godwin for his own part has no doubt that humankind will ultimately gravitate to the bedrock truth. The dark side of human interaction will be inevitably be competed away by the progressive unveiling of the *dharshan*. Negativity is nearing its end: 'The state of society we have been describing must, at some time, arrive' (PJ 660).

It *must* arrive. The evolution of mind is correcting the shibboleths of matter. Mankind is advancing steadily towards 'the greatest practicable advantage', 'the most solid and permanent happiness' (PJ 231). Life is getting better all the time: 'There are no obstacles to our improvement' (PJ 46). There is nothing that will not yield to the 'incessant activity' (in KP I 207) of the momentum and the process. Slow as it is, it is visible even to the naked eye. Writing in 1811, he reported that 'the human race has made larger strides...in these twenty years than perhaps in any hundred years preceding' (in KP I 208).

It *must* arrive. Betterment is the irreversible consequence of 'the progress of science and political truth' (PJ 660): 'Sophistry will vanish, and mischievous institutions sink quietly into neglect....Oppression, injustice, monarchy and vice, will tumble into a common ruin' (PJ 386).

Fleisher is not convinced: 'A fatal flaw lies at the heart of Godwin's system—an exaggerated notion of the power of reason over human conduct, an inadequate appreciation of the primal, brute forces in human nature' (Fleisher, 1951: 146). The naked ape remains the *Lord of the Flies* and not the civilised 'after you' of Socrates educating his *cognoscienti*. Godwin's anarchism, the 'conquest of pigmy evil by giant reason', clearly belongs, Fleisher says, 'to the literature of utopias' (Fleisher, 1951: 148).

Cain and Hitler had taught that even in an age of enlightenment, human psychology is a wild card. Evil in the sense of Augustine is always poised ready to strike. Caleb Williams is a good man persecuted and ultimately destroyed by a midnight force with more than its share of blood lust. Machiavelli and later Nietzsche had taught that, if 'God is dead', then 'evil is man's best strength' (Nietzsche, 1883 [1961]: 41, 299). Nice guys finish last. Godwin, however, believed that human nature in the end would come out on top. Universal benevolence is slowly but surely crowding out the death wish. Evolution is on the side of perfectibility. History-to-come will even out the bumps. Reason will make all the roads straight.

It is an opinion and an assertion. It is only one of the unsupported claims in the *Political Justice* that Philp reluctantly dismisses as 'palpably absurd': 'It seems difficult to believe that he was completely rational when he wrote the book' (Philp, 1986: 1, 6). Munro, like Philp, takes the view that 'if Godwin was sometimes right, he was right, so to speak, by accident; he was frustratingly incapable of understanding all the deeper springs of human behaviour' (Munro, 1953: 5). Munro is clearly losing patience with a self-styled magus who, declaring that he has a hotline to truth, drunkenly veers between the unverified and the unverifible: 'The whole of Godwin's moral philosophy is a mere tissue of assumptions' (Munro, 1953: 187).

Godwin's moral philosophy, Munro asserts, cannot be confirmed or refuted by any Hume-like set of facts. The truth about human nature is at best writ in water, at worst not writ at all. Godwin himself does not, however, see the stable parameters of objective reality as a perennial storm of creative destruction. Essence does not bow to impression. In the teeth of all the evidence, Godwin continued to believe that men are naturally good.

Godwin, like Marx, knew that he could not test his futurology against a data-set that did not exist. The details have yet to reveal their hand. Accepting his inability to outguess the unknowable, Godwin remains convinced that the broad lines of self-generating anarchy are falling into place. The truth, the one and only truth, is making itself heard. The rest of us are not so sure: 'For all his brave talk of progress he makes it quite clear that his ideal state is set in the extremely remote future' (Munro, 1953: 169). We know about Atlantis. We know about Malthus. We know about food and family-poverty. We know about Hobbes. We know about street mugging and get-rich-quick speculation. For now, it is a hard life. We lock our doors. We buy a very big dog.

References

By W. Godwin

Godwin, W. (1793). *Enquiry Concerning Political Justice* (abbreviated to PJ 1793) (2 Vols.). G.C.J. and J. Robinson.

Godwin, W. (1794 [1988]). *Things as They Are, or the Adventures of Caleb Williams* (abbreviated as CW). Penguin Books.

Godwin, W. (1798 [1976]). *Enquiry Concerning Political Justice* (abbreviated as PJ). Penguin Books.
Godwin, W. (1800). *Essay on Sepulchres* (abbreviated as Sepulchres). W. Miller.
Godwin, W. (1817 [1992]). *Mandeville: A Tale of the Seventeenth Century in England* (abbreviated as Mandeville), in *Collected Novels and Memoirs of William Godwin* (Vol. 4). William Pickering.
Godwin, W. (1834). *The Lives of the Necromancers* (abbreviated as Necromancers). F.J. Mason.
Godwin, W. (1873). *Essays: Never Before Published* (abbreviated as Essays). Henry S. King.

By T.R. Malthus

Malthus, T. R. (1798 [1970]). *Essay on the Principle of Population* (abbreviated as FE). Penguin.

By Other Authors

Aristotle. (2004). *The Nicomachean Ethics* (J. A. K. Thomson, Trans.). Penguin Books.
Burke, E. (1790 [1968]). *Reflections on the Revolution in France*. Penguin Books.
Commons, J. R. (1934). *Institutional Economics*. Macmillan.
de Maistre, J. (1821 [1965]). *Saint Petersburg Dialogues* (J. Lively, Trans.), in *The Works of Joseph de Maistre* (pp. 183–290). George Allen and Unwin.
de Tocqueville, A. (1835, 1840 [1961]). *Democracy in America* (H. Reeve, Trans.) (2 Vols.). Schocken Books.
Durkheim, E. (1893 [1933]). *The Division of Labor in Society* (G. Simpson, Trans.). The Free Press.
Durkheim, E. (1897 [1952]). *Suicide* (J. A. Spaulding & G. Simpson, Trans.). Routledge.
Fleisher, D. (1951). *William Godwin: A Study in Liberalism*. George Allen and Unwin.
Hartley, D. (1749 [1810]). *Observations on Man*. Richard Crutwell.
Hume, D. (1739–40 [1969]). *A Treatise of Human Nature*. Penguin Books.
James, P. (1979). *Population Malthus: His Life and Times*. Routledge and Kegan Paul.
Kegan Paul, C. (1876). *William Godwin: His Friends and Contemporaries* (abbreviated as KP) (2 Vols.). Henry S. King.
Locke, J. (1690 [1975]). *Essay concerning Human Understanding*. Oxford University Press.
Marshall, A. (1920 [1949]), *Principles of Economics*, London: Macmillan.
Marshall, P.H. (1984), *William Godwin*, New Haven: Yale University Press.

Munro, D. H. (1953). *Godwin's Moral Philosophy: An Interpretation of William Godwin*. Oxford University Press.
Nietzsche, F. (1883 [1961]). *Thus Spoke Zarathustra* (R. J. Hollingdale, Trans.). Penguin Books.
Olson, M. (1965). *The Logic of Collective Action*. Harvard University Press.
Ostrom, E. (1990). *Governing the Commons: The Evolution of Institutions for Collective Action*. Cambridge University Press.
Philp, M. (1986). *Godwin's Political Justice*. Duckworth.
Plato. (2012). *The Republic* (C. Rowe, Trans.). Penguin Books.
Pope, A. (1730 [1966]). 'Epitaph intended for Sir Isaac Newton', in his *Poetical Works* (p. 651). Oxford University Press.
Priestley, F. E. L. (1946). *Critical Introduction and Notes to Enquiry Concerning Political Justice* (3 Vols.). University of Toronto Press.
Reisman, D. A. (2018). *Thomas Robert Malthus*. Palgrave Macmillan.
Shackle, G. L. S. (1972). *The Years of High Theory*. Cambridge University Press.
Simon, H. A. (1965). *Administrative Behavior* (2nd ed.). The Free Press.
Smith, A. (1759 [1966]). *The Theory of Moral Sentiments* (abbreviated as MS). Augustus M. Kelley.
Smith, A. (1795 [1980]). *Essays on Philosophical Subjects*. Clarendon Press.
Sumner, J. B. (1816). *A Treatise on the Records of the Creation and the Moral Attributes of the Creator* (2 Vols.). J. Hatchard.
Veblen, T. (1919 [1994]). *The Place of Science in Modern Civilisation and Other Essays*. Routledge/Thoemmes Press.
Waterman, A. M. C. (1991). *Revolution, Economics and Religion: Christian Political Economy, 1798–1833*. Cambridge University Press.
Woodcock, G. (1946). *William Godwin: A Biographical Study*. The Porcupine Press.

CHAPTER 4

Justice: The State

'Government by its very nature counteracts the improvement of individual intellect' (PJ 4). Shorn of its mystique and its pomp, it is 'an evil, an usurpation upon the private judgement and individual conscience of mankind' (PJ 336). Government is a functionless fifth wheel. Reason and truth are able unassisted to solve the problem of order: 'The true supporters of government are the weak and uninformed, and not the wise. In proportion as weakness and ignorance shall diminish, the basis of government will also decay' (PJ 181–2).

The basis will decay. The 'craft and mystery of governing' (PJ 582) will wither into nothingness. The future will bear witness to 'the euthanasia of government' (PJ 182) precisely because the imperfections that made necessary the repressive state will have phased themselves out. Paine was right: 'Society is produced by our wants, and government by our wickedness.... Society in every state is a blessing. but government, even in its best state, is but a necessary evil, security being the true design and end of government' (Paine, 1776 [2000]: 5). In the lost innocence of the Garden of Eden there was no need for clothing to correct a deviation from nature's law.

In the short run, Godwin admits, we cannot do without the state. It came into being to correct a human failure. People were 'liable to error' (PJ 432). People 'suffered their apprehensions of justice to be perverted by a bias in favour of themselves' (PJ 432). Government protects their

D. Reisman, *William Godwin and Thomas Robert Malthus*,
https://doi.org/10.1007/978-3-031-62113-0_4

'tranquillity' (PJ 434). It defends them against the 'ambition and tumult' of their more aggressive fellows: 'The object of government is the suppression of such violence' (PJ 465). As individuals in society, we are able unassisted 'to supply our wants and promote our well being' (PJ 21). What we cannot do is to ensure our security. Government came into being to fill a social gap.

Like Paine, Godwin calls authority 'a necessary evil for the present' (PJ 336). In the here-and-now the anxious and the nervous must surrender some autonomy 'for the sake of general good' (PJ 338). It is the task of a good government to prepare its lost sheep for peaceable autonomy. Opting to make men wise and 'not to make them slaves' (PJ 456), it should rely on instruction rather than compulsion to set them free. In the short-run shadow of the *bellum,* it must nonetheless fill a social niche which independence and individualism, 'universal justice' (PJ 458) and 'the voice of reason' (PJ 474) are not yet mature enough to occupy.

4.1 The Constitution

There never was a 'social contract'. Hobbes, Locke and Rousseau had conjectured that there must have been an original state of statelessness from which our ancestors, fearful of civil war, had been anxious to escape. Godwin found the hypothesis facile and undocumented. There is, he reported, no evidence of a primeval non-aggression pact to which the contracting parties had given their consent.

Even if the yellowing piece of paper could be found, still it would have no moral or legal force. A grandfather generation cannot precommit its distant descendants: 'Few things can be more absurd than to talk of our having promised obedience to the laws' (PJ 163). Each person in each cohort must negotiate his own utility for himself. Even human rights are not natural but agreed-upon.

Godwin's rejection of past-dominated acquiescence seems to be an endorsement of the inperiod and the current. Promises are spot, on the principle that no parliament can bind its successor. In fact, Godwin's views are more nuanced, more conservative and more intertemporal.

For one thing, habits, lags and survivals trap all of us in a web of tacit acceptance. Convention is an implicit contract we make with each other and only then with the enforcer *ex machina*. Our relationship with our government fits into a pattern. It is not an *ab novo* calculus.

Just as important, we tie the hands of our rulers lest they overstep the limits on which our consensus has converged. We demand a multiperiod constitution that makes explicit the *what*, the *who*, the *for-how-long*. We are drawn to governance because we do not trust one other. It is no reason to give our governors a *carte blanche*.

We fear that our fellow citizens will be tempted to invade our space. We suspect that our state will be more of the same. History confirms the clear and present danger from despots and dictators, 'arbitrary and capricious' (PJ 528). Leaders who ride roughshod over the needs of their people are violating the very *raison d'être* of their monopoly of force: 'The only legitimate object of political institution is the advantage of individuals' (PJ 462). The individual is the ultimate sovereign. That is why the right to control is embedded not in 'temporary' stop-gaps but in 'fundamental' inflexibilities (PJ 526). The multiperiod constitution walls in the Leviathan. It limits his discretion. Carried forward from the past, binding even of the future, the aura of permanence is intended to stop bad governance in its tracks.

The ideal constitution lays down the rule-making rules. They will often extend to intra-government regulations. Montesquieu in 1748 had praised the British for including the separation of the executive, legislative and judiciary in their unwritten charter (Montesquieu, 1748 [1949]: 151–162). The Americans in 1787 had incorporated checks and balances into their tripartite division of function. Godwin felt that, while some insurance was essential, an excess of restrictions would be counterproductive (PJ 460). Speaking for himself, even a bicameral legislature would be an unnecessary precaution. An upper alongside a lower house would only 'divide a nation against itself' (PJ 458). The same would be true of a clause making participation in politics contingent on income, wealth, religion or education.

The postcode is the exception. An ideal constitution will do well to regionalise its rules to devolved assemblies. A Scotsman's meat is an Irishman's poison. Defence has economies of size. The iron dome must remain the monopoly of the centre. Other functions can more easily be fine-tuned to grassroots politics in dialogue with insular attitudes. Local law 'best corresponds to the real nature and wants of a human being' (PJ 533). Crucially, however, even the subordinate sub-states must not be free to decide on every issue afresh. For the 'dictates of reason' (PJ 532) to prevail, there must be a hard core of multiperiod absolutes, both local and central, that survive the merry-go-round of fancy and fashion.

Constitutions do what they can to bind the Leviathan. It is never enough. All government by its very nature is 'the principal vehicle of extensive and permanent evil to mankind' (PJ 479–80). In post expressly to 'check those excesses which threaten the general security' (PJ 481), governments drift inexorably into the superintendence of public opinion for which they are manifestly unfitted (PJ 481). Sheltering behind the objective of good order, government make their power into 'the means of subduing and undermining the virtues of its subjects' (PJ 464).

All governments drive their obedient subjects into the 'motionless inactivity and the basest cowardice' (PJ 481) of 'despicable slaves' (PJ 482). They impose their own prejudices. They blue-pencil original thought. They never listen and learn. Ideas and practices deviate increasingly from those that, through 'gradual revolution' (PJ 482), are the most favourable to the blossoming of communitarian anarchy. Command is pollution. It is not benevolent.

Constitutions are violated. Loopholes are found. No document can provide for every eventuality. Skewness, bias and irresponsibility are inseparable from state intervention: 'It is possible for the most odious injustice to be perpetuated by the best constituted legislature that ever was framed' (PJ 530). Later constitutionalists have called for specific clauses such as a gold standard, fixed exchange rate, money-supply ceiling, balanced-budget amendment or a statutory electoral period that would cap the *akrasia* and precommit the Leviathan. Godwin sees the multiplication of bulwarks as an exercise in futility. A minimal agenda would in the short run eliminate the temptations that try the officeholders' weakness of will. Licences cannot be sold if trade is free. Self-safeguarding anarchy would in the long run obviate the need for wheels within wheels. Automaticity would take on the job that no constitution can fulfil.

Aristotle identified three healthy constitutions. Each of the three was at risk of turning insidious and malign over time (Aristotle, 1981: para. 1283b). Godwin situated his politics within the framework of The Philosopher's tripartite schema: 'No form of government can be devised which does not partake of monarchy, aristocracy or democracy' (PJ 413). Although the framework was the same, still the social democrat expected it to be permanent. The anarchist saw it as no more than a short-run second best.

Godwin did not put any real faith in any one of Aristotle's ideal types. Aristotle's kingship of the wise, his aristocracy of talent and his twinning compromise that mixes the *demos* with the experts are eclipsed in Godwin's philosophy by Aristotle's perverse and aberrant sunspots (Reisman, 2024: 142–152). Each of the three cases is an inadequate stopgap. Each is an evil that drives pragmatic consequentialism ever further from the rule of reason. Half full versus half empty, it all depends on your point of view.

4.2 Monarchy and Aristocracy

The first constitutional order is monarchy. Multiperiod in the sense that the title is inherited and the bloodline continuous, still it is not excellence but birth that gives legitimacy to the throne. Aristotle had an open mind: while bad kings are always bad, good kings will be 'benevolent and philanthropic' (PJ 357), 'judicious and useful', imbued with 'a real and genuine conviction of truth' (PJ 339). Godwin did not cut good kings any slack. The monarch to Godwin is 'by unavoidable necessity, the enemy of the human race' (PJ 349). The proposition is general: 'Royalty inevitably allies itself to vice' (PJ 352).

Godwin does not confine his condemnation to the British monarch alone. All government discredits itself. Mono-archy is especially adept in calling itself into disrepute. Arrogant and indifferent, susceptible to 'false refinement' (PJ 345), inclined to extravagance, ostentation, appetite, amusement, 'sensuality and selfishness' (PJ 350), the monarch is 'exposed to a hundredfold more seductions than ordinary men' (PJ 349). He has no reason not to yield. 'Debauched from their birth' (PJ 352), over-indulged and self-centred, kings are taught that they have a right, sometimes even divine, to put their own happiness before the well-being of their subjects.

Kings 'subsist only under favour of error and oppression' (PJ 391). Justice, wisdom and truth are not needed where secrecy, violence and a direct line to the police is enough to protect the authority of a Caligula at once 'unacquainted' (PJ 357) with the situation of his people and 'unfriendly to their happiness' (PJ 352). Monarchy is always 'unnatural' (PJ 352). It makes benevolent despotism a theoretical impossibility.

Lacking information and perspective, even the absolutist is easily deceived by the 'adulation and servility' (PJ 349) of unscrupulous advisers and 'vindictive cabals' (PJ 358). Even an honest and incorruptible ruler will be considered a sitting target by ministers and administrators trading in 'specious and superficial observations' (PJ 359).

'Avaricious, hypocritical and interested' (PJ 356), the 'profligate' will vie with one another for 'private advantage' and to 'cut down new-fledged merit' (PJ 358). No sovereign can ever be vigilant enough to block the 'capricious measures and arbitrary infliction' (PJ 357) of his wily subordinates. Nor will he necessarily be sufficiently astute to screen out the cheats and the special pleaders: 'One weak or disingenuous man will be the source of unbounded mischief' (PJ 358).

Money talks: 'A statesman in place *cannot*, but in a very limited sense, be an honest man' (Fleetwood, 145, emphasis added). A speculative projector will employ 'deceit', 'dissimulation' and 'artifice' (PJ 362) because in the 'pecuniary polity' (PJ 365) that is what the 'voluntary prostitutes' (PJ 365) are obliged to do: 'Every man is supposed to have his price' (PJ 365). A bureaucrat on salary has a comparable incentive to cut back on work. An agent will never discharge his office in 'the same spirit, as if he were the principal' (PJ 357). In a monarchy, Godwin states, it is money more than the professional ethic that accounts for the policy mix.

The monarch himself, the richest man in the country, knows that he has a personal stake in wealth. His money buys him a life of luxury and idleness that is the polar opposite of investigation and integrity. Expense and ornament overwhelm. We 'honour a man whom…we ought to despise' (PJ 367). They also create a sense of injustice and resentment. Ordinary people see the contrast between 'scanty subsistence' in the street and 'ostentatious splendour' in the palace (PJ 352).

It is not a recipe for social cohesion. Extravagance is 'absurd' (PJ 356). Inherited tenure is 'an intolerable grievance' (PJ 386). 'Universal corruption' (PJ 363) undermines the allegiance. All men are equal. Ordinary people see it less and less in their interest to be 'driven like sheep' (PJ 364). Debunking the hyperbole and the veneration—'it is of no real use' (PJ 368)—they conclude that 'monarchy is founded in imposture….It tramples upon the genuine nature of things' (PJ 366). Monarchs have no intrinsic superiority. They are the 'adversaries of the true interests of mankind' (PJ 373). The alienation of the masses can in the limit erupt into armed insurrection. 1789 is just round the corner. It always is.

Monarchy is spies and troops: 'A king is necessarily, and almost unavoidably, a despot in his heart' (PJ 360). Big Brother is watching you: 'The eye of the tyrant is never closed' (PJ 364). It is the reign of terror in which Versailles sends to the guillotine all those who dare to oppose it. It is thought-control and Newspeak in which the masses are manipulated into 'torpid dullness, in which all the energies of man are forgotten' (PJ 364). Monarchy is 'the bane and grave of human virtue' (PJ 389). Sooner or later it will yield to something else.

Godwin's first ideal type is monarchy. His second constitution is aristocracy. It is not Aristotle's aristocracy of self-regulation, education and good intentions, of 'superlative talents and uncommon genius' (PJ 375), but rather Aristotle's oligarchy of wealth. Not one man but a small group of men will share the power and the spoils.

Aristocracy, like monarchy, 'is founded in falsehood' (PJ 404). It is 'foreign to the real nature of things' (PJ 404). As it is in monarchy, information is scarce, lobbies abound and privilege is handed on (PJ 179). An elite coterie corners for the ruling *politburo* the good things in life. It has no reason to seek out the truth. The particular outweighs the general. Economically and politically, the masses remain on the outside looking in. 'Wealth is the fatal blast that destroys the hopes of a future harvest' (PJ 396).

4.3 Democracy

Godwin's third and last constitution is democracy. It is a political order, representative or direct, in which 'national opinion' on 'eminent benefit' (PJ 529) sits on the throne: 'Government could not justly flow, in the first instance, but from the choice of the people' (PJ 527).

Government follows 'the voice of the nation' (PJ 461). It leads Godwin to predict that all government will ultimately exhaust its mandate. Public opinion in the long run will predictably vote *nem con* to shut Whitehall and the White House down. In the short run, however, public opinion will gravitate to the democratic state. Although not the best sovereign, public opinion will take it to be the best attainable: 'However erroneous that opinion may be, we can do no better' (PJ 458). It is not a strong endorsement.

4.3.1 The Consensus View

Democracy tracks the consensus view: 'No assembly, though chosen with the most unexampled solemnity, is competent to impose any regulations contrary to the public apprehension of right' (PJ 529). 'Public apprehension' rules. It is factored-down private apprehension scaled up to the whole.

In a democracy, one counts as one. No one ever counts for more: 'Every man is regarded as equal' (PJ 411). Officeholders, sensitive and self-abrogating, take care to match policies to attitudes: 'The competence of any government cannot be measured by a purer standard than the extent and accuracy of its information' (PJ 358). Knowledge is imperfect. What the democrats have at least they share: 'Frankness of communication takes off bitterness' (in KP II 270).

Democracy is not anarchy. Person and property are still protected top-down by law and order. The best system—'obvious and simple' if also 'inexpedient and impracticable'—would be 'for each man to be the arbiter of his own concerns' (PJ 356). That, however, is the future. The present is still the state. Democracy has the attraction that its policy is more likely than either monarchy or aristocracy to 'bear a resemblance…to the public sentiment' (PJ 363).

The ancient Athenians practiced direct democracy (PJ 413). Larger nations are forced to rely on representative assemblies. They must trust to subsets of 'individuals selected out of the mass by the voice of their fellows, and who will speedily return to a private station' (PJ 455). There is a risk. The delegates are equal in status. They are equal in blood. They are not, however, equal in what Robert Michels was to call the 'natural greed for power': 'The desire to dominate, for good or for evil, is universal. These are elementary psychological facts' (Michels, 1911 [1949]: 205, 206).

Machiavelli, Nietzsche, Pareto, Schumpeter, all recognised that the true price of *panem et circensenses* could be the iron law of oligarchy. Retaining the old name for show, democracy could slide into the Them of a domineering elite lording it over the Us of a silent and passive majority. Mosca saw it as the natural order: 'What Aristotle called a democracy was simply an aristocracy of fairly broad membership' (Mosca, 1896 [1939]: 52). Godwin knew that it could happen. It was an argument for anarchy. Once there is no longer a state, the politics of opportunism, bullying and malversation will disappear with it.

4.3.2 Oligarchs and Intellectuals

That, however, is the future. Real-world democracy falls short of the ideal type. Factions develop. Mutual aid gives way to disunity. In the end the Assembly becomes a thing apart. No longer prepared to rubber-stamp the 'sense of the people at large' (PJ 388), the political class proclaims a 'fictitious unanimity' (PJ 469) which it reifies into the composite judgement of a 'moral individual' (PJ 471) who does not and cannot exist: 'The pretence of collective wisdom is among the most palpable of all impostures. The acts of the society can never rise above the suggestions of this or that individual, who is a member of it' (PJ 472).

Politics in real-world democracy is red in tooth and claw. The 'spirit of party', 'personal character' and the 'political machine' (PJ 474) make the common man 'the dupe of knaves', the 'blind instrument' of 'quackery' on the part of 'the state juggler that would mislead him' (PJ 473). It is the economics of politics. Hegelian statesmen, Godwin reveals, are not Plato's philosopher-rulers but merely than self-interested merchants who look after themselves. The power-hungry manipulate opinion and mutilate the mind. Ordinary citizens become apathetic and indifferent because they have been informed on good authority that the leaders will provide.

Elections are 'gigantic' and 'unwieldly' (PJ 374). The popular vote frequently goes to 'persons of notorious imbecility' (PJ 375) rather than to candidates with their ear to the ground. The aspirant of genuine merit might be too self-effacing to be spotted in the crowd: 'Ability is not always intrusive' (PJ 384).

Politics is not dentistry: 'There is no satisfactory criterion marking out any man, or set of men, to preside over the rest' (PJ 165). There is no hereditary entitlement, university diploma or recertification by peer-review. Instead, there is election bottom-up by the stakeholders who are told repeatedly that their interests are the *suprema lex*. Bottom-up can go badly wrong. Democracy can be an open invitation to a would-be trickster imbued with 'artful sophistry' (PJ 412) de facto to stand the *suprema lex* on its head.

A gifted salesman might tout the present and not the future, luxury and not investment, spend-spend and not good husbandry. In the limit, calling democracy 'a monstrous and unwieldy vessel' (PJ 412), he might promise to stabilise the 'fits of occasional insanity' (PJ 455) by increasing the power of the executive relative to the parliament. He might press for a referendum to suspend regular re-election. Such a referendum would be the revealed preference of the people. Liberty would be non-liberty as a citizen's choice. It would be democracy put on public display. It would for all the semantics be a far cry from Aristotle's, from Godwin's ideal type.

The politicians lose touch with the street (PJ 568). Compulsion takes the place of consultation. It is Michels' oligarchy. It is democracy in name only. As extensive as the freedoms of the press and of assembly might be, they would not be enough to bend the state to the will of its masters. Anarchy would eliminate the noise on the line. Repressive tolerance, however, would be blocking the advance into something new. The age of politics need not be nearing its end.

Godwin never became active in party politics. He never attempted to force-feed the transition from within. Like Malthus, Adam Smith, Schumpeter and Galbraith, unlike Burke, Ricardo and Woodrow Wilson, he preferred to remain an intellectual observer on the sidelines who ferreted out the truth. As he wrote in 1820: 'I am a philosopher: that is, a person desirous to become wise. I do not mix in the business of the world' (in KP II 266).

The truth by itself is enough. It does not 'stand in need of support from any political ally' (PJ 415). What the committed intellectual should do is to assist in the removal of 'those restraints which prevent the human mind from attaining its genuine strength' (PJ 414). Blind submission, faith, fear, concealment, a lack of self-confidence above all—enlightened teachers negate the negation. Men of 'superior education and wisdom' (PJ 415), 'the most enlightened part of the nation', come to exercise superior influence on public opinion. De facto they will 'deliberate for the whole' (PJ 455). They will serve as the spokesmen for the truth. They will make sham democracy into real democracy: 'Democracy restores to a man a consciousness of his value' (PJ 414). And they will win.

Deep thinkers uncover the grail. It is an uphill struggle. The wise are outnumbered by the unwise. Philosophers are mistrusted because mind at variance with matter is so conspicuously a minority creed. Above-average high-flyers will encounter populist resistance at the very time that the orators, the demagogues and the downright pushy are mounting a rearguard action: 'All government corresponds, in a certain degree, to...a tyranny' (PJ 472). Godwin believes that democracy is more likely than either monarchy or aristocracy to provide a springboard for change. It will be an uphill struggle.

4.3.3 *Beer and Balderdash*

Godwin's democracy is about individuals. Each citizen is and must be 'inspired with a consciousness of his own importance' (PJ 166). Each stakeholder is and must be guaranteed 'a voice in the public concerns' (PJ 166). Yet Godwin's democracy is also about social location. Birds of a feather flock together. Citizens are segmented by salient signifiers when they enter actively into the maze of accountability and consultation. Most prominent among these in the new industrial order is their economic status and stake.

Marx saw the post-feudal polity as *ipso facto* 'a committee for managing the common affairs of the whole bourgeoisie' (Marx & Engels, 1848 [2011]: 66). Godwin was more inclined to think of the manufacturing and trading estate as decisively non-political. The up-and-coming and the self-made have a class interest in laws that repeal other laws. The businessman does not want special-interest legislation so much he wants the freedom to increase his net worth: 'He is a model of ignorance. He never reads, and knows nothing beyond the topic of the day....He rarely thinks of anything beyond himself' (PJ 319).

Yet money talks and laws are licences. The self-made new-rich in common with the old-rich landowners and rentiers are 'directly or indirectly the legislators of the state' (PJ 30). Godwin cites examples such as the game laws, the combination laws, the wage-ceilings, the execution of highwaymen, to prove his point. Taxes fall 'almost exclusively' on the unenfranchised working class (PJ 544). Public offices are farmed out for a fee. The concessions are cumulative. The modern state is the architect of future inequality even as it reflects the pecuniary skewness of past and present.

Land and capital have a stake in the laws. So does labour. Here Godwin comes straight to the point. Superior to a pig (PJ 321), 'happier than a stone' (PJ 319), the farmworker or the factory operative is not in a good position to think things out. 'The range of his ideas is scanty' (PJ 319). His vacillating inconstancy is 'the reverse of political justice' (PJ 412). Plagued with 'infantine ignorance' (PJ 196), 'at the mercy of every momentary impulse' (PJ 412), frequently paralysed by illiteracy, the *hoi polloi* will only be parroting what they have been taught: 'They swallow it whole' (Essays, 286). The common people could barely be more common: 'What is it they desire? They know not....What they profess to desire is little better than what they hate' (PJ 196).

'Beer and balderdash' is all that they know. Aristotle, Adam Smith, Burke, Carlyle, the Webbs, all had serious doubts about the man in the street. Democracy is majority rule. The majority, however, is still in the process of becoming fully itself. It will fail to see and defend its stake in the laws. 1789 is the *Mahnmal* to the 'tyranny of a multitude drunk with unlimited power' (PJ 473). Mob rule is mob without rule. It all adds up to this: 'The groveling views of the great mass of mankind' (in Kegan Paul II 195) must not be allowed to lie where they fall.

The ordinary man cannot be trusted to make democracy fully representative of all interests and opinions. One man, one vote, Godwin declared in 1820, was 'pain to my heart': 'I can anticipate the most disastrous effects....England is not yet ripe for universal suffrage' (in KP II 265). The prescription would be 'too strong for the English nation' (in KP II 265). Political thinking cannot be left to the valets and the chambermaids: 'I am in principle a Republican, but in practice a Whig' (in KP II 266).

The ideal type is clearly defined. Democracy is the 'general voice' (PJ 168) in support of the 'general good' (PJ 169) and the 'common benefit' (PJ 172). Government by the people, of the people, for the people, the mandate in a democracy will 'be vested in the community' (PJ 171). That, however, is precisely the bottleneck and the bind. *Vox populi* can never be *vox dei* so long as the 'misguided millions' (PJ 169) come to the forum with nothing but a barbarian's *ba-ba* to share.

The groundswell is no swell at all. Public opinion is beer and balderdash. Majority rule has no answer to that: 'Truth cannot be made more true by the number of its votaries' (PJ 168–9). The millions do not know what they want. Evolution is on the side of the masses. Yet we start from here. The masses are unlikely to vote for the truth if they do not know what it is.

The feudal, the mercantile and the common are not likely to make Aristotle's democracy work. The moderate middle classes, educated and alert, are a better bet. They are, Hume believed, the social constituency that would most dependably stand up for the constitution: 'That middling rank of men...are the best and firmest basis of public liberty' (Hume, 1752 [1804]: I 295). Malthus, styling himself 'A Friend of the Constitution', called the 'middle regions of society' (FE 207) the 'only hope that Great Britain has' (in James, 1979: 51). Buying books, reading newspapers, conversing in coffee-house and at the Exchange, they were the 'best suited to intellectual improvement' (FE 207).

The future, Malthus said, is heavily invested in an increase in 'the proportion of the middle classes, that body on which the liberty, public spirit, and good government of every country must mainly depend' (OCL 101). Landowners, capitalists and workers are too close to economic life to see things clearly. The impartial 'middle classes', second sons of second sons in banking, education, journalism, the Church and the law, had a more general overview. It was they, Malthus believed, who could better be trusted to save the day.

Godwin had been there before. The pensive and the evidence-based have the knowledge and the inclination to move their nation ever closer to the truth. A little philosophy goes a long way. A 'man of a liberal and enlarged mind' (PJ 319), a 'man of taste and liberal accomplishments' (PJ 320), a level-headed professional able to tap into 'new senses, and a new range of enjoyment' (PJ 320) is by definition a better judge than a man who thinks only of pay and perks, profits and dividends, beer and balderdash.

In democracy as it is presently constituted, all men are not of equal worth. Some are fundamentally incapable of going beyond 'the selfish passions' (PJ 314). Others are positioned to enjoy 'a more refined and genuine happiness' (PJ 103). It is the thinkers, 'God's nobility' (Mandeville, 1817 [1992]: 89), and not the doers who must serve as the opinion-leaders. It is they who must wean the passive majority away 'from contemplating their own benefit in all that they do' (PJ 314).

Thinkers know best. The thinking estate, whether the moderate centre or the brotherhood of intellectuals, is not invariably a perfect go-to. 'Study is cold' (PJ 321) where it is not accompanied by benevolence. On balance, however, the philosophically inclined are the most likely to develop the moral muscles that will turn loose the upward drift: 'The man who has once performed an act of exalted generosity knows that there is no sensation of corporeal or intellectual taste to be compared with this' (PJ 321).

He rises above 'barter and exchange' (PJ 321). He 'ascends to the highest of human pleasures, the pleasures of disinterestedness' (PJ 321). Democracy works best where the thinking estate provides the countervailing power and enjoys the cross-class influence that it deserves. Starting from here, the far-seeing have the social function of restoring each of us to ancient Athens where every political animal was able to make his own consent informed.

4.4 The Protective State

There is the agreement. Tacit or explicit, people form communities and live by the code. There is the state: monarchy, aristocracy, democracy, the constitution imposes the apparatus until anarchy obviates the supra-social constraint. There is also the agenda. Our government is here to fulfil specific functions. Without that social shortfall, there would be no need for a state: 'The true and only adequate apology of government is necessity' (PJ 166).

Malthus confirmed to Godwin that they shared a resistance to 'the interference of Government which I know you would reprobate as well as myself' (in KP I 323). Adam Smith had assigned to the sovereign, 'all systems either of preference or of restraint...being thus completely taken away', the three residual duties of justice, defence and the correction of private underprovision through public works (WN II 208–9). Malthus and Godwin recognised that Smith's open-ended checklist was incompatible with the philosophical ideal of a minimal state. In the long run, Godwin said, top-down authority would become extinct. As for the short run, the sole function of the state would be to protect the scaled-up against the tyranny of the factored-down: 'My only justifiable ground of obedience is that I will not disturb the repose of the community' (PJ 174).

It is exclusively a matter of civil war and world peace: 'Governments can have no more than two legitimate purposes, the suppression of injustice against individuals within the community, and the common defence against external invasion' (PJ 466). Malthus left the door open for some at least of Smith's social works and public services. Godwin did not. Beyond the state's 'two legitimate purposes', the expectation must be that we will be left alone.

4.4.1 'A Formidable Enemy'

Homo homini lupus. 'Man is of all other beings the most formidable enemy to man' (PJ 21). He is willy nilly 'the ready tool of injustice, cruelty and profligacy' (PJ 178). He is an animal that like any other animal 'preys upon his fellows': 'We cannot move our foot without becoming the means of destruction' (PJ 326). We are seriously 'imperfect' (PJ 193). We are not very nice.

We are nasty, brutish and short. The cramping and the warping do not arise 'out of the nature of man, but out of the institutions by which he has been corrupted. Man is not originally vicious' (PJ 475). A social fact rather than an innate propensity, wickedness is only marginally in the essence, overwhelmingly in the life-course. Better institutions would make men 'reasonable and virtuous': 'No evils would arise...where the empire of reason was so universally acknowledged' (PJ 475). With reason would come perfectibility. With perfectibility would come the 'utter annihilation', the 'dissolution of political government' (PJ 473). The protective state would rot down. There would be no need to contain vices that had long since disappeared into the history books.

The future is acephalous. The present is the veil of tears: 'At present we have to do, not with nations of philosophers, but with nations of men whose virtues are alloyed with weakness, fluctuation and inconstancy' (PJ

585). Our social psychology in the real, existing real world does not inspire confidence: 'The human species is at present infected with a thousand vices, the offspring of established injustice' (PJ 581).

Men in the fallen present day 'meet together with the temper less of friends than enemies': 'Every member of a polished and civilized community goes armed' (PJ 247). Our conduct is the envelope of the 'factitious appetites and perverse habits' that make human beings 'headstrong in evil, inveterate in selfishness, without sympathy and forbearance for the welfare of others. In time they may become accommodated to the lessons of reason, but at present they would be found deaf to her mandates, and eager to commit every species of injustice' (PJ 581–2).

Our body politick is beset with 'every species of injustice'. The only solution is the police state: 'The ill propensities of mankind' preclude 'the abolition of coercion' (PJ 583). The disease is writ in unashamed shoplifting, Ponzi duplicity and bare-knuckle despoiliation. It is widespread but there is a cure. Not inborn nature but external conditions have made the bad man what he is: 'The assassin cannot help the murder he commits, any more than the dagger' (PJ 557). It is not his fault. Most of all it is poverty that makes him a thief. It is his soul-destroying work-function that makes him run amok.

A civilised community should be tough on crime but tough on the causes of crime. Beccaria and Howard called for prison reform because the exponential alienation of the offender trapped in the system would only escalate 'those practices to which the disease owes its most alarming symptoms' (PJ 583). Coercion, Godwin said, is itself a noxious evil, to be used 'as sparingly as possible' (PJ 480). The opposing view was that a 'strong hand' (PJ 588) was necessary to curb deviancy. It was the logic behind the 1834 Poor Law, the workhouse test and the hard line that many traced back to Malthus.

4.4.2 The Nations Fight

Aggression is a threat world-wide just as it is at home. In the quasi-Hobbesian arena of childlike tribalism the forcible redistribution of scarce endowments is a fact of life. The discrete polities become corrupted by 'an inextinguishable rage for augmenting their dominions' (PJ 584). The nations, befuddled by 'the pernicious notion of an extensive territory' (PJ 582), go to war because if I have it, then you do not.

It is Nietzsche on the *Wille zur Macht*. It is *Saint George for England*, *Rule Britannia* and *God Save the King*. Blood and soil are the true cause of 'the dreams of glory, empire and national greatness, which have hitherto proved the bane of the human species, without producing entire benefit and happiness to a single individual' (PJ 582). A non-rational *folie à plusieurs* is instilling in the flag-waving xenophobes of 'my country right or wrong' a minus-sum mindset. It is converting the ploughshares into swords first and foremost because an Englishman reacts badly to 'a supposed insult' (PJ 433) from an outsider unable to control his 'tyrannical jealousy' (PJ 435).

Conquest is discretionary. Defence is survival. The unanimity of consensus will be especially strong where our homeland itself is at risk of invasion: 'No people were ever conquered at their own doors' (PJ 441). The foreigner challenging our home and hearth does not stand a chance against our citizen militia: 'Upon our own ground his match is unequal' (PJ 463).

Wars can result from 'the most trivial causes' (PJ 433). The defence of the heartland will never be trivial. Economic use-value is of less importance. Misguided protectionists and gung-ho imperialists treat need-satisfaction as unlimited when the truth is that the material wants gravitate over time to satiety: 'No man can cultivate more than a certain portion of land' (PJ 430). Over time, as the gross national product advances to its flat-of-the-curve, no country will be driven into cross-border seizure, transfer and belligerency to relieve avoidable deprivation at home.

Conspicuous wealth is a tempting target both for non-rational hoarders and for the military that welcomes any excuse for a scrap: 'War, in all its aggravations, is the growth of unequal property' (PJ 653). Mercantilists, calling for sectional privilege, bounties, tariffs and monopolies, are especially favourable to snatch-and-grab economics. Godwin, like Smith and Ricardo, felt they had not understood the strong case for the gains from trade. Exports and imports would be a more effective way to raise living standards than would either beggar-thy-neighbour one-sidedness or an outright shooting war: 'Riches can only be created by commerce; and the greater is our neighbour's capacity to buy, the greater will be our opportunity to sell. The prosperity of all is the interest of all' (PJ 463).

Vestigial mercantilists were still in favour of foreign colonies. Godwin, writing not long after the Battle of Plessey in 1767, informed the East India Company and its acolyte special pleaders that any attempt to opt out of global free trade would be a 'fruitful source of war' (PJ 445). Rather than closing the doors, Godwin said, it would be better 'to throw open the ports of our colonies to all the world' (PJ 445). The locals would benefit: 'No people were ever either wise or happy who were not left to the fair development of their inherent powers' (PJ 444). The rest of the world would benefit as well. The commutation of superfluities would raise all nations, European and tropical alike, to a higher level of material prosperity.

Wealth is successfully grown through commerce and peace. Wars which destroy, waste and reallocate are not in the long-run best interest of any of the contenders. Mercantilists and generals are myopic. Their call to arms is not only trivial but self-defeating. Smith's absolute advantage in 1776, Ricardo's comparative advantage in 1817, supply the economic logic for Kant's *Perpetual Peace* in 1795 that in 1815 ushered in a century of accommodation and growth. Ignorance is not bliss (PJ 432). Using 'general reason' (PJ 434), late mercantilists like Davenant and Child were moving towards the liberal position that all nations through trade can move forward together.

War will be displaced by interest, nationalism by gain. Patriotism, a 'deceitful principle' (PJ 432), will go the way of all the 'specious illusions' (PJ 431) that a money-minded, power-hungry minority employs to cozen the masses into *Blut und Boden* and blinkered nativism. Loyalty will be to justice and not to race, sect, culture or tribe. A new citizenship of the world will emerge. 'Offensive war will be extirpated' (PJ 430). War gives most people less. Peace gives most people more.

Free trade is favourable to perpetual peace. The protective state should keep open the channels and ensure a level playing field. Beyond that, it should entrust to anarchic automaticity the determination of quantity, quality and price. Laissez-faire: 'Commerce never flourishes so much as when it is delivered from the guardianship of legislators and ministers' (PJ 485). Intervention and regulation create vested interest. It is all for nothing. 'The rivalship of nations is a creature of the imagination' (PJ 463). Conflict is 'an unintelligible chimera' (PJ 463). 'Mankind are brethren' (PJ 462). Free trade will seal the deal.

In the short-run free trade and in long-run anarchy, Godwin concluded that in stateless economics one hand will successfully wash the other: 'The more accurately we understand our own advantage, the less shall we be disposed to disturb the peace of our neighbour. The same principle is applicable to him in return....Wisdom is the growth of equality and independence, not of injury and oppression' (PJ 463). Alliances, blocs and leagues of nations will no longer have any function: 'The whole human species would constitute, in some sense, one great republic' (PJ 465). It will be market and not state. It will be peace and not war. The nations will not fight.

4.5 The Rule of Law

The function of the state is to defend the citizen against the force and fraud of 'domestic or foreign invaders' (PJ 17): 'Government is a contrivance instituted for the security of individuals' (PJ 165). That is its only function. All other functions can safely be left to private individuals pursuing utility-seeking initiatives of their own.

Individuals interfacing with the lawmakers and the enforcers accept some coercion in the expectation that the gain will be greater than the loss: 'Men at present live under any particular form because they conceive it their interest to do so' (PJ 117). Each man in society knows that his 'sphere of discretion' will of necessity be 'limited by the co-ordinate sphere of his neighbour' (PJ 167). Ego's fist must keep clear of Alter's nose. Most frequently the neighbours will be able to settle their differences on their own. Sometimes the distance will be too great without laws and lawcourts able to adjudicate the dispute: 'The maintenance of this limitation…is the first business of government' (PJ 167).

The first. The last. Anarchy does not emerge fully formed from its chrysalis. Statelessness evolves from status quo regularities, pre-existent expectations and third-party enforcement. We start from here. Future advantages 'cannot be effectually procured if we be inattentive to the present security' (PJ 584).

Most of our people most of the time are on the side of the law. Outside control presupposes a threshold measure of de facto consent. There must be a strong consensus that each citizen has had 'some share', implicit or formal, 'in the selection of its measures' (PJ 165). Not abstaining, not revolting, not emigrating, each player is revealing his overall acceptance of 'that which the nature of things has already decreed' (PJ 170). Jack fits in. Jill conforms. Man-made constraint is the insurance they buy to defend themselves one against the other.

The law glues down the loose ends. In doing so, however, it reconvenes the constitutional convention. *Quid custodiet custodes* was not resolved for all time when the rule-making rules were first adopted. Office holders have a personal incentive to twist the constitution into their own narrow shop. Their 'watchful and intolerant jealousy' (PJ 81) is at variance with the *raison d'être* of the protective state. The laws that they propose should be approached by the public 'with great caution and unwillingness' (PJ 460). Anything other than the minimum bid should be regarded as ultra vires.

Some observers discount the likelihood that the apprentice will turn against the sorcerer. Subsuming the partial in the general, they argue that the third party exists wholly for 'the safety of the community' (PJ 597). Its rights and duties are strictly delimited by the mandate 'which society exercises in its corporate capacity' (PJ 571). Godwin is less optimistic about the tail that wags the dog. Ordinary people are even now seeing through the work-arounds and the half-truths: 'There is no state of mankind that renders them incapable of the exercise of reason' (PJ 85). The great majority are fully aware that 'the real enemies of liberty' are 'those higher orders who find their imaginary profit in a contrary system' (PJ 85). The Establishment is corseting the constitution into its own private game. Monarchy, aristocracy, democracy itself, absolute power corrupts and even the bias becomes skewed.

Law is the new despotism. Godwin is not taken in by the rhetoric. The lawmakers are an interested minority with an estate identity of their own: 'The rich and titled members of the community, proud of their fancied eminence, behold, with total unconcern, the destruction of the destitute and the wretched' (PJ 595). There are more lawbreakers because there are more laws. There are more laws because there is more property: 'The more there is in any country of inequality and oppression, the more punishments are multiplied' (PJ 595).

The law is an ass. The government is an ass. 'Grand moral evils' (PJ 19) can result where the public interest is being 'sacrificed at the shrine of positive law and political institution' (PJ 25). Warlords like Alexander the Great and Julius Caesar had demonstrated that irresponsible edict 'lays nations waste, and thins the population of the world' (PJ 21). World-historical mouldbreakers never kowtow to rule-making rules that perpetually kowtow to great kings. What Godwin is saying is that even an agreed-upon constitution is not enough to protect the people against anti-social legislation that violates the spirit but not the letter of the multiperiod constraint. Malthus on propagation and privation will not be put to rest. Unjust laws propagated by unjust lawmakers will do nothing for equity and equality.

Godwin proclaims it 'an institution of the most pernicious tendency' (PJ 609) when incumbents pass laws that benefit no more than their own narrow clique. There are laws which circumscribe the freedom of speech. Presumptive sedition threatens traditional privilege. There are laws which curtail path-breaking innovation. Novelty of any kind is always Pandora's Box. All laws by their very nature tend 'to fix the human mind in a stagnant condition' (PJ 609). They tend 'to substitute a principle of permanence in the room of...unceasing progress' (PJ 609). Argument is release. Citizens think for themselves. Decree is repression. It 'annihilates the understanding' (PJ 563). Countries where there is a surfeit of laws make their citizens into 'mere phantoms of men' (PJ 139).

Laws do not treat like as like. Since 'no two crimes were ever alike', it would be an 'absurdity' and an 'inequity' Procrustes-like to categorise the disparate as if they were the same (PJ 573). Intention and motive are impossible to document. Evidence is ambiguous and incomplete. Official Secrets Acts bury vital parameters. As for the outcomes, reformation is thin on the ground: 'The proper object of political superintendence is not the past, but the future' (PJ 603). The proper object is to discourage reoffending. The more likely outcome is for the offender to take care not to be caught.

State aggression does not persuade and convert. Hardened criminals will treat state violence as just another contender in the ongoing tug-of-war for control: 'Oppression stimulates them to mischief and piracy' (PJ 588). If His Lordship can commit murder, then so can Bill Sykes. 'Coercion cannot convince' (PJ 568). 'All coercion sours the mind' (PJ 569). Every ruffian is thoroughly sour. Macheath was gay about everything but coercion: 'Since Laws were made for ev'ry degree/I wonder we hadn't better Company/Upon Tyburn Tree' (Gay, 1728 [1983]: II 61).

'Mountains of parchment' (PJ 613) perpetuate ignorance. Laws are 'a cloak for oppression' (PJ 613). The assemblies and the courts, the policemen and the prisons, do not speak for the nation as a whole: 'A lawyer can scarcely fail to be a dishonest man' (PJ 609). Protection is essential. A protective state is not. In the short run, and 'as a temporary expedient' (PJ 581), the rule of law must be slimmed down to the protective function that neutralises the threat from 'men as we now find them' (PJ 581). It will not be for all time. In the long run even the rule of law must pass the sceptre to a better and more lasting order.

4.6 Rules Without Rulers

Visiting Nowhere, William Morris was told that truth, tolerance and benevolence had taken the place of the Commons and the Lords: 'We are very well off as to politics—because we have none….The whole people is our parliament' (Morris, 1890 [1993]: 107, 116). Automaticity, homeostasis and 'spontaneous justice' (PJ 613) had succeeded to the artificial constraint of Sir who said he knew best. He did not know best. The laws were gone. The constitution was gone. Rules without rulers had become the norm. Nowhere was an-archy. It had negated the negation.

Hobbes believed that the *bellum* was the default equilibrium. Godwin replied that evidence-based discrimination was the more natural order: 'Reason is a thousand times more explicit and intelligible than law' (PJ 619). Innate essence pales into insignificance compared with mutable circumstance: 'Nothing can be more unreasonable than to argue from men as we now find them to men as they may hereafter be made' (PJ 414). Progress is taking its course.

Godwin predicted that, 'as men advance in improvement' (PJ 461), so any tendency to dislocation and caprice would be competed away by the superior happiness that accrues to integration, interdependence and moral suasion. Life in common exposes the team-player to the sanctions of the real and the impartial spectator. He learns from experience, and 'without the teaching of law' (PJ 539), that theft, violence and dishonesty are narrow-minded and counterproductive. Not self-interested but self-denying, they deplete the felt well-being of an articulated whole.

The truth is strong. 'The principles of reason' (PJ 583) will succeed where the laws and the punishments will fail: 'Legislation…is not an affair of human competence. Immutable reason is the true legislator' (PJ 170). State-less anarchy is the unstoppable result of the law of gravity and the invisible hand. If individuals are 'imbued with a love of freedom' (PJ 197), if they are endowed with 'a tranquil and dispassionate temper' (PJ 205), if 'the system of independence and equality be the truth' (PJ 196), if the national culture assigns a high priority to 'security and permanence' (PJ 205), it follows from the logic of Godwin's four 'ifs' that the Nowhere of self-stabilising reason 'may be expected hourly to gain converts' (PJ 196).

Godwin is using 'if' as a synonym for 'since'. He is treating a value judgement as a strong axiom. He is conflating his *is* with his *ought-to-be* to an extent that makes him more nearly a moral philosopher than a positive scientist. Godwin himself would, however, not have accepted that his fact-gathering was selective and his predictions all but prescription. Godwin was convinced that 'freedom', 'tranquillity', 'independence', 'equality', 'security' and 'permanence' appeal so strongly to reason that no further proof of their integrity was required. Ethics is 'stronger than a host of foes' (PJ 441). Men are 'eminently capable of justice and virtue' (PJ 463). To Godwin at least the truth was unambiguously happy-end.

Godwin by temperament is an Enlightenment optimist. Rational assessment is coming in. Unthinking spontaneity is going out. It is a multiplier process in which contemplation holds the winning hand: 'Make men wise, and by that very operation you make them free....No usurped power can stand against the artillery of opinion' (PJ 198). The advancement of science, *by that very operation*, closes the door to myth and delusion. The blood donors and the intellectuals are every hour gaining converts. The street thugs and the margin traders are being relegated to the Dark Ages where only the fringe, the quaint and the eccentric will feel at home. The process is unstoppable. There will never be an upper turning point.

The truth comes first: 'Nothing can be improved but in conformity to its nature' (PJ 611). The thinking citizen, rejecting any truth-denying edict that compels a dog to be a cat, filters the natural order through the medium of conscious choice: 'Man is the ornament of the universe only in proportion as he consults his judgment' (PJ 178). No man will sign off on a rule unless he believes it to be 'coincident with his private judgment' (PJ 181). Scaling up from the one to the many, no rule will ever be validated bottom up if it 'contradicts the propensities and spirit of the nation' (PJ 483). Where, however, the citizens, increasingly 'enlightened and virtuous' (PJ 181), agree that the rule is just, they will give it their stamp of approval. Public opinion will take over from the man-made artificialities of the protective state. It will mean 'the gradual extinction of law' (PJ 533).

The process of de-legalisation is self-reinforcing. As individuals gain in self-confidence, they will be freeing themselves from their childlike dependence on a God, a *Führer* or a Parliament that takes over from them the labour of thought: 'Men are weak at present, because they have always been told they are weak, and must not be trusted with themselves. Take them out of their shackles, bid them enquire, reason and judge, and you will soon find them very different beings' (PJ 613). Thinking makes them different beings. They go to bed a swarm. They wake up individuals, free-standing and self-aware.

The individual grows into himself. His society, inevitably, does so as well. Individual-ism is not the polar opposite of social-ism but rather the precondition for echo-chamber magnification. I respect you. You respect me. I help you. You help me. True independence engenders a common culture without the need for statist social engineering: 'Human beings are partakers of a common nature; what conduces to the benefit or pleasure of one man will conduce to the benefit or pleasure of another' (PJ 625).

Perfectibility comes with practice. People who 'cultivate a more frequent and cultivated intercourse' are better placed to share each other's moral sentiments (PJ 464). Interaction has the capacity is 'to draw men nearer to each other, not to separate them' (PJ 464). Herbert Spencer, paraphrasing Mackintosh on the unwritten constitution, says that 'society is a growth and not a manufacture' (Spencer, 1891: I 269). Evolution will do what revolution cannot. It will generate a state of affairs in which the government and its laws will no longer have any role to play in the 'political improvement of mankind' (PJ 209). Force, a vestigial organ like the appendix, will fade away. Its historic function will fall to thee and me: 'Each man should be wise enough to govern himself, without the intervention of any compulsory restraint' (PJ 187).

'Government, even in its best state, is an evil' (PJ 187). Warm-blooded comrades, never costing their benefits, will have no need of the state to keep the peace: 'The love of our neighbour is the great ornament of a moral nature; the perception of truth is the most solid improvement of an intellectual nature. He that sees nothing in the universe deserving of regard but himself, is a consummate stranger to the dictates of general and impartial reason' (PJ 542–3). Love is on board at last. Even for a being of an 'intellectual nature', the exercise of reason will have to be leavened by sentiment and passion.

The non-rational as well as the rational is the cause and effect of the self-governed society. A suicide bomber does not demand a danger differential: 'If a thousand men are to be benefited, I ought to recollect that I am only an atom in the comparison' (PJ 543). A public servant driven by 'zeal' (PJ 547) does not expect a merit bonus. Honours are permissible. Money is not. Altruists who volunteer at a charity clinic would withdraw their labour if their service ethic were to be debased. Nowhere, like Utopia, is the land of feel-good. Non-rational or rational, one thing is clear. We do not need the state.

4.7 Mind and Matter

Marx and Engels made perceptions and paradigms the '*historical and transitory products*' (Marx, 1847 [1976]: 166, emphasis in original) of an economic system driven by class: 'The ruling ideas are nothing more than the ideal expression of the dominant material relations' (Marx & Engels, 1845–1846 [1976]: 59). The ruling laws are the practical embodiment of the wealth and power. As we act, so we think.

Godwin reversed the chicken and the egg: 'The voluntary actions of men originate in their opinions' (PJ 209). The evidence is persuasive: 'Reflection and enquiry must have gone before' (PJ 588). The thought precedes the deed. Ideas are the 'operative principle of action' (PJ 487). As we think, so we act.

Godwin made thought the senior partner: 'The extravagant sallies of mind are the prelude of the highest wisdom' (PJ 499). It is 'impossible' (PJ 209) that a man will turn to crime or a free rider default if he understands the ramifications of his choice. Rules without rulers are many times more 'conducive to the welfare of the whole' (PJ 100) than toffee noses dressed up as laws. Events are powered by ideas: 'The supreme power in a state ought not, in the strictest sense, to require anything of its members that an understanding sufficiently enlightened would not prescribe without such interference' (PJ 100).

Marx looks to the momentum inherent in matter to make history happen. Godwin turns to 'an understanding sufficiently enlightened' to think its way out of the box. Malthus, objecting to the 'old mode of philosophising' that made 'facts bend to systems', had little patience with 'wild and eccentric hypotheses' (FE 126) such as those of Descartes. In the beginning it had been the deed and not the word, not disembodied conjecture but the 'book of nature', that provided the unbreakable link between matter and mind. As it was then, so it is now. Malthus is likely to have seen Godwin as the creature of the *cogito*. Godwin to him was a modern monastic too often afraid to stray from the godsend of his a priori.

Godwin as a philosophical idealist was convinced that, as we think, so we act. What critics like Malthus failed to see is that Godwin situated the mind not in an intellectual vacuum but in the restless disequilibration of material circumstance. God, dwelling outside the specificity of time and place, had first-mover advantage when he trusted to his reason to conjure up the best-possible design. Man in situation no longer has that freedom. The 'vicious habits of a corrupt society' (PJ 601) have levied a toll. The clay has been moulded. The track is not ab initio. Philosopher or commoner, we today have no choice but to think from here.

It is the tyranny of the status quo. We know what we see. We see what we are accustomed to see. Matter is in place. Philosophers are wise enough to question the legitimacy of the *fait accompli*. Even so, mind is not in a position to depose an existing nexus at the stroke of a pen. Matter has unequal wealth and the rule-making rulers on its side. To rob a bank is illegal. To found a bank is subsidised. The majority of our people do not even know that something is amiss. 'Unforced concurrence' (PJ 182) has them by the throat.

Conventions and statutes are the product not of single-valued truth but of property and factor-reward. The laws are 'relative to the exercise of political force' (PJ 615). It is matter and not mind that gives the Pitts and the Grenvilles the opportunity to impose their dominance on the community as a whole. The message is clear. Man-made laws 'must perish when the necessity for that force ceases' (PJ 615). They will not, however, perish so long as a biased and unnatural economic basis survives.

The old-rich landowners and the new-rich capitalists are in possession of assets 'entitling one man to dispose of the produce of another's industry' (PJ 544). The aristocrats and the businessmen fulfil no useful economic function: 'Both these classes, in the form in which they now appear, might, under a different mode of society, be dispensed with' (PJ 544). Rents and profits are 'iniquity' (PJ 544). Yet they are here. Money talks. Politics listens. In present-day conditions, the privileged are able to impose their done thing and their normative constraint on the rest of us. Our consensus is their consensus. Our government is their executive committee. The tail is wagging the dog.

Low pay, glaring inequalities and exhausting toil might generate the perception that the workers are badly treated. In that way the basis might be producing a superstructure that will be incompatible with the survival of the existing order. Matter might be the cause of a new and more rational state of mind.

Marx felt that it was material failure that would trigger the new 1789. Godwin looked not so much to failure as to success for the unwinding of the existing economic order. Food, clothing and shelter are the necessary condition if our people are to have time for contemplation and sociability. A people 'must…have arrived at some degree of leisure and prosperity, before the love of letters can take root among them' (PJ 394). The growth in the gross national product is the precondition for the growth in the gross national truth. Only after Beveridge's giant evils have been rooted out through material progress will ordinary people become aware that there is a better economic order beyond the unsatisfying nine-to-five.

Mind arrives *post festum*. It gets there in the end. Liberal capitalists demand an unwinding of true-blue repression: permissive licence better favours their narrow material interest. The bees in Mandeville's *Fable* are 'instruments of providence' (PJ 313): they demonstrate the success of natural anarchy. The new economic basis has an unintended outcome. 'Liberty and justice…awakens thought' (PJ 432, 587). It 'diffuses energy and enterprise through the community' (PJ 587). 'Thought', 'energy' and 'enterprise' will make all of us, and not just some of us, leisured, happy and wise. They give ordinary people the freedom to think. Prosperity and markets in the sense of Smith even more than deprivation and alienation in the sense of Marx are the invisible hand. They make anarchy inevitable.

The owl of Minerva flies at dusk: 'The progressive nature…of the human mind' is 'unquestionable' (PJ 490). It is a two-way process. Matter causes mind which causes matter. Godwin felt that it was mind and not matter that would be the senior partner. One way or another, the truth would make its way into public view. It might not be so.

Market capitalism takes as its success indicators not the libraries and laboratories of the non-acquisitive society so much as the airconditioned cinemas, the indoor bathrooms and the whirlwind fashions of exponential growth. Mind might vote against Godwin's flat-of-the-curve and in favour of sustained progress in affluence. With a stronger moral consensus and weaker state control, anarcho-capitalists might contend that utopia is a good place to do business.

Malthusians at the same time would be warning that levelling up in Godwin's idyllic anarchism would disappear into population and poverty, misery and vice. Deprivation would go up. Lawlessness and Leviathan would come back. Godwin put his faith in the truth. Better people, wiser people would never let knowledge gained slip backward into the dark. Ordinary people *want* to be philosophers. It is the guarantee that mind will for all time keep anything but the best-case scenario out.

References

By W. Godwin

Godwin, W. (1798 [1976]). *Enquiry Concerning Political Justice* (abbreviated as PJ). Penguin Books.

Godwin, W. (1805 [1992]). *Fleetwood, or the New Man or Feeling* (abbreviated as Fleetwood), in *Collected Novels and Memoirs of William Godwin* (Vol. 5). William Pickering.

Godwin, W. (1817 [1992]). *Mandeville: A Tale of the Seventeenth Century in England* (abbreviated as Mandeville), in *Collected Novels and Memoirs of William Godwin* (Vol. 4). William Pickering.

Godwin, W. (1873). *Essays: Never Before Published* (abbreviated as Essays). Henry S. King.

By T.R. Malthus

Malthus, T. R. (1798 [1970]). *Essay on the Principle of Population, as it affects the Future Improvement of Society, with Remarks on the Speculations of Mr. Godwin, M. Condorcet, and Other Writers* (abbreviated as FE). Penguin.

Malthus, T. R. (1814 [1986]). *Observations on the Effects of the Corn Laws, and of a Rise or Fall in the Price of Corn on the Agriculture and General Wealth of the Country* (abbreviated as OCL), reprinted in *The Works of Thomas Robert Malthus* (Vol. 7, pp. 87–109). Pickering and Chatto.

By Other Authors

Aristotle. (1981). *The Politics*. Penguin Books.

Gay, J. (1728 [1983]). *The Beggar's Opera*, in his *Dramatic Works* (Vol. II, pp. 1–65). Clarendon Press.

Hume, D. (1752 [1804]). *Essays and Treatises on Several Subjects* (2 Vols.). Bell and Bradfute.

Kegan Paul, C. (1876). *William Godwin: His Friends and Contemporaries* (abbreviated as KP) (2 Vols.). Henry S. King.

Marx, K. (1847 [1976]). *The Poverty of Philosophy*, in *Karl Marx and Friedrich Engels: Collected Works* (Vol. 6, pp. 105–212). Lawrence & Wishart.

Marx, K., & Engels, F. (1845–1846 [1976]). *The German Ideology*, in *Karl Marx and Friedrich Engels: Collected Works* (Vol. 5, pp. 19–540). Lawrence & Wishart.

Marx, K., & Engels, F. (1848 [2011]). *The Communist Manifesto*. Penguin Books.

Michels, R. (1911 [1949]). *Political Parties: A Sociological Study of the Oligarchical Tendencies of Modern Democracy* (E. and C. Paul, Trans.). The Free Press.

Montesquieu, C.-L. de Secondat (1748 [1949]). *The Spirit of the Laws* (T. Nugent, Trans.). Hafner Press.

Morris, W. (1890 [1993]). *News from Nowhere*, in *News from Nowhere and Other Writings* (pp. 41–228). Penguin Books.

Mosca, C. (1896 [1939]). *The Ruling Class* (H. D. Kahn, Trans.). McGraw-Hill.

Paine, T. (1776 [2000]). *Common Sense*. In T. Benn (Ed.), *Common Sense and The Rights of Man* (pp. 1–52). Phoenix Press.

Reisman, D. A. (2024). *Aristotle's Economics: Ethics and Exchange*. Edward Elgar.

Smith, A. (1776 [1961]). *The Wealth of Nations* (abbreviated as WN) (2 Vols.). Methuen.

Spencer, H. (1891). *Essays: Scientific, Political, and Speculative*. Williams and Norgate.

CHAPTER 5

Justice: Origins and Destinations

The real world is falling short. One householder in seven is receiving money from the poor rates. Ninety-five out of a hundred Englishmen are consuming less than the citizenship minimum (PJ 409). The supply of grain is at the mercy of wartime blockades, bad harvests and underutilised estates. A large family is becoming a proxy for 'poverty and wretchedness' (PJ 28).

Bad times were testing the truce on inequality. Civil society in the years immediately after 1789 was moving ever closer to a 'state of war' (PJ 28). The underlying reason had been an unsupportable disparity in ownership, function, opportunity and consumption. Nature was not to blame. It had been man-made artificialities and not the invisible hand that had been separating one nation into its mistrustful sheep and goats. It had been profit-seeking economics and class-based politics and not Malthusian childbearing racing ahead of niggardly land that had excluded some of our people from the bounteous feast. Matter was not living up to mind. If amicable and tolerant intercourse were to be restored, then the excesses of distance and appetite would have brought into line with a popular consensus that man is not made to bowl alone.

D. Reisman, *William Godwin and Thomas Robert Malthus*,
https://doi.org/10.1007/978-3-031-62113-0_5

5.1 Ownership

As with all law, the origins of the claims are buried in 'doubtfulness' (PJ 614) and lost in 'obscurity' (PJ 615). They are never fully documented due to the 'jargon', the 'complexity' and the 'imbecility' of the records (PJ 615). Appropriated, purchased, stolen or inherited, it serves no useful purpose to dwell in the past: 'It is of no consequence…how I came into possession' (PJ 631). It is a 'gross imposition' for endowment-holders to pride themselves on 'property bequeathed to them by their ancestors' (PJ 632) or created for them by their government through land-grants and subsidised patents. The past is not the present. Whether in the state of nature like the American frontier or in an old country like England that carefully papers over its Cromwells, its sequestrated monasteries and its mercantilist monopolies, this much is clear. Today is the first day of all the history that is not bunk.

Function comes first. Property is 'the keystone that completes the fabric of political justice' (PJ 623). It is conducive to 'the benefit or pleasure of man' (PJ 624). 'Every man has a right to…exclusive possession' (PJ 624) provided that individual happiness and social stability can be shown to result from his claim. No man, however, has a right to continuing ownership if the consequence of his exclusivity is 'abuses' (PJ 623).

Your property 'belongs to you' (PJ 632). Every man has an 'absolute right' (PJ 632) to do as he pleases with his own. Yet your property also belongs to us. Quintessentially relative, every man's title is contingent on its validation by the All. To be legitimate my claim must be 'generally acquiesced in by the community in which I live' (PJ 631). My claim is perpetually on trial before the court of public opinion. Property Register or self-signposted squat, if the general will is opposed to my deed, no Court of Equity will decide in its favour.

Pleading for 'some permanence of external possession' (PJ 630), the asset holder must take his stand on the principle of social utility. He must demonstrate that 'a greater sum of benefit or pleasure' (PJ 631) is being generated than would accrue to the next-best mode of ownership. Property belongs to the person who 'most wants it', to whom 'the possession of it will be most beneficial' (PJ 1793, 790). It belongs to the person who will use it best (PJ 132). It does not belong to the person who will use it worst: 'Nothing can be more iniquitous, than for one man to possess superfluities, while there is a human being in existence that is not adequately supplied' (PJ 1793, 790–1). It is not the over-fed but the hungry that have the superior claim to a loaf of bread. Every magistrate must come to see that survival comes before any deed or title.

Basic needs are sacrosanct. So are the modest indulgences that top up the iron rations with butter and jam: 'Every man is entitled, so far as the general stock will suffice, not only to the means of being, but of well being' (PJ 1793, 791). It is writ in the natural law. Every member of a stable and self-perpetuating community has a common claim on a common harvest. No sitting tenant has first-comer's entitlement to more meals that he can ever eat or to clothes that he will never wear: 'Does any man doubt that, when I employ a sum of money small or great in the purchase of an absolute luxury for myself, I am guilty of vice?' (PJ 1793, 796). No man will deny it. That is the proof. The landowner does not own his land. We all own his land.

Social-ist groupthink corrects Malthusian doublethink at a stroke: 'If land were perpetually open to him who was willing to cultivate it, it is not to be believed but that it would be cultivated in proportion to the wants of the community, nor by the same reason would there be *any efficient check* to the increase of population' (PJ 1793, 816, emphasis added). The arithmetical ratio would not represent *any* real barrier to the increase of population. Malthus reading Godwin by the light of the burning hayricks would have seen precisely what this meant. Population is not a threat to sustained well-being. Functionless ownership is the greater danger to need satisfaction.

Time-out-of-mind is no defence. Locke says that the underlying objective of civil society is 'the mutual preservation of...property' (Locke, 1690 [1947]: para.123). Godwin replies that past arrangements are a dead-cat bounce. Entitlements wear out. Legitimacy comes and goes. The collectivity, weighing tenure against obligation, must keep the claims and the counterclaims perpetually under review.

Property is a social fact. It is 'appropriated only by convention' (PJ 519). Whenever or however it is acquired, the registered privateer has 'no right to dispose of a shilling of it at the suggestion of his caprice' (PJ 108). He has no right to withhold any part of it from community service. His personal assets, his land and his capital belong in the last instance to the Whole (*New Testament, Mark*: 10, xxi): 'All who believed were together and had all things in common' (*New Testament, Acts*: 2, xliv). Private property is public property. Private holdings cannot be seized and redistributed simply because they are there. Subject to due process, however, there is no reason why they should not be transferred from one asset-owner to another.

His property is never his alone. The same is true of his person: 'I hold my person as a trust in behalf of mankind. I am bound to employ my talents, my understanding, my strength and my time, for the production of the greatest quantity of general good' (PJ 108). Each man is 'bound to consider himself as a debtor in all his faculties, his opportunities, and his industry, to the general welfare' (PJ 257). He is forever repaying his bond. Our nation needs doctors and not poets. Square pegs, round holes, individual choice must be subordinated to collective choice. Our fellow citizens have laid down the priorities. Refuseniks factor down when they are bound to scale up. They should mind their own business. Pretty verses do not set a broken leg.

Society is not one individual but 'an aggregation of individuals' (PJ 109). Each of us must do 'everything that is requisite for their welfare' (PJ 109). Each of us must contribute his quota to the common stock. Even his life is discretionary. A man 'has no right to his life when his duty calls him to resign it' (PJ 131). Nor does he have a right to resign it without a chit from the pool. Death in the service of the Fatherland is meritorious. Suicide is default on a debt that the one-off owes to his team. Duelling is 'despicable' (PJ 113): it squanders useful lives that are not ours to spend. Godwin does not explore the status of non-useful lives that take from the common pot but put nothing in. The value of life is the value of livelihood if that is what our fellow citizens decree. There is no right to welfare. The old, the infirm and the unemployable, like the rest of us, live from one short-term allocation to the next.

Justice is reciprocal. To prevent a greater evil or to promote a greater good, what is clear to societal totalitarians from Meninius Agrippa to Herbert Spencer is that the stomach can never declare itself independent of the heart, the lungs or the brain: 'I am myself a part of the whole' (PJ 107). A single cell in an embedding organism, it is 'incumbent on me to maintain my body and mind in the utmost vigour, and in the best condition for service' (PJ 108).

Plato had said it in ancient Athens: 'Neither you nor this property of yours belongs to yourselves' but rather, and 'even more absolutely, to the state' (Plato, 1970: para. 923b). T.H. Marshall was to say it in welfare-state Britain: 'Your body is part of the national capital, and must be looked after, and sickness causes a loss of national income' (Marshall, 1965 [1981]: 91). Lunchtime o'Booze is attacking not just his individual liver but our Treasury, our British Museum and our White Cliffs as well. His fellow citizens will regard him as a renegade who skives and shirks. They will make clear to him that there will always be an England but that an Englishman in exchange must confine himself to tea.

Godwin was only one among many to warn that beer and balderdash impose a tax on us all. I have, he said, no right to waste 'the means of future usefulness' that would otherwise be of 'advantage to the public' (PJ 258). My life is leasehold only. It is never an unencumbered freehold in the service of my narrow, my self-ish advantage.

Property or person, England expects every man to do his duty. My *freedom from* cannot be detached from your *freedom to*. The exchange of the stranger gift for the privilege of membership is as 'complete' (PJ 108) as it would have been if the circular flow had been a paid-for market transaction: 'It is therefore impossible for me to confer upon any man a favour; I can only do him right' (PJ 109).

Denial is not an option. It is not pity or compassion so much as the prosperity and even the perpetuation of the social whole that impels the top-of-the-heap to share their subsistence with the down-at-heel. The haves have a social duty to pass over a part of their consensually legitimated endowment. Yet the have-nots have a counterpart duty to rescue themselves from their dependency. All of us expect each of us to do his best (PJ 120). We do not regard the gift relationship as a scrounger's charter. Voluntary undersupply is antisocial default. It is, as St. Paul says, an implicit betrayal of an implicit covenant: 'If anyone is not willing to work, let him not eat' (*New Testament, 2 Thessalonians*: 3, x).

Virtue is a red line blooded by agreement. The asset holder and the welfare recipient are both obliged to fit in. Whether helping or being helped, each is fully accountable to 'that portion of mankind among whom he resides': 'He is only the steward' (PJ 631, 632). We are all in it together. Freedom without duty is a horse designed by a donkey.

Strict constructionists say 'my home is my castle'. Statutes and precedents legitimise their claim. Godwin is attracted not to yesterday's legislation but to the current consensus. Status, he contends, must be ranked beneath contract. We are all brothers and sisters under the skin. Justice, he argues, is not being served so long as the pecuniary distance between our fellow bowlers is so great as to threaten the superordinate principle of equal moral worth: 'Equality of conditions, or, in other words, an equal admission to the means of improvement and pleasure, is a law rigorously enjoined upon mankind by the voice of justice. All other changes in society are good, *only as* they are fragments of this, or steps to its attainment' (PJ 655, emphasis added). *Only as.* In the words of R.H. Tawney, there are duties that a decent Englishman or passing Samaritan simply cannot refuse: 'One can't look a gift cherub in the mouth' (Tawney, 1972: 53–4).

The baseline standard is equality of access to the wider middle ground. Each cherub takes home an identical bowl of lentils and even an identical piece of cake. *Only as* is the exception that adds an extra clause to the rule. Godwin's *only as* is the first cousin of John Rawls's first principle. It is social justice pinpointed by a real-world near-unanimity stranded, as if in Plato's cave, behind a thick veil of ignorance: 'Each person is to have an equal right to the most extensive basic liberty compatible with a similar liberty for others' (Rawls, 1971: 60). *Only as* the departure from an across-the-board basketful is 'reasonably expected to be to everyone's advantage' (Rawls, 1971: 60) will a rational citizen be convinced that a social or an economic disparity is in the common interest.

Godwin's ideal is flatline equality in the basics and the indulgences. As with Rawls, however, he makes clear that the middle ground is a broad church. His *only as* is a reminder that, so long as the starts are dead level and the race unqueered by favouritism, the finishes can and must be shaded by differential contribution and non-standard need. Justice as fairness does not dictate that mine and thine must be an identical 'three acres and a cow'. Godwin is not saying that the outturns and the entitlements must conform precisely to the median. What he is arguing is that the stock and flow of assets should be levelled on to the wider centre ground. A change in matter will in that way be both the cause and effect of a change in mind.

As we become more equal, so we become more contented: 'Justice…is coincident with utility. I am myself a part of the greater whole, and my happiness is a part' (PJ 134). More bunching and fewer extremes bring the gift cherubs closer together. They are more equal. But they are not all the same.

5.2 The Factors of Production

How much is one dimension of social equality. *What* and *which* is another. Land and capital are not only assets in their own right but the means to an additional tranche of income and wealth. Combined with the active ingredient of human labour, they grow in value by virtue of the input that has nothing but itself to monetise. Godwin was insistent that any discussion of origins and destinations had to build upon the qualitative distinction between the three factors of production that were the unintended pillars of an unnatural economic system.

5.2.1 *Labour*

Locke saw the present through the prism of the past. Good title is acquired by labour: 'As much land as a man tills, plants, improves, cultivates and can use the product of, so much is his property' (Locke, 1690 [1947]: para. 38).

Labour legitimises the fences and the locks. An entitlement is made untouchable and irreversible by the first mover's toil and trouble. He has conquered his external reality by the sweat of his brow. Locke imposes the complementary condition that the pioneer engrosser must leave behind 'enough and as good' (Locke, 1690 [1947]: para. 33) for the next cohort to make its own. Zero sum is not a problem in the state of nature. New settlers moving into virgin territory can always stake out a new property. They are not obliged to compete with old settlers for the right to enclose.

Godwin on the first settler ever to sight the daisies that were later to be privatised into premium Piccadilly followed in the footsteps of Locke on the original state of nature: 'The good things of the world are a common stock, upon which one man has as valid a title as another to draw for what he wants....Each man has a sphere the limit and termination of which is marked out by the equal sphere of his neighbour. I have a right to the means of subsistence; he has an equal right. I have a right to every pleasure I can participate without injury to myself or others; his title in this respect is of similar extent' (PJ 625). So long as my equal right does not infringe on his equal right (PJ 630), my asset has a putative claim to full protection from the 'momentary caprice' (PJ 624) of envious interlopers.

Locke, anchoring his natural right in conjectural history, traced his absolute entitlement to labour embodied. Godwin shared with him the recognition that living labour is the necessary condition if the acorns on the ground are to acquire an economic value: 'Those things which are necessary for the accommodation of man in society cannot be obtained without the labour of man' (PJ 630). As, however, Locke had done, Godwin saw that labour expended was no longer sufficient to make either the acorns or the ground into good and ethical title. Second movers were arriving too late at the bounteous feast. Nature bids them pay a forfeit to the first movers or else move on to a more satisfactory game.

5.2.2 *Land and Capital*

Economics and politics have moved on. Starting not from Adam Smith's 'early and rude state' (WN I 53) but from North-West London in 1793, Godwin presents himself as a revisionist who knows that even Locke must be kept to date. The means of production, no longer a free lunch, occupy a material bottleneck. Labour is obliged to rent out its productive potential to a private proprietor who regards the anonymous lump not as a cherub in the sense of Tawney or an end-in-itself in the sense of Kant but as a means to the mercantile objective of surplus value in the sense of Proudhon who said that property was theft.

The peaks and troughs in earning and spending are only a part of story. The private ownership of land and capital is the greater problem. The mass of mankind, Godwin writes, have become 'slaves and cattle for the service of a few' (PJ 646). The factory system is a threat to the full flowering of the mind. It deprives the operative of the capacity to think: 'Put him into a mill, and his understanding will improve no more than that of the horse which turns it' (Fleetwood, 90).

Treated as 'beasts of burden' (PJ 409), crushed by their masterful betters into 'a servile and truckling spirit' (PJ 645), the workers are 'benumbed with toil' and 'invaded with infirmities' (PJ 650). They are subject to 'the severest and most incessant labour' (PJ 372). They are forced into an alienating job function which 'annihilates so much thought' and so much happiness (PJ 409). They are 'condemned to slavery and sweat, incessant drudgery, unwholesome food, continual hardships, deplorable ignorance, and brutal insensibility' (PJ 631). They are exposed to 'the miseries, the agonies of pain, the anguish of heart, and the dreadful paroxysms of despair' (Mandeville, 1817 [1992]: 86). Even that is not the end of their woes. The worker is exploited through a wage that falls short of his productive contribution. It is a poverty wage, not even 'in the precise proportion necessary for his consumption' (PJ 630). Marx said it in 1844 and 1867. Godwin said in 1793 when the English industrial revolution was less than 20 years old.

Consumption restricted, creativity repressed, denied equal respect, the workers are at the mercy of robber landowners and maximising capitalists who pocket 'that which, in strict justice, is the right of another' (PJ 627). The propertied elite add nothing to the wealth of nations: 'The earth supplies us freely with her productions, and industry multiplies them' (Mandeville, 86). It is power and not productivity that make the rich into robber barons who 'with niggard hand' seize the surplus to which 'the whole was indebted for existence': 'One man gets the share of ten thousand, which he wastes and dissipates in thoughtless profusion....Every costly morsel that he eats, is mixed with the tears and the curses of the poor by *whose labours it was procured*' (Mandeville, 86, emphasis added).

Engels could not have said it better. Godwin, he announced, was supreme among the 'practical philosophers of recent times', even if 'virtually studied only by the workers' (Engels, 1845 [1958]: 273). The workers know enough to distance themselves from the 'incredible savagery', the 'most flagrant warlike aggression' (Engels, 1845 [1958]: 320, 323), of Parson Malthus and his running dogs. The Malthusians, speaking for the comfortable middle classes, deny that the workers possess any 'inalienable right to food, clothing and shelter' (Engels, 1845 [1958]: 321). Their shopkeeper economics sets at nought the moral entitlement of every human being to the means of survival, improvement and happiness. The proletariat is not bamboozled by their humbug economics of supply and demand. Like Godwin, in defiance of Malthus, the proletariat knows precisely how profits are made and by whom.

The wretched make the free gifts of nature into economic tradeables. The workers look on while the owner class, boastfully showing off 'the badge of extortion' (PJ 663) made manifest in its stately homes and Paris fashions, is publicly 'revelling in the fruits of their labours' (PJ 29). All wealth is the envelope of a 'certain quantity of human labour' (Mandeville, 150). Man the maker is by virtue of that contribution 'entitled to the benefit' (Mandeville, 150). It is a cheque that he is finding it impossible to encash. Private property has split the community into posh and steerage. Locke's original state of justice and equality has been left behind by appropriation.

However much it is Veblen and Goffman in the wrappings, it is Marx and Engels at the core. Godwin's 'rich' spend and outspend. Godwin's 'poor' dwell in a 'state of abject poverty' (PJ 24). The disparity can only get worse. 'The growth of unequal property' (PJ 653) and the 'unrelenting avarice' that fuels the 'torpid luxury' of money-grubbing land and capital (PJ 595) must inevitably force the three-factor society into a change of direction. Hard-working labour is becoming less willing to share its value added with the non-productive few. An alternative will have to emerge from the restless tectonics.

5.2.3 *One-Factor Economics*

Godwin starts where he means to finish. The supplier of labour has an irrevocable entitlement to 'the produce of his own industry' (PJ 631). Three factors are two factors too many. Both ethics and economics point to a single-factor economic system.

Adam Smith had experimented with a labour theory of value: 'It is natural that what is usually the produce of two days' or two hours' labour, should be worth double of what is usually the produce of one day's or one hour's labour' (WN I 53). Smith had explicitly restricted his single-input theory of new value added to that basepoint economic order 'which precedes both the accumulation of stock and the appropriation of land' (WN I 53). Godwin, ignoring Smith's reservations, brought it up to date: 'All wealth, in a state of civilized society, is the produce of human industry' (PJ 544). In the developed First World as it is in the backward South, the proposition is set in stone. There is 'scarcely any species of wealth' that is not 'produced by the express manual labour' (PJ 632).

Labour made it. Labour should keep it. The labour theory of entitlement is often traced back to John Gray in 1825 and John Bray in 1839. Anton Menger in 1886 declared that it was all in Godwin: 'The first scientific advocate of the right to the whole produce of labour, known to me, is William Godwin....Godwin may be regarded as the first scientific socialist of modern times' (Menger, 1886 [1899]: 40). Godwin was a socialist in his economics: sweat and tears by natural law make the acorns my own. Godwin was also a social-ist in his equity: if your need is greater than mine, then it is not a 'contradiction' (Menger, 1886 [1899]: 42) but a step upward in the hierarchy of moral principles for even a Malthusian to share his earned endowment. The labour theory of entitlement, necessary but not sufficient, is not the last word on obligation.

Godwin identified both a rich-poor and an owner-labour dyad. The two dyads are all but the same due to the distinction between the productive who make and the sterile who take. One prediction from the dialectical incompatibility would have been a new 1789, red in tooth and claw. Pulled by Marx on the underlying conditions of production, pushed by Veblen on the veneer of signs and symbols, the expropriation of the expropriators might be just round the corner.

Marx in the *Manifesto*, Morris in *News from Nowhere*, envisaged a revolution on the model of the Great 1789. Godwin did not. Godwin, an evolutionist, a gradualist, did not expect that the conversion from ownership to anarchy would occur at the flick of a switch. The present day is a veil of tears. It is an interregnum in which the parasitism of cream-skimming, 'monopolizing' (PJ 634), 'force and fraud' (PJ 633), are tragically being given a free pass by an enforcer state in symbiosis with the economic elite.

The *lumpenproletariat*, ignorant, credulous, lacking in leadership, is not about to take matters into its own hands. *Natura non facit saltum.* Only a naïve utopian would deny that mind must be given the time it needs to move matter on to a higher plane: 'Vicious conduct is always the result of narrow views' (PJ 239). Narrow views are doomed. Not, however, at one stroke. Like Lenin, like Engels, Godwin anticipated that the state would not be abolished but would simply wither away once there was 'nothing more to be repressed which would make a special repressive force, a state, necessary' (Engels, 1880 [1942]: I 182).

Progress is inevitable. Godwin, relying on anecdotes and impressions, asserts that change for the better is taking its course. As mankind has moved steadily upward from 'barbarism' to 'refinement', so there has been a 'tendency towards the equalization of conditions' (PJ 709). What has emerged from the unstoppable march of ideas sparking events has been a more equitable distribution of 'the good things in life' (PJ 645). Yesterday it was feudalism. Today it is commerce. Tomorrow it will be one-class, one-factor social-ism. Labour alone will reap the harvest that labour alone has sowed. Theory and evidence, the *why* and the *what*, are thin on the ground. Godwin can afford to fall back on conjecture. He is confident that he has the truth on his side.

The destination is not in doubt. The non-producing minority will be absorbed into the Marxists' 'vast association of the whole nation' (Marx & Engels, 1848 [2011]: 89). The progress of one will become the progress of all (PJ 711). Costly consumables will no longer have the power to divide: 'No man will have the least desire, for purposes of ostentation or luxury, to possess more than his neighbours' (PJ 133).

In the long run the private ownership of land and capital will have disappeared into prehistory. In the short run mankind must coexist with the rough edges while the functionless survivals slowly but surely make their way to the exit. It is a counsel of patience. There is unlikely to be an early 'change in men's dispositions and sentiments' (PJ 634). No organ ever withers away overnight. The most that can be expected in the short run is the halfway house of land and capital with a more human face.

At the end of the journey the three factors will be absorbed into one. In the short run it will be the Smithian, Malthusian economics of wealth creation through social class. Godwin, in making peace, however provisional, with the status quo, is showing a remarkably conservative reluctance to look horizontally at the multiplicity of permutations that could be injecting new ideas from within. He could have proposed socialism nested within private ownership in the form of profit-linked pay, worker directors or employee buyouts. He could have proposed producer cooperatives. In fact, he was strongly opposed.

Godwin, eulogising the independent self-determination of the romantic self, made clear to Shelley that 'associations, organised societies, I firmly condemn' (Brown, 1926: 262): 'Everything that is usually understood by the term co-operation is, in some degree, an evil' (PJ 678). Godwin was not on a direct line to Robert Owen, Fourier's *phalanstères*, Christian socialism, Ricardian socialism, the Israeli *kibbutz* or trade unionism that exercises countervailing power. In the short run at least, the shop floor would continue to hew and draw.

Small-scale corporatism was not the answer. The labour-owned, labour-managed enterprise was not a viable step up. Just as 'miserable' as before, the workers 'would have gained nothing' (PJ 634). As citizens, they would actually have made a loss. It is not in the social interest to declare war on outstanding captains 'of greater ingenuity or more indefatigable industry' (PJ 636). Economic advance relies upon exceptional alertness. Business stagnates where it becomes a bureaucracy. Outcomes matter. It would be a mistake to throw out the baby with the bathwater.

Schumpeter's entrepreneurs are a persuasive argument for private ownership. Without the individual discretion and time-tested judgement of Marshall's owner-undertakers, there would be, Godwin states, 'no independence, no improvement, no virtue and no happiness' (PJ 642). It would be 'pernicious' (PJ 634) unnecessarily to depress the productive potential of the nation: 'No well informed community will interfere with the quantity of any man's industry' (PJ 636).

Outcomes aside, even a businessman is a moral entity. Every individual deserves an equal opportunity to do his best: 'We should set bounds to no man's accumulation' (PJ 638). To advocate the forcible invasion of a going concern that has imposed no external costs—except, of course, inequality and exploitation—is to reveal oneself 'an enemy to the whole' (PJ 642). A minor slip-up is 'not an evil to be corrected by the interposition of government' (PJ 637). Given enough time, given adequate security from premature intervention, 'ill conceived and abortive' (PJ 636), a minor slip-up will heal itself as guided by an invisible hand.

5.3 Opportunity

Godwin was a meritocrat: 'Of all the principles of justice, there is none so material to the moral rectitude of mankind as that no man can be distinguished but by his personal merit' (PJ 399). The levelling down of undeserved inequality is one step in the direction of the *carrière ouverte aux talents*. The levelling up of blocked potential is another.

5.3.1 An Equitable Start

People differ in their capacities and propensities. The just society prides itself on the citizenship guarantee of an equitable start: 'The thing really to be desired is the removing as much as possible [of] arbitrary distinctions….We should endeavour to afford to all the same opportunities and the same encouragements' (PJ 118). The just society offers each player an equal chance to become unequal. An unjust society pulls up the drawbridge to protect the claim of Royal Ascot on the House of Lords.

Some of our people are 'possessed of higher faculties' (PJ 103). They bring above-average strength and intelligence to the table. Some make a less glittering contribution to the well-being of the whole. What is essential is that the high-flyers should not be prevented by artificial stumbling blocks from achieving the deserts to which they are entitled by virtue of their excellence and assiduity. Social location based not on privilege but on potential is, Godwin says, 'the true equalization of mankind. Not to pull down those who are exalted, and reduce all to a naked and savage equality. But to raise those who are abased' (PJ 321–2). Godwin wanted to open the flood gates. He wanted to level up the underachievers who never had a chance.

Godwin was in favour of an equal start and an open road. Unequal outcomes are that much less divisive where each runner is fairly treated. Identical hurdles for non-identical meritocrats defuse the latent frustration that 'kills all liberal ambition in the rest of mankind' (PJ 398). Godwin knew of the new wedge that might appear should Marx's proletariat be succeeded by Michael Young's idiotariat, forever on the outside looking in. He recognised that an impartial sift had to be complemented by a common culture if both the sagacious Fénélon and his slow-witted valet were to see themselves as members of a single club.

The curate becomes a bishop. His chambermaid remains a chambermaid. Irrespective of the rises and the falls, Godwin says, what matters most to nation-building is a collective commitment 'to communicate to every man all genuine pleasures, to elevate every man to all true wisdom and to make all men participators of a liberal and comprehensive benevolence' (PJ 322). As Tawney puts it: 'Civilization is not the business of an élite alone, but a common enterprise which is the concern of all' (Tawney, 1931 [1964]: 43). It is Disraeli, Coleridge and T.S. Eliot. It is Eliza and Higgins. It is the Nürnberg rallies. It is the Dunkirk evacuation.

Social levelling to a social-ist like Godwin means something more than an equal opportunity to declare oneself a stakeholder in the unenclosed commons. It also means a one-nation value system and a shared code of conduct. If our polis is to be harmonious and united, our fellow citizens must regard one another not as incomprehensible *ba-ba* but as the member-participants of a single team. We all have the common faculties of perception and reason, pleasure and pain: 'We are partakers of a common nature' (PJ 117). It is only one step further to say that we all apply 'one unalterable rule of justice to every case that may arise' (PJ 117). We are Manchester *United*. We do not bowl alone.

5.3.2 Education: A Case Study

The British Fabians argued that the state has a duty to supply not only the protective services of policemen and lawcourts but also the enabling services of healthcare, housing and education. Without the scaffold and the escalator, a fair chance in law would be profoundly unequal in practice. Godwin saw no need to turn to depots like Pitt, Grenville and George III for a helping hand. The private sector will provide. Education shows that choice and competition can get the job done.

Godwin, P.H. Marshall says, 'always remained a preacher' (Marshall, 1984: 55). Transiting from the clergy, continuing to dress like a Calvinist, he contemplated a small school for 12 boys at Epsom. In *An Account of the Seminary at Epsom* (1783) and the *Letter of Advice to a Young American* (1818), in novels such as *Fleetwood* (1805) and *Mandeville* (1817), in *Political Justice* (1793), in *The Enquirer* (1797) that will be considered in Chapter 7.2, below, Godwin returned repeatedly to the value of learning in its broadest and fullest sense. We learn from a named teacher. We learn from the social environment. Either way, we never cease to refine our stock of wisdom.

At birth the infant is Locke's white sheet of promise on which experience writes: 'The human mind is pure and spotless, as it came from the hands of God' (Seminary, 24). Education stands at the crossroads of life. Its mission, 'infinitely important', is 'to mould those pliant dispositions, upon which the happiness of multitudes may one day depend' (Seminary, 3). False education condemns its impressionable charges through jargon and memory-work to a rigid slavery that undermines their reason. True education empowers the malleable lump of wax to develop his own character and talents through a self-motivated voyage of discovery.

The child 'from the moment of his birth' is 'an experimental philosopher': 'He essays his organs and his limbs, and learns the use of his muscles' (Fleetwood, 90). Experience is habit-forming, life the ultimate seminary, liberty the top-ranked 'school of understanding': 'Every boy learns more in his hours of play than in his hours of leisure....In his sports he actually thinks' (Fleetwood, 90). The child of a savage never-read-a-book 'can run like lapwings, and climb trees with the squirrel' (Fleetwood, 90). That is not to disparage the contribution of formal education: 'In school he lays in the materials of thinking' (Fleetwood, 90). The pupil must be given a structure to his private and personal search (Seminary, 36). School emancipates the mind precisely because it disciplines the focus. At the same time, it should leave the child the freedom to explore. The school is in the party of repression where it stultifies original initiative and straitjackets the reflexes.

Malthus, inspired by Smith, was in favour of state schooling. Correcting market underprovision, national education would ensure a bedrock of transferable skills and mainstream values. Godwin in contrast saw only harm in the iron fist false-flagged as liberation. A vast propaganda machine, a nationalised system would land its victims in a treacle of 'superstitious veneration' (PJ 537), 'supineness and indifference', 'formal dullness' (PJ 538), 'exploded errors', 'permanence' and 'aversion to change' (PJ 536). The schools 'actively restrain the flights of mind' (PJ 536). The universities stifle boat-rocking discovery: 'The knowledge taught there is a century behind the knowledge which exists among the unshackled and unprejudiced' (PJ 536). No one goes to Oxbridge to learn about breakthrough technology or, still less, tradesman's entrance economics.

Real intellectual improvement entails both an advance to the state-of-the-art frontier and an eagerness to 'start from thence in the pursuit of further acquisitions' (PJ 536). The schools and the universities, peddling 'pedantry' that is 'not learning' (PJ 395), are mere sausage machines. They force their charges into surrendering 'the best attribute of man' in exchange for 'fixed principles' learned by rote (PJ 537). Such education is not education at all but 'intellectual *decease*' (PJ 537, emphasis added). Its victim is left 'no longer a man; he is the ghost of departed man' (PJ 537).

State education hands on 'absurdities' such as the hegemony of the established Church and the custom 'to bow to every man in a handsome coat': 'All this is directly contrary to the true interests of mankind. All this must be unlearned before we can begin to be wise' (PJ 537). Creeds and ideologies will have to be bred out: 'No vice can be more destructive than that which teaches us to regard any judgment as final, and not open to review' (PJ 537).

State education is antithetical to personal and social development. In its place there ought to be child-centred learning that channels natural curiosity into understanding and only then into action. The child should be guided towards the 'elegance of civilization' and the 'manliness of virtue' (Seminary, 5). Proclivities rather than facts, they will empower him to find his own way to the truth: 'Great energies cannot flow but from a powerful sense of fitness and justice' (PJ 241).

People must find their 'own means of being happy' (PJ 538). The most the mentor can do is to remove artificial sunshades that would impede independent investigation: 'Whatever each man does for himself is done well; whatever his neighbours or his country undertake to do for him is done ill' (PJ 538). Schooling should awaken the child's imagination (Letter, 4). It should make use of discussion, debate, observation and openness to protect the child against the soul-destroying stagnation of 'perpetual pupillage' (PJ 538). It should challenge the tricks and templates of state-manufactured indoctrination. The government will no longer be able to control its subjects by means of a minoritarian consensus aligned to the rigidities of 'an arbitrary will, stimulated by the possession of power' (PJ 568).

The freedom of speech will be the by-product of the freedom to learn. A plurality of schools is conducive to a plurality of thoughts. It can just as easily be convergence on the common culture as it can be the dissonance of 'do your own thing'. Referring to the plethora of sects which might undermine the monolithic Catholic Church, Adam Smith predicted that the outcome of perfect competition would be a 'pure and rational' body of belief (WN II 315). Godwin, treating small schools as secular chapels, is applying the same logic to the multiplication of educational establishments. Underlying the differences there is, after all, but a single objective. Both as an individual and as a part of a wider whole, the child goes to school to open his eyes: 'It is the truly enlightened man, that is best qualified to be truly useful' (Letter, 15).

As with Rousseau and Helvétius in the restless *ancien régime*, Illich and Goodman in the permissive 1960s, Godwin believed that education had to provide an entry-level platform upon which the child can build in order to manage his subsequent take-off into self-sustaining idiosyncrasy. At birth we are all on a par: 'The state of society is incontrovertibly artificial....By nature we are all equal' (Seminary, 2). Rejecting 'the artificial distinctions of civilised life', Godwin says, there is not much in Arcadia to separate a distinguished philosopher from a common street porter: 'Every man in the savage state is in the main...like any other man' (Mandeville, 214).

Progressive education is the road to *Walden*. As with all institutions, however, there is always the danger of extremes. De-schoolers make it their mission to draw out from each schoolboy his unique and non-social essence. Godwin, following Locke, replies that the release of some innate *I am* is both philosophically impossible and socially divisive. The inward-looking liberty of the schoolboy to round out his own sacred self is insignificant compared with the outward-looking convergence of private and public opinion on the single-valued truth.

Education, in its broadest sense, must ensure that social sanctions are such as to make the community into a well-oiled machine. Sympathy is what education is all about. Do unto others is the ultimate text: 'The noblest part of man is his moral nature; and I hold morality principally to depend...upon our putting ourselves in the place of another, feeling his feelings, and apprehending his desires' (Letter, 4). Education is not individual-ism but social-ism. Child-centred education is more than Emile's right to rock any boat he wishes.

Jesus on the golden rule, Smith on the moral sentiments, Durkheim on the *conscience collective* will keep the peace. Even Emile must be taught that sincerity in the sense of 'to thine own self be true' must be enriched with a devotee's commitment to the norms and values of the wider orchestra that plays from an agreed-upon score. The schoolboy does not need a Machiavellian *domine* to sergeant-major him into shape. A general's certificate of education only proves that the throughput has been drilled down into role-play. What the young person does require is a developed sensitivity to the common code. The real and the impartial spectator are well suited to the task of social approximation. Their good counsel is the price of membership and integration. Emile, true to himself, would be a misfit. Anarchism would not be viable if each free spirit refused the moral education that came to him from outside.

Godwin believed that the intrinsic distance between ego and alter was not an insuperable barrier: 'The points in which human beings resemble are infinitely more considerable than those in which they differ' (PJ 183). Even so, the heterogeneity is there. It is the remit of the protective state to ensure that individual dispositions and self-regarding conduct do not in the short run stray too far from the 'common good'. In the long run even that protection will not be needed. Social cohesion will emerge spontaneously from the unseen hand of the seamless web.

5.4 Consumption

We are separated not only by what we own and earn, by our factors of production and the life chances we enjoy, but also by our patterns of expenditure. Consumption alongside property, function and opportunity is a topic in origins and destinations. Bowler hats, cloth caps, diamond tiaras and military uniforms are the currency in which we trade. Superstructure but not basis, mind soaring over matter, the presentation of self will frequently be the difference that divides: 'Consumption goods are most definitely not mere messages; they constitute the very system itself' (Douglas & Isherwood, 1979: 72). The 'good things of the world' separate the sheep from the goats. They do so immediately our fellow citizens put themselves on public display.

The 'good things of the world', Godwin says, are widely taken to be (1) 'subsistence'; (2) 'the means of intellectual and moral improvement'; (3) 'inexpensive gratifications' and (4) 'such gratifications as are by no means essential to healthful and vigorous existence' (PJ 625). The fourth class, 'superfluities', is the cuckoo in the nest: 'Without it we may enjoy to a great extent activity, contentment and cheerfulness' (PJ 625). We do not need class 4. Class 4 is a negative externality for us all.

5.4.1 *Absolute and Relative Utility*

Absolute deprivation can never be a good thing: 'Every man should be impressed with the consciousness of his independence, and rescued from the influence of extreme want' (PJ 452). There is nothing noble in starvation: 'The life of a savage is...a miserable life' (OP 468). Physical subsistence and moderate indulgence accompanied by adequate leisure for mindful contemplation and neighbourly *Gemeinschaft* are the sine qua non. They are the bedrock imperatives without which the human being cannot fully develop into himself.

They are the material hard core. Important as they are, they can nonetheless be satisfied at a relatively low level of economic prosperity. In terms of human need, the intrinsic difference in 'the pleasures of the palate, between a simple and wholesome diet on the one hand, and all the complexities of the most splendid table on the other, is...small' (PJ 626). It is so small that 'few men would even think it worth the tedium' (PJ 626) of exchanging exhausting grind for flat-of-the-curve shopping. The backward bending supply curve of labour is more than Third World traditionalism. It is a rational choice.

'Solitary sensualism' (PJ 626) has an upper limit. No man can obtain real utility from things 'trivial in themselves' (PJ 626) that service 'artificial desires' (PJ 452). Paley had used his common sense to declare a moratorium on unashamed gluttony and new-rich flamboyance: 'The luxurious receive no greater pleasure from their dainties, than the peasant does from his bread and cheese' (Paley, 1785: I 41–2). Adam Smith had warned against the 'deception' of meaningless shop-till-you-drop: 'To what purpose is all the toil and bustle of the world?....Is it to supply the necessities of nature? The wages of the meanest labourer can supply them' (MS 70, 263). Paley and Smith had said it. 'Frugal fare and a cheerful poverty' (PJ 546) are enough. They are as good as a feast.

Consumer sovereignty is a prison. Pushpin is *not* as good as poetry. There is a hierarchy of pleasures that the informed and the integrated are morally obliged to respect. Economics is ethics through and through. None of us as economic actors would continue to earn and spend once our basic needs for food and shelter had been met. Yet we do, and the reason is invidious comparison. Incremental consumables serve us 'only as instruments for satisfying our love of distinction' (PJ 626). We buy them not for the 'direct pleasure' (PJ 626) they provide so much as for the pecuniary position that they put on public display.

'Every human mind' is open to the 'love of distinction' (PJ 626). That is why, having satisfied his basic human needs, the social actor moves on to the 'gay attire' and the 'handsome habitation' that would not 'engage his attention if he lived in a desert island': 'There is scarcely an article that is not in some respect an appeal to the good will of our neighbours, or a refuge against their contempt. It is for this that the merchant braves the perils of the ocean, and the mechanical inventor brings forth the treasures of his meditation....He cannot bear to pass through life without distinction and esteem....This is the purpose of all the great exertions of mankind' (PJ 627).

There is 'scarcely an article' that is not a prop, a pawn or a means. So long as the classes are stratified and the players unequal, each participant in the social game of predatory one-upmanship will be compelled to invest in 'gaudy ostentation' that he would never have contemplated 'if he had no spectators' (PJ 1793, 792, 795). It is the spectators and not the self that are forcing us into lavish expenditure.

Veblen-like, the winners in life's race are obliged to publicise their pre-eminence through 'the splendour of their equipage, the magnificence of their retinue and the sumptuousness of their entertainments' (PJ 29). Utilitarian individualists have got it back to front. 'Wealth is not pursued for its own sake' or for the 'sensual gratification' (PJ 30) that it makes possible but most of all because of the hunger for applause and the counterpart 'fear of contempt' (PJ 31). We live in the shadow of the Other. Blinded by the symbols and the signifiers, the bystander must be made 'to convert that wonder into an adulation of the owner' (PJ 31). We love the gain because we love the love. We do not prize a trophy if we are all alone.

High-end luxuries are positional goods. Money is 'the great requisite' that makes the dreams come true: 'Distinction, the homage and esteem of mankind, are to be bought, not earned....Rarely indeed does it happen that there is any crime that gold cannot expiate....Money therefore is the only object worthy of your pursuit' (PJ 372). It is all in Guizot: '*Enrichissez-vous*' Otherwise you will be cellophane man, invisible in the lonely crowd.

Money is the gatekeeper: 'The man with the longest purse is proverbially victorious' (PJ 29). The man with the shortest purse, observing him from outside, will often be mistaking splendour for felicity: 'He cannot persuade himself that an embroidered garment may frequently cover an aching heart' (PJ 29). Bystanders might not grasp the real cost of the first-class carriage. Yet it is there. The poor little rich girl may have lost more than she has gained. She should have known when to stop.

Obliged to 'make a certain figure, and to live in a style calculated to excite respect' (PJ 546), the insecure and the envious travel to the margin for the gaze. It is a mirage. The intrinsic happiness that accrues to increasing consumption declines steadily to zero and thereafter still further into pain. The incremental standing that is put in the public domain by Smith's 'trinkets and baubles' (WN I 183), by Godwin's 'baubles and splendour' (PJ 340), is a different matter: 'The great incitement to the acquisition of wealth is the love of distinction' (PJ 658). Public approbation is the true reason why men earn and spend even when the intrinsic utility from their status symbols has gone into the red: 'Ambition is, of all the passions of the human mind, the most extensive in its ravages' (PJ 652).

The rich man has passed the break-even point. It is what it means to be rich: 'Every man is in reality rich who has more than his just occasions demand' (PJ 109). It was never the bank balance, always the name recognition, that his efforts and gambles were being called upon to service. They will not do him any lasting good. In a race to do and outdo, utility is a musical chair. Paper-thin and skin-deep, evanescent relativity is a weak justification for an eternity of harried competition.

What one can do, all cannot. Flash, dash and cash are trapped in an upward spiral of show-trumping show. Unanchored and unrooted in the monetised order, social actors struggle to squeeze 'deference' and 'slavish attention' (PJ 628) from their costly mansions and their yachts. Self-advertisement becomes their 'ruling passion' (PJ 627). To them, Veblen says, self-preservation through self-promotion has become 'the pervading trait of human nature' (Veblen, 1899 [1970]: 84). A 'mean appearance' (PJ 30), relative or absolute, condemns the also-ran to the ravages of spoiled identity. He who does not go up goes down. No one wants to be snubbed or treated with contempt. No one wants to be 'shut out from the real benefits of society' (PJ 340).

5.4.2 Convergence and Moderation

At one extreme there is the shame and squalor of five-to-a-room Shadwell. Great deprivation makes it all but impossible for a man 'to be honest, virtuous, and honourable' (in KP I 198). A reallocation of existing endowments accompanied by economic growth to expand the national product is essential if all of our people are to be integrated into a citizenship-class standard of life,

At the opposite extreme there is the self-advertised debauchery of Park Lane opulence. Great riches 'corrupt the morals and harden the heart' (in KP I 198). The 'superfluity of wealth' (PJ 340) makes no Midas happy. The 'most exquisite viands' washed down by 'the most highly flavoured wines' rapidly lose their intrinsic attraction (PJ 1793, 792). What does not go out of fashion is the capacity of *haute couture* and breakfast at Tiffany's to put superior income and wealth on public display. The indolent flaunt. The collateral look on. Huckstered intemperance divides what ought to be one nation into a cacophony of badged identities. The front is a threat to us all. It 'deprives us of all intercourse with our fellow men upon equal terms' (PJ 340).

Wardrobes are weapons. Clothes make the man. Squire Ferdinando Falkland, a country gentleman 'of considerable opulence' (CW 6), 'distinction and fortune' (CW 130), 'the fool of honour and fame' (CW 106) in Godwin's novel *Caleb Williams*, all but commits the perfect murder. His 'imperious carriage' (CW 160) guarantees his reputation. Falkland has made himself 'an object of wonder, and that which excites our wonder we scarcely suppose ourselves competent to analyse' (CW 307). Razzle-dazzle 'em and they will make you a star.

The competition for standing leads directly to division, resentment and in the limit violence. It 'cannot be beneficial to the community' (PJ 430). A man's a man. Bond Street bling is not. The new commercial way rat-races to 'count the value of a man by pounds, shillings, and pence' (in KP II 329). It is mere dross and dirt compared with a more inclusive, less judgemental window on the world: 'That form of society, perhaps, is the best which shall make individual man feel most generous and most noble' (in KP II 329). It will be a form of society in which each of us will be valued for himself alone and not for his showy appurtenances: 'I have been all my life accustomed to regard man as everything….and property as comparatively mere dross and dirt' (in KP II 329).

'Prosperity is pernicious' (PJ 339). Poverty is pernicious. *Proverbs* 30, viii, is right: 'Give me neither poverty nor riches'. Rather than the nakedness of absolute destitution cheek-by-jowl with the wastefulness of silly show, the standard of living should gravitate to the middle ground. Each median member of a single polis should enjoy 'a moderate supply of the good things of this life' (Essays, 64). No integrated member should enjoy significantly more or less.

The representative citizen should have unrationed access to a basketful of commodities conducive to his physical survival and personal development. He should be in a position to tap into a modest tranche of discretionary happiness in the form of 'considerable accommodation', 'copiousness' and even some 'splendour' (PJ 673). Not every consumable need be 'absolutely necessary to maintain us in sound and healthful existence' (PJ 672). A moderate surplus above the bodily basics is a good thing. An Englishman is not a monk.

The real threat to the good society does not come from consumption classes 1 and 2 or even from consumption class 3. It is consumption class 4 that is the devil in church. Consumption class 4, 'superfluities', is not something in which our people ought to indulge. Zero-sum chimeras leave the diner just as hungry as before (PJ 431). They are will-o'-the-wisp enticements to 'avarice and ambition' (PJ 482) that drive the citizen into the deadweight overhead of relative standing. Unhealthy in themselves, divisive in society, our people should not be squandering resources on fool's gold comparisons. *Ecclesiastes* 6, viii, is right: 'Vanity…is a grievous evil'. Godwin's ideal is a community in which each of us is good, *and* better, *and* best. None of us will be Ferdinando Falkland who threw his weight around.

Godwin writes that sensible consumers in a rational society will do well to 'be content with a little' (PJ 482). The cynics, the stoics, the medieval ascetics, the puritans and the evangelicals had all inveighed against the undammed flood of non-satiety. Godwin, however, was not Diogenes. Superfluities could not be condoned. It was not an argument for life in a barrel.

Godwin believed in convergence and moderation. His two-pronged advance did not imply a stationary state. Slow growth remained a policy option. Zero growth, zero innovation was not in the national interest. Material advance was a necessary even if not a sufficient condition for self-perpetuating progress.

Malthus felt the same. The national product should continue to rise, he said, at least until 'the two great causes of the degradation of man, misery, and too great riches' (FE 124) had been eliminated. 'Misery', Adam Smith had contended, would be challenged by full employment and occupational upgrading. 'Too great riches' is more elusive. Godwin looked to an inevitable remoralisation of social usages. Malthus was more reticent about the logic behind the income elasticity of seemliness and self-regulation. Malthus proposed and possibly even predicted that not just *too little* but also *too much* would be squeezed out of the system in the course of moderate expansion. Ongoing betterment, purified of emulation, need not be a curse. It might be a blessing.

If the national product is to grow, then consumption too must grow. Want-containment in the sense of Godwin is the paradox of thrift in the sense of Keynes. Moral values can lead to secular stagnation, unemployment and poverty. Malthus says that 'the final object in saving is expenditure and enjoyment' (PPE 467). Godwin is on the same page. Expenditure is an indispensable component in the circular flow. We must do our bit as consumers to ensure that a convergent but also a moderate rise in living standards does not run out of steam.

5.4.3 The Transition

The invisible hand is on Godwin's side. Automaticity is his star witness. Conspicuous inequality is legitimising force and fraud. Abundance side by side with penury is undermining good fellowship. Venal politicians in league with self-seeking businessmen are making a cash cow of their nation. The status quo is discrediting itself. It is bringing into focus the need for something new. Godwin knows which way the wind is blowing. He believes that an amicable middle ground is emerging where convergence and self-control will strike directly at the separate tables that keep the fellow citizens apart: 'No man would be an enemy to his neighbour, for they would have no subject of contention' (PJ 652).

The transition has already begun. Casual empiricism confirms it. At the same time as the nation has become more affluent, the would-be big spender has increasingly been deterred by 'the censure of every beholder' (PJ 711) from counterproductive 'splendour and ostentation' (PJ 664): 'His conduct would appear too absurd to excite imitation' (PJ 659). 'Rooted habits' (PJ 661) are being challenged by the man in the street. Ordinary people are even now restricting their approbation to 'genuine wants' (PJ 662). They are gravitating to 'the means of healthful existence, and of unexpensive pleasure' (PJ 662). They are finding 'the highest gratification in promoting and contemplating the general happiness' (PJ 662). They are regarding the stock and display of class 4 superfluities with increasing disdain.

Convergence and moderation are a Say's Law that creates its own demand. The destitute have less of a need to beg, the dissipated to boast. An unexpected consequence is the victory of the authentic over the fake: 'The improvement of mankind rests upon nothing so essentially as upon the habitual practice of candour, frankness and sincerity' (PJ 158). Hypocrisy and prevarication undermine the self-image of the deceitful: 'All falsehood has a tendency to enervate the individual that practices it' (PJ 258).

It cannot be very satisfying for an actor to be judged by his costumes and not his performance. No one, rich or poor, is today entirely content at the margin to let his commodities speak on his behalf. Lies are going out. The 'sacred armour of truth' (PJ 525) is conquering new ground. 'Thought begets thought' (PJ 665). It begets 'ardour and improvement' (PJ 665). It begets admiration. It does not beget superfluities. In touch with the truth, consumers are nowadays preferring to 'replenish existence with the greatest number of unallayed, exquisite and substantial enjoyments' (PJ 672).

As invidious comparison fades with satiety into 'bad form', as pecuniary proxies cease to be paramount, so, Godwin deduces, will visible living standards become more similar: 'Every man would have a frugal, yet wholesome diet' (PJ 650). Differential diligence and equal opportunities will lend legitimacy to the disparities that survive: 'Men will be estimated for what they are, and not for their accidental appendages' (PJ 710).

The decline in shallow appearance takes the edge off material inequality. Disparities in property and income will decline over time. Land and capital will not leverage, and 'to a deplorable degree', on the 'oppression of multitudes' (PJ 626). That is in the future. What is closer to home is the competitive display of 'sumptuous yet…insignificant luxuries' (PJ 625). Where the rich conform to the broad citizenship middle, they will look like the rest of us. Their bank accounts and share certificates are unseen and invisible. Material distance, out of sight, is out of mind. No one need ever know the truth.

Godwin's critics will object that his transition is in danger of stopping short at the superstructure when the underlying cause of the injustice is the basis. Godwin is aware that to equalise the consumables is not to equalise the assets. Discontent may become less but exploitation will carry on as before. The broad citizenship middle has a lot to answer for. It makes us two nations in all *but* the presentation of self.

Godwin's critics will say that mind without matter is only half the story. They will complain that Godwin has marched them up to a transition only to march them down again. Godwin's answer is that they should not lose their nerve. Consumption changes first. Production takes time. Rome was not built in a day. Anarchy has much to learn from Rome.

5.4.4 The New Distinction

Psychology has uncovered the truth. Man by nature is distinction-seeking. As a rising proportion of our people nears the upper limit of consumption classes 1, 2 and 3, a status-conscious society will have to identify a workable alternative to the pecuniary motive. That new incentive will be the distinction that accrues to socially validated achievement: 'The man who has nothing to provide for but his animal wants scarcely ever shakes off the lethargy of his mind; but the love of honour hurries us on to the most incredible achievements' (PJ 627). The love of honour keeps achievement on track even when Robinson on his island, fed and watered, would have a Malthus-type propensity to sleep under a tree.

There is no virtue in the mere 'exhibition of wealth' (PJ 628). There is no deep satisfaction in the obsequious fawning expected by 'the man who possesses and disburses money' (PJ 627). It is, however, a different matter where the appreciation is the merited reward that accrues to the especially skilled or the genuinely philanthropic. Assiduity, generosity and ingenuity improve the well-being of the community. Public opinion is united in a desire to express its gratitude.

It would clearly be in keeping with 'good sense' and 'correct perceptions' if 'the persons who possess these talents were as conspicuously treated with affection and esteem as the wealthy are now treated' (PJ 628). The acknowledgement would take the form of thanks, smiles, voiced appreciation, a pat on the back, a seat in the Lords or a Royal Medal rather than cash on the table. For all the pluralisation it remains a payment and a quid pro quo. A secular saint is able to 'derive his happiness from within' (PJ 524). Most people welcome non-pecuniary remuneration for a service performed well.

Differential contributions are reliably rewarded with differentiated gratefulness: 'Every man is *laudably* employed who procures to himself or his neighbour a real accession of pleasure' (PJ 672, emphasis added). Such praise is a distance factor. In contrast to a first-class carriage, it is, however, a distance factor which links the winner more closely to his community. There is no peak or upper turning point. Distinction in the post-acquisitive society does not disappear into the *bono publico*. Simply, it is diverted from 'servility and terror' (PJ 664) to a superior maximand that better serves the nation's needs.

5.4.5 *Work and Leisure*

Once the class 4 superfluities have been back-burnered into 'bad form', 'the necessity for the greater part of the manual industry of mankind would be superseded' (PJ 649). What survives of the less pleasant tasks, kept within 'narrow limits' (PJ 633), 'amicably shared among the active and vigorous members of the community', would be 'burdensome to none' (PJ 649–50). In the *Political Justice* Godwin estimates that no more than 'half an hour's industry *per diem*' (PJ 667) would be required. In the *Enquirer* he raises the figure to 'a tenth, perhaps a twentieth part of the labour now imposed' (EQ 163). Even two to four hours' drudgery is not an impossible burden. The cows must be milked and the clothes washed and pressed. After that, multi-dimensional man would be free to develop into himself.

It would be leisure but it would not be indolence. Activity, Marx says, is 'not just a means of keeping alive' but 'a vital need' (Marx, 1875 [1974]: 347). Alienation in the pin factory having given way to *homo faber* and true freedom of choice, self-actualising man will be in a position to 'do one thing today and another tomorrow, to hunt in the morning, fish in the afternoon, rear cattle in the evening, criticise after dinner, just as I have a mind' (Marx & Engels, 1845–1846 [1976]: 47). It would, as Godwin describes it, be a post-industrial, post-capitalist paradise in which essential chores would no longer be a serious barrier to *mens sana in corpore sano.*

To work is to be. 'The healthy exercise of faculties', Marshall says, 'is the aim of life, is life itself' (Marshall, 1873 [1925]: 115). Godwin, like Marshall, was looking forward to a post-economic future in which man would fill his days with literature, philosophy, family, philanthropy, sport and community. Labour would be transformed from work into play. Activity, properly channelled, would in itself be 'pure pleasure' (TM 308): 'Man has a natural delight in the exercise of his active powers' (Mandeville, 216). The supply curve for cooking, decorating, gardening, debating, learning, experimenting, childcare, eldercare, the draining of Hume's waterlogged meadow would no longer slope upward to the right. No rational person abstains from activity that lends 'hilarity to the spirits' (PJ 650).

Work would be voluntary, useful and purposive. A 'new stock of cheerfulness and energy' would be called into being once men 'feel that they are men' (PJ 666). A new service ethic would develop: 'A labour of this sort is perhaps not inconsistent with the most desirable state of human existence' (PJ 673). Industriousness in the sense of Morris would not yield to lethargy in the sense of Malthus. Other-orientated creativity would keep good communitarians up-and-doing. Economic growth will not grind to a halt. It will, however, be a superior mode of economic growth.

5.5 The State in the Transition

In the long run there will be no state. Experience and interest will make us good friends and enthusiastic collaborators. Origins and destinations will be determined by factored-down freedom in dialogue with the collective consciousness: 'The distribution of wealth in every community must be left to depend upon the sentiments of the individuals of that community' (PJ 636).

In the long run, pay and prices, endowments and opportunities, rights and duties, will reflect 'the good sense of the community, and the inspection of all exercised upon all' (PJ 637). The real and the impartial spectator will keep the buyers and the sellers in line. Consensus will harmonise the expectations. Where the people believe that a subset of origins and destinations is not doing all that it can for the common good, they will make a collective choice to move to a more satisfactory equilibrium (PJ 637).

In the short run the position is different. Mutual aid to develop citizenship capacity has a tendency to degenerate into civil war. Unbounded self-seeking, unanimously regarded as a threat to person and property, forces the anxious to appoint an enforcer. Security is 'the true end of civil institution' (PJ 642). The watchdog serves as the 'guardian of the rights of private judgment' (PJ 642). Without the protector state full factoring down would collapse into chaos.

We start from here. Locke calls upon the third party to uphold the existing entitlements. Godwin acknowledges the long arm of the past. Simultaneously, he deplores its lasting legacy: 'This injustice, unequal distribution of property, the grasping and selfish spirit of individuals, is… one of the original sources of government' (PJ 638). The status quo is another name for privilege baked in. Citizens today are fully aware that many of the rigidities in the present day are the unwanted baggage of class-biased rules adopted in time gone by. Primogeniture, entailing and inheritance are man-made multipliers which it is difficult to defend against the 'silent hostility of opinion' (PJ 640). They were never in the public interest: 'It would be difficult to show that feudality and aristocracy ever produced an overbalance of good' (PJ 641). They are not in the public interest now.

Most of us have serious doubts about an inherited code. Protecting handed-on assets and openings, it 'turns the stream of property out of its natural course' (PJ 409). It concentrates the ancient rights to a good life 'in the hands of a very few persons' (PJ 409). It acts as 'a premium paid to idleness' (PJ 649) which has outlived its function. The nobs have things all their own way: 'Accumulated property treads the powers of thought in the dust, extinguishes the sparks of genius, and reduces the great mass of mankind to be immersed in sordid care' (PJ 649).

Most of us know that functionless survivals are wrong. That does not, however, mean that we are looking to our state to cancel the established expectations. Plato's philosopher-rulers and Steuart's fair-minded statesmen, omniscient and beneficent, might be in a position to bring past-dominated artificialities up to date. They might be able to make government into a 'treasury of public wisdom', a deus ex machina that 'might actively lead us, with greater certainty, in the path of happiness' (PJ 642). Not so the real, existing monarchs and aristocrats of England in 1793. Tyrants and despots like Pitt, Grenville and George III have neither the will nor the skill to lean against the prevailing endowments that are so conspicuously in the hands of a conservative minority. As much as today's portfolio is a functionless survival, still the biased and the partial continue to use their stranglehold on the state to protect the interests of their own. Their power is in itself a strong reason to call for a minimal state.

There is a further reason why our people, negative as we are to man-made origins and destinations, are reluctant to invite the state as it *is* to do battle with the state as it *was*. Most of us have been socialised time-out-of-mind into 'the sacred and indefeasible right of private judgment' (PJ 642). Most of us believe that, inherited or earned, what is mine is mine and that thine comes under the same blanket rule. Most of us are convinced that incumbent inequities 'cannot be prevented without exposing us to still greater iniquities' (PJ 639). Most of us deny that they should or can be destroyed on the spot.

Most of us are torn between yes-but and but-yes. Godwin shares that ambivalence. The bulk of existing claims should be left where they are. Private property is, he insists, 'the palladium of all that ought to be dear to us' (PJ 642). Commune-ists and Marxists will throw up their hands in horror. Malthus and Ricardo will, however, regard Godwin's palladium as little more than common sense. While a periphery of entitlements may legitimately be restructured, the majority must be regarded as a palladium that is consonant with the 'general weal' (PJ 104), the 'common good' (PJ 652). Possession is nine-tenths of the law. It is all in Locke.

Time will provide. History-to-come, gradually and seamlessly, will reallocate the origins and destinations from within. In the long run the starts and finishes will become more equitable. Each man, as if guided an invisible hand, will 'be united to his neighbour, in love and mutual kindness' (PJ 653). Emancipated from the 'unresisted sway over multitudes of others' that is exercised by the rich and powerful, he will learn to 'think and judge for himself' (PJ 653). It will be anarchism. It will not be the state.

Godwin does not look to Pitt, Grenvillle or George III to remove the stumbling blocks. Adam Smith was more favourable to the state. Latter-day social engineers have continued the search for a hands-on solution to unacceptable peaks and troughs. Social democrats have made the state in the short run an input in the social production function that in the long run will bring the good society into being.

Progressive income tax, capital gains tax, estate duties and land reform level down the accumulation and transmission of property. Welfare levers such as subsidised education and the National Health put teeth into equal opportunities. Universal conscription, affirmative action and public service broadcasting diffuse the common culture. Sumptuary taxes attack the consumption of socially divisive consumables. Evolution takes too long. Provided that the democratic groundswell is on its side, the broad middle ground can be nudged into place by a wise and thinking state: 'Government must always depend upon the opinion of the governed' (Seminary, 2). So long as the governed are on side, dysfunctional excess and deficiency can be put to rout by the proactive deployment of public facilities and regulations in the service of interpersonal overlap: 'A revolution of opinions is the only means of attaining to this inestimable benefit' (PJ 636).

Godwin, minimaxing Castlereagh more than he would have trusted Attlee, did not contemplate the possibility that perfectibility and universal benevolence could be advanced by the state. To him the state was manipulation, persuasion and serfdom rather than pump-priming in the cause of moderation. If, however, there were to be bilateral communication between the state and its people, then the managed order might tick all or most of his boxes. There might be no need either for frightened libertarianism in the present or for undocumented anarchism in the future. That nice Mr. Attlee can be trusted to be the Minister of Bliss. It might be enough.

References

By W. Godwin

Godwin, W. (1783). *An Account of the Seminary at Epsom in Surrey* (abbreviated as Seminary). T. Cadell.

Godwin, W. (1793). *Enquiry Concerning Political Justice* (abbreviated as PJ 1793) (2 Vols.). G.C.J. and J. Robinson.

Godwin, W. (1794 [1988]). *Things as They Are, or the Adventures of Caleb Williams* (abbreviated as CW). Penguin Books.

Godwin, W. (1797 [1965]). *The Enquirer* (abbreviated as EQ). Augustus M. Kelley.

Godwin, W. (1798 [1976]). *Enquiry Concerning Political Justice* (abbreviated as PJ). Penguin Books.

Godwin, W. (1805 [1992]). *Fleetwood, or the New Man of Feeling* (abbreviated as Fleetwood), in *Collected Novels and Memoirs of William Godwin* (Vol. 5). William Pickering.

Godwin, W. (1817 [1992]). *Mandeville: A Tale of the Seventeenth Century in England* (abbreviated as Mandeville), in *Collected Novels and Memoirs of William Godwin* (Vol. 6). William Pickering.

Godwin, W. (1818). *A Letter of Advice to a Young American* (abbreviated as Letter). M.J. Godwin.

Godwin, W. (1873). *Essays: Never Before Published* (abbreviated as Essays). Henry S. King.

By Other Authors

Brown, F. K. (1926). *The Life of William Godwin*. J.M. Dent and Sons.

Douglas, M., & Isherwood, B. (1979). *The World of Goods*. Allen Lane.

Engels, F. (1880 [1942]). *Socialism: Utopian and Scientific*, in Karl Marx, *Selected Works* (2 Vols.). Lawrence and Wishart.

Engels, F. (1845 [1958]). *The Condition of the Working Class in England*, tr. by W. H. Henderson and W. O. Chaloner. Basil Blackwell.

Locke, J. (1690 [1947]). *Second Treatise on Civil Government*. In E. Barker (Ed.), *Social Contract* (pp. 1–206). Oxford University Press.

Marshall, A. (1873 [1925]). The future of the working classes. In A. C. Pigou (Ed.), *Memorals of Alfred Marshall* (pp. 101–118). Macmillan.

Marshall, T. H. (1965 [1981]). *The Right to Welfare and Other Essays*. Heinemann Educational Books.

Marx, K. (1875 [1974]). *Critique of the Gotha Programmne*. In D. Fernbach (Ed.), *Karl Marx: Political Writings* (Vol. 3, pp. 338–359). Penguin Books.

Marshall, P. H. (1984). *William Godwin*. Yale University Press.

Marx, K., & Engels, F. (1845–1846 [1976]). *The German Ideology*, in *Karl Marx and Friedrich Engels: Collected Works* (Vol. 5, pp. 19–540). Lawrence and Wishart.

Marx, K., & Engels, F. (1848 [2011]). *The Communist Manifesto* (S. Moore, Trans.). Penguin Books.

Menger, A. (1886 [1899]). *The Right to the Whole Produce of Labour* (M. E. Tanner, Trans.). Macmillan.

Paley, W. (1785). *Principles of Moral and Political Philosophy* (2 Vols.). Exshaw, White and Others.

Plato. (1970). *The Laws* (T. J. Saunders, Trans.). Penguin Books.

Rawls, J. (1971). *A Theory of Justice*. Oxford University Press.

Smith, A. (1759 [1966]). *The Theory of Moral Sentiments* (abbreviated as MS). Augustus M. Kelley.

Smith, A. (1776 [1961]). *The Wealth of Nations* (abbreviated as WN) (2 Vols.). Methuen.

Tawney, R. H. (1931 [1964]). *Equality*. George Allen and Unwin.

Tawney, R. H. (1972). In J. M. Winter & D. M. Joslin (Eds.), *R.H. Tawney's Commonplace Book*. Cambridge University Press.

Veblen, T. (1899 [1970]). *The Theory of the Leisure Class*. Unwin Books.

CHAPTER 6

Justice and Population

Malthus in 1798 had compared humankind to 'a noxious species of vermin', forever poised to 'overthrow the earth' (in OP 596). It was a position, Godwin said, that 'had scarcely been heard of, till the appearance of the first edition of the Essay on Population' (OP 596). Godwin believed that Malthus had been the first to poison the well. He saw himself as the frontrunner theorist who, five years before the *Essay*, had attempted 'by actual and patient investigations' to reveal the truth that Malthus had subsequently distorted and discredited: 'All that I have delivered on this head is new' (OP 323). No one before Godwin had done so much to set the record straight. After that it was the Pretender, and all was night.

Godwin's contribution in the *Political Justice* is discussed in the second part of this chapter. The first part shows that neither Godwin nor Malthus had been the first into the field. God had enjoined the community-spirited to 'be fruitful and multiply' in order to populate the empty stage (*Old Testament, Genesis*: 1: xxiii). God came before Godwin. So did Botero (1588), Bacon (1625), Graunt (1662), King (1696), Süssmilch (1741) and Ortes (1790). Both Godwin and Malthus appeal to great books such as Plato's *Republic*, Aristotle's *Politics*, More's *Utopia* (1516), Swift's *Gulliver's Travels* (1726) and Mably's *De la Législation* (1776) (PJ 649n). It is easy to accuse them of exaggerating their own importance. The truth is that they were standing on the shoulders of mentors and authorities who, starting with *Genesis*, were impatient to be heard.

D. Reisman, *William Godwin and Thomas Robert Malthus*,
https://doi.org/10.1007/978-3-031-62113-0_6

All that ever *was*, *is* or *will be* affords a good choice of research topics. It is not obvious why two morally minded scholars should have spilt so much ink on the *numerus clausus*. Godwin and Malthus made economics and justice the trunk of their respective systems. Copulation and farming could have been left to the branches and the *obiter dicta*. Godwin viewed headcount as the little finger but certainly not the heart. Malthus moved population and poverty to the very centre of his worldview.

Some thinkers, before and after, have regarded Malthus's cliff-edge as an exaggeration. Others have seen in famine-stricken, war-torn Ponderovka the lasting hard-core of his lifesaving message. Tendencies, assumptions, leads, lags, flavours in fashion and the mutation in matter forever compound the blur (Reisman, 2021: 4–18). Presumably, the perspective that wins the most promotions for its devotees is the right one. But it is not certain.

6.1 Shoulders of Giants

Plato, Malthus said, 'fully saw the tendency of population to increase beyond the means of subsistence' (SE I 137). Plato had known that rational people 'take care not to produce offspring out of proportion to their wealth, in order to protect themselves against poverty or war' (Plato, 2012: 372). After Plato there had been Aristotle. He 'appears to have seen this necessity still more clearly' (SE I 137). Natural increase, preventive checks, it had all been said before. Godwin and Malthus, hardly pioneers, were accommodating their arguments to an existing debate. Neither author was as original as he in an unguarded moment was wont to maintain.

No one at the time of Godwin's *Political Justice* and Malthus's first *Essay* knew the facts. Occasionally there was opportunistic sampling of births and deaths in the parish registers. More commonly, demography was an exercise in conjecture and guesstimate. *Too many* or *too few*, it could have gone either way. In the event, the authorities, mainly English, on whom Godwin and Malthus drew tended to argue that not overpopulation but underpopulation was the greater concern.

Petty in his 1679 *Treatise on Taxes and Contributions* had emphasised the contribution made by living labour to the national income: 'Labour is the Father and active principle of Wealth, as Lands are the Mother' (Petty, 1679: 47). 'Fewness of people', he said, 'is real poverty' (Petty, 1679: 16). No one who holds a labour theory of growth can afford to point to the active ingredient with his left hand.

In 1686, in his *Essay Concerning the Multiplication of Mankind*, Petty suggested that a law of geometric progression (Petty, 1686: 6, 12, 20, 27) governs the rate of increase. The population is growing. So long as there remain 'many Acres of unimproved improvable Land' (Petty, 1686: 43), there is no immediate danger that the supply of food will be unable to keep pace. There is no reason to be complacent about the future. That the good times would one day peter out is, Petty concedes, a mathematical inevitability: 'The World will be fully Peopled within the next two Thousand Years' (Petty, 1686: 7).

In two thousand years or even less, Malthus will be proven right. Godwin will have been eclipsed by famine and beggary. Cantillon in the *Essay* in 1755 was to warn that the natural increase of all animals proceeds inexorably to the iron ceiling set by food: 'Men multiply like Mice in a barn if they have unlimited Means of Subsistence' (Cantillon, 1755 [1759]: 83). Before him Hobbes, after him Darwin, Cantillon saw that history could let its passengers down. As with Petty, he did not think the end was nigh.

Davenant, in *An Essay on Ways and Means of Supplying the War* in 1695, shared Petty's positive attitude to people: 'People are the real Strength and Riches of a Country' (Davenant, 1695: 144). Soldiers in times of war, workers in times of peace, numbers and interactions are an important social asset. A thickly populated country is a beehive of 'Invention, Frugality and Industry' while in a thinly populated country 'there is nothing but Sloath and Poverty' (Davenant, 1695: 144). In 1622 in *Consuetudo vel Lex Mercatoria*, Malynes had said what every merchant knows that 'traffic and commerce' are a function of demand as well as supply: 'The concourse of people causeth the greater consumption of all things' (Malynes, 1622 [1979]: 235). The circular flow is always there. Thence the warm welcome. Buying or selling, people are wealth: 'No Country can be truly accounted great and powerful...but by the Multitude of its Inhabitants' (Davenant, 1695: 145). A decline in population would be the road to ruin.

Child in 1693, in *A New Discourse of Trade*, said it loud and clear: 'The Riches of a City, as of a Nation', consist 'in the multitude of Inhabitants'. Low interest rates, more thrift and less luxury are elements of the national production function. So are assiduous workers, ambitious immigrants and the elimination of unemployment that wastes scarce potential.

High wages are 'infallible evidence' that our nation is doing well: they 'cause an encrease of People, which principally enrich any Country'. High wages are favourable to marriage and thus to the workers of the future: 'A trading Country, affording comfortable Subsistences to more families...is the reason that many do Marry, who otherwise must be forced to live single'. Food, Child decided, is not a problem: produce is 'not yet advanced to the one fifth part of Improvement that this Land is capable of' (Child, 1693: Preface, 58). Godwin came from a family of 13 children, and Malthus of 8. They knew at first hand what a large family meant.

David Hume in the *Treatise* had ventured into the 'amorous passions' (Hume, 1739–40 [1969]: 441). He had seen no reason to fear that 'the appetite of generation, when confin'd to a certain degree' (Hume, 1739–40 [1969]: 442), would inevitably put intolerable pressure on the stock of grain. In his essay 'On the Populousness of Ancient Nations' he stated in 1752 that there was no reliable data on population in either classical or modern times but that deductive logic had suggested to him that the numbers must have been going up: 'Almost every man, who thinks he can maintain a family, will have one; and the human species, at this rate of propagation, would more than double every generation' (Hume, 1752 [1804]: I 400). Provided that the climate is propitious and the soil good, it is a virtuous circle that is fully in the public interest: 'Wherever there are most happiness and virtue, and the wisest institutions, there will also be most people' (Hume, 1752 [1804]: I 401).

Adam Smith in 1776 welcomed the numbers. More input produces more output. A growing workforce nurtures a growing economy which demands more labour to generate more supply. Natural increase is the effect and cause of national well-being: 'The liberal reward of labour...as it is the effect of increasing wealth, so it is the cause of increasing population. To complain of it, is to lament over the necessary effect and cause of the greatest public prosperity' (WN I 90).

It is a virtuous circle but the precondition is food. It is, Schumpeter says, 'a stale truism' (Schumpeter, 1954: 257) that, in Adam Smith's words, 'countries are populous' in proportion to 'those whom it can feed' (WN I 182): 'Every species of animals naturally multiplies in proportion to the means of their subsistence, and no species can ever multiply beyond it' (WN I 89). In stationary China where growth had stalled, the population mechanism had pushed living standards to the bare minimum. In growing New England, more people and more output had evolved into a symbiosis which would not be forced by hunger into decline and fall.

Benjamin Franklin in his *Observations* in 1755 had shown that high wages and cheap land were enabling the population in the American colonies to double every 20 years: 'People increase in Proportion to the Number of the Marriages, and that is greater in proportion to the Ease and Convenience of supporting a Family' (Franklin, 1755: 42). Births in excess of deaths were inexorably filling up a vast continent, rich in plants and animals but waiting patiently for the human input.

Montesquieu, surveying the world as a whole, was less optimistic. In 1721 and later in 1748, he expressed his concern as a pro-natalist that the trajectory was deplorably reversing itself into oblivion: 'I have come to the conclusion that there is scarcely a tenth of numbers of men on earth that there was in former times....The world is constantly becoming less populous, and, if this continues, in ten centuries it will be nothing more than a desert' (Montesquieu, 1721 [1973]: Letter 112). Individual freedom would not be enough to arrest the downward trend. Laws and bounties to accelerate procreation might be necessary to ensure that the nation obtains the numbers that it requires (Montesquieu, 1748 [1949]: II 24–5).

The real wealth of nations is its people. More is better. Less is worse. William Paley in 1785 in his *Principles of Moral and Political Philosophy* argued strongly that total utility and not just the national product is a linear function of population stock: 'In comparing adjoining periods, in the same country, the collective happiness will be nearly in the exact proportion of their numbers, that is, twice the number of inhabitants will produce double the quantity of happiness' (Paley, 1785: II 368). Paley, a Christian utilitarian, believed that brute headcount opened all the doors: 'The quantity of happiness...depends on the number of inhabitants' (Paley, 1785: II 368). Anxious Montesquieu had been right to exhort the policymakers both to stimulate an increase and, crucially, to stem a fall: 'The decay of population is the greatest evil that a state can suffer' (Paley, 1785: II 369).

Economic growth is the effect and cause. With affluence, however, is likely to come moral restraint. Luxuries, 'habitual superfluities', are becoming 'real wants' (Paley, 1785: II 375). Red wall turning blue, they are becoming an essential part of the 'accustomed mode of life' even of the 'common people' (Paley, 1785: II 375). Although in principle people should not own more than they can use, Paley had no objection to a moderate amount of comfort. It was the feedback effect on numbers that he feared. As the economy grows and incomes rise, the danger is that the materially minded will opt for later marriage lest a large family 'reduce their mode of living' (Paley, 1785: II 375). Paley was determined that expansion should not tail off. Only people can experience utility. People are a necessity. They are not a luxury consumer durable.

Malthus in 1796 in his unpublished *The Crisis* indicated that there was much in Paley's *Principles* that made sense: 'On the subject of population, I concur with Archdeacon Paley, who says that the quality of happiness in any country is best measured by the number of people. Increasing population is the most certain possible sign of the happiness and prosperity of a state' (in Keynes, 1933 [1972]: 83). Even Paley had, however, seen that it would not last. Food would one day become the lion in the path.

So great is 'the fecundity of the soil' (Paley, 1785: II 372), Paley wrote, that farm produce can increase as much as fivefold (the number has a familiar ring) to accommodate the rise in population. It is a reserve upon which the present day has no need to draw. The 'limits fixed by nature…are not yet attained, nor even approximated, in any country of the world' (Paley, 1785: II 332). For all that, a boundary is patiently waiting out the fullness of time. 'Not yet attained', not 'even approximated', still Smith's China remains a real-world probability. It can happen here.

In 1729 Swift, in 'A Modest Proposal', had solved the China problem at a stroke when he suggested that the poor, rather than petitioning for relief, should take matters into their own hands. They should fatten up their starving offspring and either eat them (one plump one-year-old feeding two standard-size adults) or else sell them to pay the rent. Children are 'a most delicious, nourishing, and wholesome food, whether stewed, roasted, baked, or boiled' (Swift, 1729 [1897]: 476). Since Catholics have larger families than Protestants, a decent fricassée or ragout would unintendedly address the Irish-Papist overhang. Swift in his modest satire had argued that population was not the ticking time bomb but that food was. It was land that was returning the prophets of progress to the drawing board.

Paley in the *Principles* had been, although cautiously, a prophet of betterment. In 1798 there was Malthus's *Essay* and he changed his mind. In Chapter 26 of his *Natural Theology* Paley warned in 1802 of 'superfecundity' that ends in 'destruction': 'There is no species of terrestrial animals whatever, that would not overrun the earth, if it were allowed to multiply in perfect safety' (Paley, 1802 [1809]: 479). Paley's 'thinnings' are Malthus 'checks'. An excessive population undermines the living standards of the common people. Misery, vice, civil war and the megalomaniac Napoleon are writ in the natural law.

Even Condorcet admitted that food was in finite supply. In the *Sketch* in 1795 he identified the burden of population on subsistence as, however distant, a point 'beyond which all future improvement is impossible'

(Condorcet, 1795 [2012]: 137). It would be a buffer to the 'indefinite' perfectibility of man even if a fall from grace were 'still very far from us' (Condorcet, 1795 [2012]: 2, 137). Science would raise average productivity in the primary as well as the secondary sector. Birth control would resolve any excess due to Cantillon's mice in the barn.

Malthus found Condorcet's invocation of science profoundly unconvincing, his argument for contraception and 'promiscuous concubinage' (FE 124) a barefaced invitation to vice. Condorcet, like Paley, had not understood the most fundamental truth about population. Not 'distant', the day of judgement 'has long since arrived' (FE 124). The excess, not 'remote' but 'imminent and immediate' (SE I 306), was already pressing on the means of subsistence (SE I 10). Progress is even now degenerating into pessimism and melancholy.

The Age of Reason was going wrong. Robert Wallace in his *Various Prospects of Mankind, Nature, and Providence* had predicted in 1761 that there would ultimately be standing room only on the surface of the earth: 'Mankind would encrease so prodigiously, that the earth would be overstocked at last, and become unable to support its numerous inhabitants' (Wallace, 1761: 115–6). It would be a physical impossibility. It is not now but the 'miserable catastrophe', the 'dreadful time' (Wallace, 1761: 116, 117), must eventually come. The human race is increasing without limit. The provisions are not. The mice in the barn are not dead but only sleeping.

Positive checks such as abortion, infanticide, sickness, plague, monasteries, cloisters, a statutory life span, 'force and fraud' would, Wallace said, not be enough. Men would be 'laid under the cruel necessity of killing one another' (Wallace, 1761: 121). Wallace, unlike Swift, did not think that cannibalism was a joke. A Christian clergyman, Wallace was philosophically on the side of More's utopia, shared ownership, labour in common: 'The whole earth would become a paradise, and mankind be universally wise and happy' (Wallace, 1761: 105). It would be Godwin's anarchy, but it would be shattered by scarcity. With equality comes numbers. A swelling population would return the world to 'the same calamitous condition as at present' (Wallace, 1761: 120). Wallace does not say how imminent or remote the final reckoning will be. Malthus saw it as here and now. There are already people living in indigence.

Sir James Steuart in his *Principles* of *Political Economy* in 1767 acknowledged the strong possibility of an incoming tide. Steuart compared the 'generative faculty' to a spring restrained by a weight. When the growth in population exceeds the growth in subsistence, 'the spring is overloaded' and 'inhabitants will diminish…in proportion to the overcharge' (Steuart, 1767 [1966]: I 32). Population, provided that 'there be a demand for men', 'has ever been, and must ever be, in proportion to the food produced': 'Whatever gives food gives numbers' (Steuart, 1767 [1966]: I 20, 40, 94).

Wealth depends on food. Agriculture is the staff of life. It does not, of course, 'follow from this, that every body almost in the state should be employed in it' (Steuart, 1767 [1966]: I 37). Steuart knew about Quesnay and the *Tableau Oeconomique*. While more a cameralist and a mercantilist than a physiocrat, he recognised that agriculture has to be in balance with the other sectors of the economy if it is to be viable. If the demand is not there, the farmers' superfluity 'will perish like their cherries in a year of plenty; and consequently the farmers will immediately give over working' (Steuart, 1767 [1966]: I 39).

Demand is the precondition for supply, but it must be *effective* demand. Market automaticity is not enough. Needed as well is the visible hand of an astute statesman, 'sagacious', 'virtuous', 'constantly awake', like those Steuart believed he had seen while in exile in Germany (Steuart, 1767 [1966]: I 64, 291; II 703). Steuart believed that aggregate demand was a function of pragmatic intervention in support of supply-side microeconomics. The government must eliminate internal barriers to trade and ensure the built infrastructure. It must manage sudden inventions lest they cause unemployment that destroys purchasing power. It is clearly in the national interest to get the relativities right: 'Agriculture among a free people will augment population, in proportion only as the necessitous are put in a situation to purchase subsistence with their labour' (Steuart, 1767 [1966]: I 48).

Godwin as an anarchist saw little need for a hands-on state. Malthus was more receptive to Steuart on politics, numbers, food and the ability to pay. Malthus says that Steuart 'has explained many parts of the subject of population very ably' (SE I 23). Marx, calling Malthus a 'master in plagiarism' who 'often copies whole pages', reveals that Malthus 'borrowed the greater part of his doctrine from Sir James Steuart' (Marx, 1867 [1961]: 507n, 647n). Schumpeter was no less dismissive of an overrated clergyman whose dire predictions had made him famous but whose ideas were hardly new: 'There was nothing left for Malthus to say that had not been said before….Malthus really did no more than repeat it' (Schumpeter, 1954: 255). In advance of census data from Sweden in the late eighteenth century, from America after 1790 and from Britain after 1801, there was not, however, much more that Malthus and Godwin could do but refine the insights of distinguished pioneers from Maynes to Steuart.

Population was logic. Food was conjecture. No one knew for certain the 'number, weight, or measure' of the ratios. Some authors had nonetheless made preliminary estimates of the citizenship stock.

Richard Price was a non-conformist clergyman, political radical and mould-breaking speaker at Old Jewry in 1789. In his *Observations on Reversionary Payments* in 1771, Price calculated that the population of England and Wales had fallen by a quarter since 1688 (Price, 1771: II 311). Such a fall was not sustainable. Steuart's statesman would have to reverse the trend: 'The encouragement of population, therefore, ought to be one of the first objectives of policy in every state' (Price, 1771: I 280).

Arable had been enclosed into pasture. Sheep, once meek and tame, had begun to 'eat up and swallow down the very men themselves' (More, 1516 [1910]: 26). Thomas More, more than two centuries earlier, had formed the impression that his fellow Englishmen were becoming thin on the ground. Richard Price knew the reason. The price of food had been increasing more rapidly than the money wage. Misery and vice had been shrinking the circular flow.

John Howlett in *An Examination of Dr. Price's Essay* in 1781 stood Dr. Price on his head. Howlett calculated that the population of England and Wales had not shrunk since 1688 but, 'greatly advancing', had actually increased by as much as a third (Howlett, 1781: 152). Such a rise could not be sustained. Up, down, William Godwin in 1793 knew that the empirical evidence was hardly speaking with a single voice. Then he gave his own assessment. Both Price and Howlett had lost sleep for nothing. There was no problem at all: 'In ordinary cases, the standard of population is held, in a manner, stationary for centuries' (PJ 654).

6.2 Godwin on Flow and Stock

Too many or too few, population was not, Godwin felt, a live issue. In the massive two volumes of his *Political Justice*, he devotes less than ten pages to the balance between the mouths that eat and the hands that work. Setting Price's underpopulation to one side despite the need for fighting men in the European war, he devotes his attention to Howlett's overpopulation. He concludes that the possibility is 'remote', the danger 'at a great distance', the debate best reopened, if at all, in 'myriads of centuries': 'It were idle therefore to conceive discouragement from so distant a contingency' (PJ 689).

6.2.1 Tendencies and Laws

The tendency law is not wrong: 'There is a principle in human society by which population is perpetually kept down to the level of the means of subsistence' (PJ 653). It is true by definition that, 'if the population became overstocked, the lower ranks of the inhabitants would be still more incapable of procuring for themselves the necessaries of life' (PJ 654). It is a logical deduction, a hypothetical 'if'. It is not a fact. Bad things are imminent. Overpopulation, however, is not one of them.

The law of progress favours reason over impulse, mind over matter. Mind, 'the ruler of the system', is capable infinitely of 'extending its empire' (PJ 1793, 865). It is already scoring triumph over triumph in the field. Couples in all social classes are coming to 'prefer the pleasures of intellect to the pleasures of sense' (PJ 681). Even without the intimacy of the body that overbreeds the race, men and women are learning to enjoy the 'purest friendship', unsullied by the 'extreme depravity of our present habits' (PJ 684). The passions are in decline: 'They no longer excite the ardour of the mind' (PJ 695).

Sexual intercourse is becoming less frequent: 'One tendency of a cultivated and virtuous mind is to diminish our eagerness for the gratification of the senses....We soon learn to despise the mere animal function' (PJ 695). In time to come, the sex act, like mutton soup, is likely to go out of fashion. People 'will probably cease to propagate' (PJ 696). Loss of interest is a means of contraception that no major religion has ever banned. So, for that matter, is economics. Education, affluence, social subsistence and moral restraint all point to later marriage. Vice and misery can be capped at source. Children are expensive. Consumption yields a higher return.

England, other things being equal, will sink into the ghost-town status of Goldsmith's *Deserted Village*. Godwin, despite his 'probably' (PJ 696), is unlikely to have thought that it would really happen. Reasonable people rely on 'the due exercise of the understanding' (PJ 71) to keep their unrestrained propensities in line with external circumstances. If England is becoming overcrowded, the socially sensitive will marry late as their gift to the whole. If England is shrinking and sinking, they will renounce their selfish celibacy to do their patriotic chore: 'Reasonable men now eat and drink, not from the love of pleasure, but because eating and drinking are essential to our healthful existence. Reasonable men will then propagate their species, not because a certain sensible pleasure is annexed to this action, but because it is right the species should be propagated' (PJ 1793, 851–2). Either way, there is an automatic self-stabilising mechanism that

Malthus, attracted to the invisible hand, ought to have found a source of reassurance.

Godwin could have involved the visible hand in the form of taxes and subsidies, laws and controls. Instead, he turned to the real and the impartial spectator to assure the delivery of an essential public good. Hazlitt comments that, transparently under the influence of 'some of the most beautiful and striking texts of Scripture', Godwin relied not on man as he *is* but on man as he *ought to be* to solve a potential mismatch: 'He raised the standards of morality above the reach of humanity' (Hazlitt, 1825 [1971]: 33, 36).

Godwin relied in the first instance on a qualitative rather than a quantitative standard: 'It is of more importance that a man should be a virtuous and an honourable creature, than that he should merely be' (Sepulchres, 23). Impractical and uncertain as such a devolution of authority may have been, it is fully in keeping with Godwin's reliance on individual ethics rather than a non-ego enforcer to keep progress on course. Factored-down homeostasis would guarantee a number of pregnancies just sufficient to keep Great Britain great. Grenville and Pitt need not apply.

Duty was a preventive check that stood in the way of depopulation. Science was another. Advances in medicine reduce infant mortality and prolong human life (PJ 695). Birth and death in that way become topics not just in biology but in conscious choice and consent as well (PJ 1793, 869). A longer lifespan acting as a de facto elixir is an alternative to the moral imperative that calls upon every man to think of England.

6.2.2 Marriage and Family

Marriage itself is pro-natal. It is 'most favourable to population' (PJ 683). A stable union keeps the numbers up. Malthus, logically speaking, should have spoken out for free love since promiscuity limits the number of births. While Godwin does not demystify the two cultures in the gynaecological ward, what he does assert is that Cantillon was poorly informed about mice. Where the problem is *too many* and not *too few*, what is needed to contain the geometrical ratio is not lifetime pairing but the permissive society. It is 'extremely hostile' (PJ 688) to procreation. Overbirthing in the sense of Malthus would never occur if the community recognised, with Godwin, that all marriage is an 'evil' (PJ 682), 'an irretrievable mistake' (PJ 682). Even cohabitation is bound to be more trouble than it is worth (PJ 681).

Marriage is bilateral monopoly. Closing the door to interlopers, it encourages immoral practices such as 'odious selfishness' and intolerable possessiveness (PJ 682). The fact that the state is the third signatory to the deed politicises the contract into a by-your-leave from Sir. The fact that the union is for life fences off the potential happiness that would accrue to a pair, voluntarily linked, who simply want to change their mind. Malthus as a clergyman was properly disapproving (FE 135). Not only did he predict an expanding population, he could not be expected to give his approval to living in sin without the sacrament.

Godwin had no such reservations. Marriage, he was convinced, is unfreedom. In anarchy it will cease to exist. In the first edition of *Political Justice* Godwin went so far as to hypothesise that children once born will be the responsibility of the community and not of their biological parents: 'It cannot be definitely affirmed whether it be known in such a society who is the father of each individual child. But it may be affirmed that such knowledge will be of no importance' (PJ 1793, 852). The paternal bent will disappear. Given that there will be open marriage, it is unlikely that many fathers will be able to identify their sons. Godwin does not discuss the mothers and their attachments.

Surnames will disappear once the intergenerational transmission of property has become impossible. Arranged marriages will no longer be needed to keep capital in the bloodline. The downgrading of family ties will take the edge off the privateness that is so great an obstacle to anarchistic sharing. Together with the new moderation in commodity consumption, it will defuse the latent aggression and with it the need for an enforcer state. No man will steal my house if he has a house just as good of his own (PJ 1793: 857).

With the disappearance of the state-within-the-state kinship group, with the termination of runaway ostentation in trophy consumables, the communalisation of assets will take its course: 'Bolts and locks would be unknown. Every man would be welcome to make every use of my accommodations, that did not interfere with my own use of them' (PJ 1793: 857). Hobbes's Leviathan will lose his function once the family has withdrawn its insistence on property rights. Malthus would have seen that there was more to promiscuity than population alone. Godwin was attacking the very basis of economic justice itself.

More offspring or fewer offspring, the proposal in 1793 that it takes a village to bring up a child was deleted from the later editions of *Political Justice*. His own marriage in 1798 may have persuaded Godwin that monogamy, sexuality, emotional attachment and a stable family unit have deep roots in human nature. They are a 'little gleam of pure sunshine, which compensates for a thousand other hardships and calamities' (OP 555). Relationships were back. They did not alter Godwin's attitude to population. Human beings are not mice in a barn. They are not about to overpopulate the planet.

6.2.3 *Subsistence*

What is of greater concern is the supply of food. It is the thermostat: 'The number of inhabitants' increases up to but cannot increase 'beyond the facility of subsistence' (PJ 688). Automaticity is always on the lookout for a weak link. It would, however, be premature to exaggerate the risk. The earth is rich, and its potential is barely tapped: 'The average cultivation of Europe might be so improved as to maintain five times her present number of inhabitants' (PJ 653). Godwin, like Child and Paley, saw that humanity might still be able to win the caucus race.

Coke at Holkham had demonstrated the beneficial impact on per acre productivity of manures and machines. Scientific farming would push outward the possibilities frontier. So would the conversion of existing plots from pleasure grounds for the rich to the production of meat and grain for the people: 'The established administration of property may be considered as strangling a considerable portion of our children in their cradle' (PJ 654).

It is true by definition that nature cannot service an infinite demand. The silent partner in scarcity economics is, however, the ceteris paribus. Sub-optimal cultivation and class-based conventions indicate that it is not just the land but also the landowners that must be held to account. Rousseau had said: 'Man is born free, and everywhere he is in chains.... What can make it legitimate?' (Rousseau, 1762 [1947]: 240). Godwin's reply was that nothing could make it legitimate. In the civilised countries of Europe, 'the sources of subsistence are kept within a certain limit' (PJ 653). It is not natural law but man-made law that is leaving the great majority at the mercy of the toffs. Three-quarters of the 'habitable globe' is currently uncultivated and unimproved (PJ 689). Convert the grouse moors from hunting to food. Tear down the fences that privatise the commons. No one then will go hungry.

In a 'free and equal state of society' (PJ 654) the land will meet the social need. In the unfree and unequal present day, misdirected property 'may be considered as arresting, upon the threshold of existence, four fifths of that value and that happiness' (PJ 654). 'That value'—it is Smith. 'That happiness'—it is Paley. Idle land is unable to feed idle people. It is social class and not irresponsible procreation that is the real threat to a decent standard of living.

The agricultural revolution could begin at the bottom with the rick-burners and the Jacqueries: 'Men of England wherefore plough/For the lords who lay ye low?... Sow seed—but let no tyrant reap' (Shelley, 1819 [2002]: 405). It could also begin at the top, with an enlightened aristocracy that recognises in the voluntary 'cession by him that has' (PJ 656) the truth of Jesus's instruction to the rich man to divide and share (*New Testament*, *Mark*: 10, xxi). The Quakers in Pennsylvania had freed their slaves. It is all in Adam Smith.

Compulsion, Godwin says, is not the answer. The way forward can only be the conversion of public opinion from costly superfluities to the revived sense of duty that Beatrice Webb called 'a new consciousness of sin among men of intellect and men of property' (Webb, 1926 [1979]: 179). Social sanctions can make self-love and social be the same. So, although Godwin does not say so, can pure-blood mercenary capitalism. An estate that sells more food generates more profit. Reason and understanding point to planting, harvesting, feeding and cashing in.

6.2.4 Deprivation

Population is demand. Food is supply. There is also the fringe. Excluded from the feast, unable to meet their basic needs, the rejected have no fall-back but parish relief and private charity. Of the options, Godwin makes clear which one he prefers: 'Mildness and an unbounded philanthropy are the most effectual instruments of public welfare' (PJ 410).

Gesellschaft is impersonal: 'Justice measures by one unalterable standard the claims of all' (PJ 240). *Gemeinschaft* cares. Philanthropy, 'rather an unreflecting feeling than a rational principle' (PJ 239), is an emotive response. Our neighbours do not count or calculate before they react ad hominem to a good Samaritan in distress.

The haves have a duty to share. The have-nots have, however, a concomitant duty to pull themselves out of their passing dependency. In the circular flow of gift-giving, the donor has an implicit lien on the recipient's full recovery. Untied aid is 'frequently more injurious than beneficial': 'It leads to a blind partiality, inflicting calamity without remorse, upon many perhaps, in order to promote the imagined interest of a few' (PJ 240). Godwin is not a soft touch. In his view, both the donor and the recipient must be in no doubt about the expectations that circumscribe their de facto quid pro quo: 'More than justice it would be disgraceful for me to ask, and for you to bestow. I stand upon the foundation of right' (PJ 619).

Ebenezer Scrooge cuts corners on his duty. Mary Sunshine, however, is the greater enemy to an 'erect and unembarrassed mien': 'If you bestow upon me unmerited advantage, you are a recreant from the general good' (PJ 619). Just as the fortunate should not abandon the hard cases to lie where they fall, so the residual should take only 'what I deem necessary for the supply of my wants' (PJ 545). Bounty and obligation are two sides of a single coin. 'Each man would be united to his neighbour, in love and mutual kindness' (PJ 653). The precondition is that his neighbour plays by the rules irrespective of whether he is rich or poor.

Scroungers and free riders will always take what they can. They are the deadweight cost of doing good. What matters more than the outlier is the median. It is 'the highest and most indispensable business of man to study and promote his neighbour's welfare' (PJ 251). All of us have a moral duty to do that which is 'conducive to the happiness of mankind' (PJ 253). We expect that our fellow donors will be doing the same and that our dependent favour-seekers will not be exploiting our kindliness. We anticipate that the median couple will not be overbreeding recklessly in the confidence that a compassionate community will not leave it to war, famine, pestilence and plague to cull the population surplus. We expect that Malthus will know that he has lost the debate.

References

By W. Godwin

Godwin, W. (1793). *Enquiry Concerning Political Justice* (abbreviated as PJ 1793). G.C.J. and J. Robinson.

Godwin, W. (1798 [1976]). *Enquiry Concerning Political Justice* (abbreviated as PJ). Penguin Books.

Godwin, W. (1800). *Essay on Sepulchres* (abbreviated as Sepulchres). W. Miller.

Godwin, W. (1820 [1964]). *Of Population: An Enquiry Concerning the Power of Increase in the Numbers of Mankind, Being An Answer to Mr. Malthus's Essay on That Subject* (abbreviated as OP). Augustus M. Kelley.

By T.R. Malthus

Malthus, T. R. (1798 [1970]). *Essay on the Principle of Population, as it affects the Future Improvement of Society, with Remarks on the Speculations of Mr. Godwin, M. Condorcet, and Other Writers* (abbreviated as FE). Penguin.

Malthus, T. R. (1803 et seq. [1989]). *An Essay on the Principle of Population: Or A View of its past and present Effects on Human Happiness, with an Inquiry into our Prospects respecting the Removal of the Evils which it occasions* (2nd ed., 1803; further editions in 1806, 1807, 1817, 1826) (abbreviated as SE I and SE II) (2 Vols.). Cambridge University Press.

By Other Authors

Cantillon, R. (1755 [1959]). *Essai sur la Nature du Commerce en Général* (H. Higgs, Trans.). Frank Cass.

Child, J. (1693). *A New Discourse of Trade*. T. Soule.

Condorcet, Marquis de (1795 [2012]). *The Sketch (Esquisse d'un tableau historique des progrès de l'espirit humain)* (J. Barraclough, Trans.), in *Condorcet: Political Writings* (pp. 1–147). Cambridge University Press.

Davenant, C. (1695). *An Essay Upon Ways and Means of Supplying the War*. Jacob Tonson.

Franklin, B. (1755). *Observations Concerning the Increase of Mankind, Peopling of Countries, etc.* John Clarke.

Hazlitt, W. (1825 [1971]). *The Spirit of the Age*. Scolar Press.

Howlett, J. (1781). *An Examination of Dr. Price's Essay on the Population of England and Wales*. J. Black.

Hume, D. (1739–40 [1969]). *A Treatise of Human Nature*. Penguin Books.

Hume, D. (1752 [1804]). *Essays and Treatises on Several Subjects* (2 Vols.). Bell and Bradfute.

Keynes, J. M. (1933 [1972]). *Essays in Biography*, reprinted in *The Collected Writings of John Maynard* Keynes (Vol. 10). Macmillan.

Malynes, G. de (1622 [1979]). *Consuetudo vel Lex Mercatoria*. Walter J. Johnson.

Marx, K. (1867 [1961]). *Capital* (Vol. I). Foreign Languages Publishing House.

Montesquieu, C.-L. de Secondat (1721 [1973]). *Persian Letters* (C. J. Betts, Trans.). Penguin Books.

Montesquieu, C.-L. de Secondat (1748 [1949]). *The Spirit of the Laws* (T. Nugent, Trans.). Hafner Press.

More, T. (1516 [1910]). *Utopia*. J.M. Dent.

Paley, W. (1785). *Principles of Moral and Political Philosophy* (2 Vols.). Exshaw, White and Others.

Paley, W. (1802 [1809]). *Natural Theology*. J. Faulder.

Petty, W. (1679). *A Treatise on Taxes and Contributions*. Obadiah Blagrave.

Petty, W. (1686). *An Essay Concerning the Multiplication of Mankind*. Rob. Midgley.

Plato. (2012). *The Republic* (C. Rowe, Trans.). Penguin.

Price, R. (1771). *Observations on Reversionary Payments* (2 Vols.). Cadell.

Reisman, D. A. (2021). *Ideology: Conservatives, Liberals and Socialists*. Edward Elgar.

Rousseau, J.-J. (1762 [1947]). *The Social Contract* (G. Hopkins, Trans.). In E. Barker (Ed.), *Social Contract* (pp. 237–440). Oxford University Press.

Schumpeter, J. A. (1954). *History of Economic Analysis*. George Allen and Unwin.

Shelley, P. B. (1819 [2002]). Song to the men of England. In *The Selected Poetry and Prose of Shelley* (pp. 405–406). Wordsworth.

Smith, A. (1776 [1961]). *The Wealth of Nations* (abbreviated as WN) (2 Vols.). Methuen.

Steuart, J. (1767 [1966]). *An Inquiry into the Principles of Political Oeconomy* (2 Vols.). Oliver and Boyd.

Swift, J. (1729 [1897]). A modest proposal for preventing the children of poor people in Ireland from being a burden to their parents or country. In *The Works of the Rev. Jonathan Swift* (pp. 475–478). W.P. Nimmo, Hay and Mitchell.

Wallace, R. (1761). *Various Prospects of Mankind, Nature, and Providence*. A. Millar.

Webb, B. (1926 [1979]). *My Apprenticeship*. Cambridge University Press.

CHAPTER 7

Godwin's *Enquirer*

Malthus said that it had been the *Enquirer* in 1797 that led him to write his *Essay* in 1798. The *Enquiry* had contended that the world was evolving from feudalism through liberal democracy into peaceable anarchy. The *Enquirer* continued the examination of social change in response to an unsatisfactory status quo. The economy is unjust. The poor are in need. Godwin does not say that population is the problem. Malthus was quick to identify the missing variable. There are too many people. Godwin had failed to see that the mice in the barn would renounce exchange and consensus for civil war when there was not enough food to go round.

The *Enquirer* is a collection of 27 loosely connected essays on social patterning in a state of flux. The topics range from gain-seeking economics and the science of society to normative constraint and the pathways from the past. There is also the short chapter on 'Avarice and Profusion'. It lit the spark that became the *Essay on Population*.

The *Enquirer*, sandwiched between the second and third editions of the *Enquiry*, amplifies what Godwin was saying in his big book. 'Gallic republicanism' (EQ ix) had been a blind alley. Rootless profiteering was no better. Present-day institutions do not meet man's needs: 'I weep over the madness of artificial society' (EQ 209). The *Enquirer* like the *Enquiry* looks forward to a higher social order that is more in keeping with virtue and need.

D. Reisman, *William Godwin and Thomas Robert Malthus*,
https://doi.org/10.1007/978-3-031-62113-0_7

7.1 Business Economics

The maximising mindset spindles warm-hearted good-neighbourliness into the pre-scripted categories of competitors, consumers and helots. The shopkeeper posts a price of which 'the generality of his customers are incompetent to judge' (EQ 218). The wheeler-dealer delights in another's wheeler-dealer's loss when he practises that 'most odious and accursed contrivance' (EQ 267) of cut-throat underselling. The tradesman resorts to concealment and misrepresentation to cozen his way through a zero-sum game: 'His whole mind is buried in the sordid care of adding another guinea' (EQ 217). The good society ought to provide an outlet for the 'expansive affections, that open the human soul, and cause one man to identify himself with the pleasure and pains of his fellows' (EQ 238). Our commercial mindset is not propelling us upwards into Aristotle's Athenian *polis*. Rather, it is making us into an unstructured mass that respects no value but the casino of market exchange.

Profit-seeking and aimless spending are unworthy and inefficient. Fortunately, and even in the new commercial state, there is an alternative ethos. Alongside the free marketeers who never gift what they can sell, there is a minority of productive agents who live by a professional ethic of quality workmanship and disinterested service. The doctor, teacher, policeman and firefighter never haggle about pay and conditions. They do their duty in accordance with 'maxims previously promulgated and made known to all' (EQ 221). Income is a necessary but not a sufficient condition when, motivated by commitment and empathy, they swear a quasi-Hippocratic Oath to contribute what they can to the 'welfare of the whole' (EQ 220). They are, as Tawney said, the exemplars of the Functional Society that is to come (Tawney, 1921 [1961]: 90–1). Godwin regarded them as the harbingers of the post-business culture that was already emerging from the *bellum* of self-centred economics.

The supreme aim of production, consumption, distribution and exchange is to 'contribute to the welfare of mankind. The most essential attribute of right conduct therefore is, that it shall have a beneficent and salutary tendency' (EQ 252). Consequences, as in the *Enquiry*, are the Supreme Court. The 'happiest effects' (EQ 317) are the best. They are the most likely to be the external manifestation of 'liberal and generous habits of thinking and acting' that are themselves the internal manifestation of 'a high degree of civilisation and refinement' (EQ 215).

It is not 1789 or 1917 but rather the glacier of obligation that is the guarantor of the common welfare. The butcher, the brewer and the baker will serve us not from pecuniary self-interest but from benevolence, fellowship, intellectual curiosity, job satisfaction and the pursuit of a good name. Our character and conduct will be role-modelled on the district nurse and not the venal property-agent whose time centre-stage is nearing its end.

7.2 A Science of Society

Godwin sees man as an empiricist and a calculator. We rely on remembered regularities, sequences and conjunctions to make predictions about an unknown future: 'If one billiard-ball strike another in a particular manner, we have great reason to suppose that the result will be similar to what we have already observed in like instances' (EQ 19). It is the *Enquiry* (PJ 280–1). It is the *Enquirer*. We do not give up. We learn from experience and 'dispassionate enquiry' (PJ 331) to anticipate a probable succession of events. We make careful observation of 'the pole-star of truth' (EQ vi): 'All our refined and abstracted notions are compounded from ideas of sense' (EQ 246). We leave superstition behind. If there is no evidence, there is no truth.

7.2.1 Perceptions and Facts

Sensory perception, 'concurring circumstances' (EQ 361) and substantive 'habit' (EQ 312) allow us to extrapolate an unknowable future from familiar associations that we believe to have been that much better than random. Free will is an all-too-human conceit. The truth is that will is only free within the boundaries that mind and matter have built up over time: 'All the actions of men are necessary' (PJ 266).

The senses are the window to the world: 'All knowledge makes its approach through the senses' (EQ 360). The facts must be brought to light: 'Let every thing be examined, as far as circumstances will possibly admit, before it is affirmed for true' (EQ 292). The examination will never be 100 per cent: 'Human life, in every one of its parts, is a calculation of probabilities' (EQ 273). Outcomes are 'capricious and uncertain' (EQ 273). Errors abound: 'All men are fallible' (PJ 132). Black swans and billiard balls are susceptible to deviation and surprise. Change is a gamble (EQ 268). We examine the data. We affirm the sequence. We do the best we can. It is never good enough. No one on the eve of Bosworth Field could have said with certainty which horse would win.

Horses have a will of their own. Prediction is an art as much as a science. Everything is related to everything else (EQ 312) Action leads to reaction which triggers the unanticipated knock-ons which unleash the unintended spin-offs which Pigou-like can enrich but also pollute: 'We cannot exist without generating evil' (EQ 72). Morally minded human beings should seek to make themselves the 'authors of the greatest overbalance of good' (EQ 73). The intentions are positive but the outcomes for all that opaque. The future is a black box. The evidence only goes so far.

The mission statement of the investigation is laid down by moral philosophy. Non-testable, non-refutable, the ultimate goal is 'the generation of happiness', the proximate objective to make each man 'useful' (EQ 1). Induction reconstructs the means to the end. Science sets aside the *ought-to-be* in order to focus its attention on the *is*: 'To make a man virtuous we must make him wise' (EQ 2). We must make him aware of the external realities that exist outside his ungrounded imaginings. We must make him curious about the vast *terra incognita* that remains to be explored.

Curiosity is the first step on the road to discovery. On that journey, it is likely to be the 'men of genius' (EQ 10), schooled into 'habits of intellectual activity' (EQ 5), who will take the lead. The Academy and the Lyceum are able to draw upon 'the wisdom of a cultivated intellect' (EQ 2). Ordinary citizens are not. Thinking is not their strongest suit: 'They are brutified by immoderate and unintermitted labour. Their hearts are hardened, and their spirits broken' (EQ 17).

Mind-numbing manual toil unmakes men: 'It is the great slaughterhouse of genius and of mind. It is the unrelenting murderer of hope and gaiety, of the love of reflection and the love of life' (EQ 17). The man in the street is not intellectually equipped to conduct a sequential probe. Physically exhausted and mentally unchallenged, life in the pin factory has left him 'as stupid and ignorant as it is possible for a human creature to become' (WN II 303). He would be well advised, ignorant and impulsive, to follow in the footsteps of the skilled thinkers who have had a head start.

It will not always be so. While the 'men of genius' will always have a comparative advantage, the manual classes can look forward to steady upgrading in a post-capitalist future. In anarchy the working week will shrink to its 'smallest practicable portion' (EQ 176). It will be much less than the stultifying toil needed to sustain present-day growth and consumption. Those hours released from the 'importunate pressure of the first wants of our nature' (EQ 335) will be devoted, as in the *Political Justice*, to 'the cultivation of the understanding' (EQ 175). Philosophy is coming home. Gross domestic happiness is going up.

A state of 'cultivated equality' is the 'most consonant to the nature of man' (EQ 176). Godwin believes that Aristotelian contemplation will in time to come crowd out the capitalistic division of labour. He does not explore expedients such as job rotation, team-tasking or straightforward robotisation that might make the employee's latent creativity an input in his employer's production function. Godwin's future extends to token hours but not a radical redesign of work. The 'delicate and evanescent touches of the soul' (EQ 335) will disappear from economics only to reappear in the newly liberated areas of human life.

7.2.2 Education

Mind and matter will no longer be held back by gain-seeking activity. Moral values will take the place of economic values. It is not work alone that must be moved on to a higher plane but also man's capacity to see and search. Education, broadly defined, should do what the economy cannot. Cut loose from the state, its objective must be to empower, to equalise and to integrate.

Education was discussed in Chap. 5. The *Enquirer* returned to an investigation that Godwin felt the *Enquiry* had not entirely exhausted. Later as earlier, Godwin begins his discussion with Locke. Children are born with different but not excessively different talents. Young people are 'ductile and pliant' (EQ 143): 'Their minds are like a sheet of white paper, which takes any impression' (EQ 70). The innate, the original and the immutable make up 'a very insignificant catalogue' (EQ 12) of the potential that is theirs to develop. Even genius 'is not born with us, but generated subsequent to birth' (EQ 17).

Content and syllabus must be selected with care. The child must read the classics. In his proposed seminary at Epsom, the four languages of Greek, Latin, English and French were to make up the core. Great books widen the perspectives: 'From the Greek and Roman authors the moderns learned to think' (EQ 38). The same is true of geometry: 'It cultivates the powers of the mind, and generates the most excellent habits' (EQ 48). History is its natural pendant. There is no time in geometry. Reality, however, is a never-ceasing process of development.

Apart from the subjects themselves, there is the invisible curriculum. Studying is a challenge: 'Left to ourselves, we are apt to sink into effeminacy and error' (EQ 41). Without education the mind would be 'a wilderness' (EQ 49). Exposed to education, it is sensitised to the constraint of 'inflexible laws' (EQ 49) that limit the freedom of choice. Education teaches the child that there are non-ego boundaries to autonomy and whim.

Education is mentoring. For that reason alone, the pupil-teacher relationship is of necessity unequal. As with the state-citizen nexus, it will normally be the authority figure who takes the lead: 'All education is despotism', a 'tyranny of implicit obedience' (EQ 60). It is not slavery, nor is it liberty: 'The pupil is the clay in the hands of the artificer' (EQ 74).

Rousseau in *Emile* had proposed that the discovery process should be pupil-led: 'Nature provides for the child's growth in her own fashion, and this should never be thwarted' (Rousseau, 1762 [1972]: 50). An individualist, he argued for de-institutionalised learning that would leave it to nature to grasp the chalk: 'The indifference of children towards meat is one proof that the taste for meat in unnatural....Beware of changing this natural taste and making children flesh-eaters' (Rousseau, 1762 [1972]: 118). Ego knows best.

That was Rousseau. It was not Godwin. Godwin describes Rousseau as 'the most eloquent and delightful madman that ever existed' (in KP I 328–9). He praises Rousseau for the 'irresistible energy of his writings' and the 'magnanimity and originality of his speculations' (EQ 106). Rousseau's *Emile*, Godwin declares, had been a 'most valuable treatise' in clarifying his personal vision of education for life: 'I have borrowed many of my ideas from this admirable writer' (Seminary, 4). In spite of that, Rousseau had let undirected laissez-faire ride roughshod over warm-hearted social-ism. Rousseau lived, Godwin declared, 'in a world of his own, and saw nothing as it really was' (Fleetwood, 159). Children must be guided. The expert knows best. Emile has not yet acquired the wisdom he needs to manage autonomy on his own.

Natura non facit saltum. Godwin was reasoning that children, initially dependent on their parents, their teachers and their state, would in time mature into self-determining adults. They would not need a leaderly instructor to pre-select their reading matter or censor their expression. The Jesuits and the Freudians know better. Godwin may have underestimated the risk of arrested development picked up on the way. Thought control is addictive. Rewards and punishments at an impressionable age condition a knee-jerk reflex into a self-perpetuating rut. Educator-led instruction can be a danger both to individual sense-perception and to individual initiative. The shadow of authority might never fade away.

7.3 A Social Animal

Man in society is not Wild Peter in isolation. Individuals interact. They experience empathy. They desire validation. They want their fellows to think well of them.

Other people are the benchmark and the context: 'The social affections are the chief awakeners of man' (EQ 57). They are the sounding board, the mirror and the echo: 'It is difficult for me to feel much eagerness in the pursuit of that by which I expect to contribute to no man's gratification or enjoyment. I cannot entertain a generous complacency in myself, unless I find that there are others that set a value on me' (EQ 57). Other people are the social market that prices each individual dear or cheap. Without that constraint, I would not know what I am worth.

Chapter 2 on the *Political Justice* described the social binding just as Chap. 5 described the non-state education that socialises and entraps. Godwin's vision of glass walls that emancipate the free and independent monad from himself is carried forward from the *Enquiry* into the *Enquirer*. Alter sets a value on ego. Ego sets a value on alter. It is all judge-and-jury out there.

Wild Peter when he settles among us adopts our dress, our language, our *mores* and our morals. He knows that the glass walls are enclosing him in a cage. Having escaped the schooled despotism of parents, teachers, the Church and the state, the sovereign self is coming under attack from the person-to-person sanctions of public opinion. He wants to be the Wild Peter that he is. Instead, he is being forced into the Procrustean template of 'others that set a value on me'. Godwin believed that the gain would more than compensate for the loss: 'The greatest pleasures of which the human mind is susceptible, are the pleasures of consciousness and sympathy' (EQ 68). I wear a bowler hat. I drink my tea. It is worth it to remain in the game.

Socially and psychologically, it is all a matter of 'voluntary transmigration': 'One of the best practical rules of morality that ever was delivered, is that of putting ourselves in the place of others' (EQ 298). We evaluate our fellow players by imagining how we ourselves would respond to an identical stimulus. They test our revealed preferences against the glass standard of non-negotiable propriety. It is all in Hutcheson, Smith and Burns. It is all in Durkheim, Goffman and Mead. Praise backed up by praiseworthiness is 'a liberal satisfaction in communicated and reciprocal pleasure' (EQ 57). We bend our sentiments and our actions in such a way as to win the ungrudging admiration of the 'disinterested spectator' (PJ 524). Impartial and informed, he knows the circumstances and the right response.

The 'magnetism of sentiment' and contact make us intellectual communists, the proprietors of a shared stock: 'It is scarcely possible for a man to adhere to an opinion or a body of opinions, which all other men agree to condemn' (EQ 273). My ideas are *our* ideas. It is scarcely possible for a man to deviate from the rules if he is 'utterly unsupported by the suffrage of his neighbours' (EQ 273).

Man is 'an imitative animal' (EQ 358). He, 'like the camelion, owes the colour he assumes, to the colour of the surrounding objects' (EQ 358). His character is moulded and shaped by his fellow travellers: 'Man taken by himself is nothing. In the first portion of his life, he is more ignorant and worthless than the beasts' (EQ 358). His behaviour patterns and the 'self-complacency' (EQ 256) that internalised norms evoke in him are contingent on the pass-through of the generalised Other.

The generalised Other is the antidote to spoiled self-esteem. Self-valuation is in the gift of the gaze: 'Who ever thought highly of his own talents, till he found those talents obtaining the approbation of his neighbour?' (EQ 57). Life with others clones our conduct. Sympathy, a 'magnetic virtue', limits our scope for discretion: 'When sympathy is strong, imitation easily engrafts itself' (EQ 124).

The precondition is free and full disclosure. Sympathy is not possible where the moves and gambits are shrouded in deception, mystery, secrecy, hypocrisy, cunning, trickery, quackery and downright falsehood. 'Empty and unmeaning cant' tends to 'poison morality' (EQ 103, 105). To avoid misunderstanding that ends in injustice, it is always better for an actor to put his cards on the table: 'Frankness is perhaps the first of virtues; or, at least, is that without which virtue of a manly and liberal dimension cannot exist' (EQ 149).

The sympathy motive modulates and even reverses the power of self-love, narrowly defined: 'To give pleasure to another produces in me the most animated and unequivocal consciousness of existence' (EQ 57). My 'consciousness of existence' is at its most vivid when my pleasure is derived from *your* pleasure and from *their* pleasure. Passion and temptation are kept in line where the neighbours are the shareholders in the common stock: 'Friendship requires that the man in whose bosom it reigns, should act, and appear to act, for the interest of the object of his friendship' (EQ 130). Your interest is my interest. I do not raise the price of snow shovels in a snowstorm. I do not charge extra because mine is the last bus home. My pecuniary self-interest and my social self-interest are not the same.

It is in the individual's social self-interest to mimic the customs and conventions of his warm-blooded surroundings: 'The habitual motive...may be emphatically selfish' (EQ 257). The 'suffrage of the world' gratifies a taste for 'inordinate self-admiration' (EQ 257). Applause will be his remuneration in kind for conspicuous philanthropy, exemplary workmanship or a just price that does not rise with an unexpected snowfall. Integrity is the best policy if an unblemished reputation gets Honest Abe elected.

Motives are mixed: 'In the majority of cases at least, a fair character seems essential to eminent success in the world' (EQ 258). A fair character is the means. Eminent success is the end. Eminent success depends on the replication of the code. Other people demand the right to put their oar in. Self-government is not what it seems. Altruism, never pure, is a calculated investment.

Other people put a new gloss on individual freedom. The collective discipline of all over each is the hard core of community and integration. Yet it also imposes a monkey-see-monkey-do which Wild Peter might regard as a prison without bars. Godwin as a social-ist gives his opinion that membership in enveloping aggregates is felt well-being: 'Who ever was satisfied with his own exertions, till they had been sanctioned by the suffrage of a bystander?' (EQ 57). Godwin as an individual-ist is, on the other hand, quick to declare that autonomy is 'the pure and genuine condition of a rational being' (EQ 77). Liberty is essential if Wild Peter is to grow into the Peter that he would like to be. You are not Peter. Why then should Peter be forced to be you?

Godwin is an individual-ist: 'The greatest of all human benefits...is independence' (EQ 240). Independence would permit each stand-alone, irreducible and authentic, to chart his own course: 'Man is a creature that loves to act from himself' (EQ 144). The product 'not of implicit faith, but of his own understanding' (EQ 77), every human being should be given the freedom to strike out on his own (EQ 116).

Godwin is an individual-ist. Like Mill in *On Liberty*, he is strongly in favour of tolerance and hands-off, of 'reverence and forbearance', of the 'consideration and deference that man owes to man' (EQ 89): 'Respect them, that they may respect themselves' (EQ 118). Yet Godwin is also a social-ist. Self-stabilising anarchy is possible only because factored down accepts the groupthink of scaled-up. I look inward to the part precisely because I look outward to the whole. I am I because We are We. None of us is a pure-breed. Each of us is a hybrid, a compromise and a mix. All of us are complements, embedded in a surrounding symbiosis that gives us a common purpose. Even a commitment to individual-ism is itself a collective choice.

Godwin, in the *Enquirer* as he did in the *Enquiry*, situates the private mind in the public ether. Yet it is Big We again. True libertarians will object to the lexical primacy of the synthesis over the self. Criticising Godwin, they will say that the unwelcome consequence of his sociological totalitarianism is in effect to excise the state and its laws only to imprison the free-standing ego in yet another Bastille. Hell is other people. They shrink the self into the standard size.

Conformity is being traded for esteem. So long as Wild Peter is something more than Ibsen's Peer Gynt, layers of an onion without an inner core, he would have done better not to nest his identity within our ongoing grid. True libertarians will express the fear that Godwin is sacrificing authenticity and novelty to tradition and community. At least it would lay the Malthusian spectre of overpopulation. No one in our village would brave the face-to-face sanctions that would spoil the self-image of a Malthusian couple that bred too many children or, of course, too few. We keep an eye on our own. Extremes are not welcome.

7.4 Past and Progress

It is yesterday today. The 'vulgar' and the 'undiscriminating' tend to 'love those things that preserve a certain level, and abhor every thing that is calculated to startle and surprise' (EQ 253). 'Moderation and mediocrity' (EQ 254) take over: 'The mass of mankind does not love…any thing that surprises or puzzles them' (EQ 262). 'Dupes of our own devices', we are taken in by our own propaganda: 'A man who habitually defends a sentiment, commonly ends with becoming a convert' (EQ 311).

Ordinary people gravitate to the 'trite and plain' which they regard as a familiar old shoe: 'Upon uncommon flights of virtue they usually put a sinister interpretation' (EQ 262). They tend to dismiss 'great delicacy of sentiment' as 'affectation and artifice' (EQ 263–4). They are deeply suspicious of 'eminent and extraordinary men' (EQ 265), of 'characters of energy, of grand and decisive features' (EQ 264), who are more likely to rock the boat. 'Moral excellencies' sight 'untried paths' (EQ 264). Ordinary people prefer the going concern.

The done thing is a safe pair of hands. The result will often be the reproduction of shared experience, prudently protected against 'any thing great, magnanimous and ardent' that might disturb the 'assigned limit' (EQ 259). The common man, eschewing what is 'most illustrious in his nature' (EQ 259), joins in 'senselessly' (EQ 261) with the herd. He does what the other lemmings do. Even if the opinions that his neighbours regard as 'most sacred and momentous…are the most ridiculously absurd, or flagrantly indefensible' (EQ 262), the natural pushover will put the usual before the aberrant. He will go with the flow because what he values even more than the truth is the 'good opinion of others' (EQ 279).

The man of 'uncommon moral endowments' (EQ 259) will be less willing to make a deal with the devil. There is more to self-image than the real spectator: 'An elevated temper will induce us to act from our own reflections, and not from the judgment of others' (EQ 280). As much as the sensitive teammate wishes to please his fellows, he must accept that all persuasion comes at a price: 'He that would conduct himself with uncommon excellence, must in all probability expect to lose the kindness of a larger portion of the vulgar' (EQ 276).

The vulgar are prone to 'stopping their ears' (EQ 278). Their opinion, 'too little discerning to be worth the courting,…degrades the man that submits to it' (EQ 280). Desiring change, it is clear that the intelligentsia must focus their proposals not on the unwashed median but on 'the suffrage of all the instructed and all the wise', on 'the approbation of the acute and the excellent', on 'the comforting judgment of impartial thinkers and profound reasoners' (EQ 276–7). The scholars road-test the ideas. The common man does not. The *demos* does not know best. Often it knows nothing at all.

The intellectual must have the courage of his convictions. He must put his faith in Adam Smith's 'man within'. Reputation 'is not the ultimate object which a generous mind would desire' (EQ 287). A genuine seeker after truth will often have no choice but to do what he alone believes to be right: 'An elevated temper will induce us to act from our own reflections, and not from the judgment of others. He that suffers himself to be governed by public opinion, substitutes the unsteadiness of a weathercock, instead of the firmness of wisdom and justice' (EQ 280).

Only the 'unmanly' would prefer 'a mistaken superiority to the promotion of truth and usefulness' (EQ 281). Popularity does not last: 'A man of generous ambition will spurn it from him with contempt' (EQ 280). History will prove him right or wrong. In the here and now at least, 'he that would gain in any valuable sense the suffrage of the world, must show himself in a certain degree superior to this suffrage' (EQ 280–1).

History will prove him right or wrong. Savages are backward. We today live better. One generation builds on the generations that went before. Plato and Aristotle are going from strength to strength even if the unabridged texts 'have no longer a place but in the brains of a few dreaming and obscure pedants' (EQ 285). The improvement in mind and matter bears witness to the 'progressive nature of man, whether as an individual, or as the member of a society' (EQ 317).

Unbiased study diffuses great ideas. Economic growth uplifts the standard of life. Fungible money takes over from clunky barter. Momentum expands the faculties. Knowledge triumphs over ignorance. 'Stationariness and sacredness of opinion' (EQ 352) are not for all seasons. All change should be gradual rather than 'precipitate and headlong' (EQ 322). Given time, however, change is bound to be progress. Automaticity will provide.

Godwin puts his faith in the invisible hand. He is confident that the dynamic of nature reinforced by the wisdom of science will be the battle that ends all battles. His critics will object that his optimism is premature and unfounded. Reformers are swimming against the tide. The majority might win. The right-thinkers might lose.

The right-thinkers know what is right. In the case of temperance, they prove that excessive drinking brings the alcoholic into 'debauched' and 'execrable company', impairs 'the intellectual faculties' and 'shortens the life', most regrettably so 'when that life is eminently a useful one' (EQ 270). In case of fornication, they demonstrate that 'promiscuous venery' goes with a 'depraved appetite' that makes Don Juan perpetually dissatisfied with himself (EQ 270–1). In the case of bad language, they show that the swearers and the blasphemers are shunned because of their 'repulsive grossness' and their conspicuous 'absence of delicacy of taste' (EQ 271).

Beer, fornication and the x-word are bastions that might conceivably fall to an 'enlightened spectator' (EQ 156) who knows what is right. They are, however, secondary targets in comparison with Godwin's more immediate Big Game. Godwin's Big Five are private property, social inequality, the marriage contract, the established Church and the nation-state. All five, Godwin said, were 'highly artificial', intrinsically at variance with 'the strongest propensities of individual man' (EQ 321). Right-thinkers will know with certainty that inherited institutions like these must surrender to unsentimental progress that has no need for the vestigial past. The masses and the classes will be more inclined to honour the wisdom of the ages that has made us what we are.

It will be a hard sell. 'Individual man' is Socrates. He is not Henry Dubb. To convince the median citizen that the alcoholic is a 'bad member of society' (EQ 272) will be an easier task than to persuade the ordinary and the common that the Archbishop of York is making the rest of us unhappy. Godwin says: 'There is nothing perhaps that has contributed more to the introduction and perpetuating of bigotry in the world, than the doctrines of the Christian religion' (EQ 322). Godwin cannot really believe that the masses will rally to a manifesto such as that. Time will tell. Optimism tempered with patience might pay off.

A nation has roots. Godwin sensed that his personal and private crusade would encounter stiff opposition in the short run from the ingrained and the entrenched: 'There is nothing, however monstrous,...to which custom does not render us callous' (EQ 207). Property is 1066 or even before. Laws 'are usually the prejudices of a barbarous age artificially kept alive and entailed upon a civilised one' (EQ 222). Sunk cost is never bygone. The horse-drawn carriage is keeping the combustion engine off the road. The past is standing in the way of progress.

The stale is ruling over the fresh. In the one corner 'unprejudiced contemplation', in the other 'long habits of intellectual slavery' (EQ 230), there is no reason to think that the median citizen will opt for intellectual uprating in preference to the 'perennial stationariness of his understanding' (EQ 231–2). It is all writ in the Oxford Street sales. Luxuries come under censure where the shopper 'glaringly pampers his appetites...*without the consent, of his neighbour*' (EQ 267, emphasis added). That is just the point. *Without the consent?* And *with the consent?* Once public opinion has carved out a groove, it is very difficult for an Isaiah or even a Godwin to shunt the Thames into a new and superior bed.

Memory hands on the done thing. New cohorts internalise the behaviours that are the lingua franca in time and place. They conform to 'what the majority of mankind has determined to be essential to a moral character' (EQ 258). They pass forward the going *ought-to-be*s. Progress is retarded. It is not stopped in its tracks. Capital, equality, family, religion, politics—history is the witness. Gradually, incrementally, Godwin was convinced that the future was on his side.

7.5 'Avarice and Profusion'

Malthus believed that *The Enquirer*, Part II, Essay 2, only 16 pages in length, had been the watershed and the catalyst in the run-up to his theory of population. It had to be refuted.

The Enquirer, Part II, Essay 2, is about justice and virtue. It is about stratification, ostentation and welfare. It is about the rise and fall of modern capitalism. There is no mention of population. Malthus nonetheless saw something in Godwin's 16 pages that frightened him into his theory of the ratios and the checks. Malthus in the *Essay* seems almost to be focusing on the smaller target because the bigger target for him was a target too far. *Gulliver's Travels* is only tangentially about Brobdingnag and Glubbdubdrib. It is possible that Malthus's *Essay* homes in on biology because Godwin had written about economics in a way that Malthus rightly perceived to be a threat.

7.5.1 Division and Distance

The country is England and the date 1797. Communal ownership is not in the social interest. Collectivisation is 'a state of slavery and imbecility' which 'deserves our fixed disapprobation' (EQ 168). Private property provides a better outlet for 'that independence and individuality, which are the genuine characteristics of an intellectual existence, and without which nothing eminently honourable, generous or delightful can in any degree subsist' (EQ 169). The personal and the private are the complements to 'an intellectual existence'. Hume's meadow is a waste of space. Pooling lets the mind grow cold.

Godwin was making policy expressly for England in 1797. It was the fallen short run. Malthus took the view that even in the long run the human condition would be just as fallen: 'The temptations to evil are too strong for human nature to resist....The whole black train of vices that belong to falsehood are immediately generated' (FE 138). Short run, long run, Malthus will have found much in Godwin on 'independence and individuality' that was to his taste. Godwin on rentiers and absentees 'maintained by the industry of others' (EQ 162) will, however, almost immediately have tripped the alarm.

Private property, Godwin wrote, is conducive to 'independence and individuality' that feeds through into efficiency and output. At the same time, he warned, it can be a licence for laziness and an architect of social distance: 'There is no reason to be found in the code of impartial justice, why one man should work, while another man is idle' (EQ 171). The workers, 'gratuitously' (EQ 171), are adding value that will enrich the non-producing proprietors of the non-labour inputs. The usufruct is for the idle. The 'weight of oppression' (EQ 178) is for the poor.

Adam Smith in advance of Ricardo and Marx had attributed all new value to living labour. Chapter 5 has shown what the *Political Justice* made of that. While Smith on value could be as obscure as his distinguished predecessors Petty and Locke, Godwin at least said in *The Enquirer* precisely what it all meant: 'Wealth consists in this only, the commodities raised and fostered by human labour' (EQ 179).

All value comes from labour. Land and capital make production possible. In and of themselves, however, they add nothing new to our national stock: 'It is a gross and ridiculous error to suppose that the rich pay for any thing. There is no wealth in the world except this, the labour of man' (EQ 177). The landowners and the capitalists ride free. The remuneration that trickles down to the class that creates is slender and small (EQ 173): 'They labour indeed; but they do not consume the commodities they produce' (EQ 171). Surplus value is being siphoned off by functionless privilege. It is bringing the logic of 'independence and individuality' into disrepute.

The terms 'rich' and 'poor' are often used to capture the 'extreme inequality of conditions' (EQ 173) that separates one true Athenian from another. Godwin in the *Enquirer*, following his procedure in the *Enquiry*, opens up the umbrella deciles to isolate the dialectic of 'employer' and 'employee'. The 'have-nots' are precisely that. Lacking a share in land or capital, they are de facto the 'slaves and cattle' (PJ 646) of the 'haves' who have the right and the wherewithal to provide them with work.

The have-nots are the downtrodden victims not just of generic oppression but of the Marxian exploitation that even pro-market Adam Smith had described as a 'deduction' (WN I 73). Locke's labour theory of entitlement has run its course. Once the original state of nature has been fully appropriated, once the workers have become dependent on the propertied for their very survival, the terms 'rich' and 'poor' cease to capture the enormity of the abuse. The asset-owners, dining out on the labour of others, are 'freed from all solicitude about the supply of tomorrow' (EQ 162). Is it just? 'Certainly not' (EQ 163). Labour is honourable. Service to The Man is not.

It is Marx on the new capitalist economy. It is as old as the slaves in ancient Rome. Wat Tyler, John Ball and Jack Cade had made their target the parasitical employers and not just the idle rich. Swift's Yahoos, 'odious', 'malicious', 'filthy, noisome, and deformed' (Swift, 1726 [1992]: 289) not only loved what Swift calls 'profusion or avarice' (the phrase that Godwin took over for himself) but, quite specifically, loved surplus value: 'The rich man enjoyed the fruit of the poor man's labour, and the latter were a thousand to one in proportion to the former....The bulk of our people was forced to live miserably, by labouring every day for small wages, to make a few live plentifully' (Swift, 1726 [1992]: 268). The love of money was the love of exploitation in the service of a 'degenerate and brutal nature' (Swift, 1726 [1992]: 254). Things will change: 'Reason will in time always prevail against brute strength' (Swift, 1726 [1992]: 257).

Service and distance are social bad. Especially bad is the case where relative poverty degenerates into absolute deprivation. Godwin was the witness to the sawtooth of cyclical fluctuation, wartime dislocation, involuntary unemployment, the 'privation of the enjoyments of life' (EQ 164), the 'want of a suitable provision for sickness, infirmity and age' (EQ 163). Dark, satanic mills were outputting dark, satanic people: 'Inordinate labour produces untimely decrepitude' (EQ 164). Industrial-age decrepitude is a uniquely modern shortcoming. It is brought on by long hours, low pay, subdivided labour, relentless speed-up and, the cause of all the other causes, the capture of the unearned surplus by The Man.

Trapped in a new *bellum* that is more than the 'rich' side by side with the 'poor', the factor labour is being stupefied by the factors land and capital into a 'neutral existence' of 'inanity and torpor' (EQ 165). 'Impelled by accident, hurried by necessity' (EQ 166), deprived of 'that leisure which is necessary for the improvement of the mind' (EQ 164), the workingman's exertions are 'fettered and drawn aside from their true direction' (EQ 167). The worker experiences 'few moments...of complacence, of exultation, of honest pride, or of joy' (EQ 165). The 'noblest conceptions of his mind' are 'rendered abortive by the ills of fortune' (EQ 166). He has a species need to become *homo sapiens*. He is marooned in interchangeable parts instead.

'Employee' and 'employer' are class-correlated categories. They will not last forever. Relatively 'rich' and comparatively 'poor' are, however, social pigeonholes which are likely to have a longer lifespan. Capacity is not the same: 'It is certain that men will differ from each other in their degrees of industry and economy' (EQ 169). Merit is not the same. Effort magnified by luck will ensure that inequality at the finishing line remains 'to a certain extent unavoidable' (EQ 169).

Capacities diverge. Yet needs converge: 'It is not less certain, that the wants of one man are similar to the wants of another, and that the same things will conduce to the improvement and happiness of each' (EQ 169). In terms of value demanded even if not of value supplied, it is in the interest of social harmony that the pillars of the arch should be brought more closely together: 'The principles of virtue require, that the advantages existing in any community should be equally administered; or that the inequalities which inevitably arise, should be repressed, and kept down within as narrow limits as possible' (EQ 169).

As narrow limits *as possible*. We are all dead-level equal before the law. The economy is more judgemental. Purchasing power must be made more even lest the disparity between fellow citizens become an unbridgeable gulf. It must not, however, be made dead-level equal. It is a central tenet of natural justice that especial service deserves a differential reward.

Outcomes should be as close together *as possible*. Cohesion is a public good. Tails sow discord. Means bring peace. Yet production is also a public good. We want comfort. We need motivation. Godwin put his faith in a future society in which the stream of convergence balanced by the stream of divergence broadly satisfied the social consensus, sensibly guided. Malthus wrote the *Essay* to show that he was wrong.

Godwin, Malthus said, had argued against communal ownership but in support of collective tinkering. It was Jacobinism. It was Tom Paine. It was pragmatism without principle. Good people do not invade each other's endowments. Ethics aside, levelling has unintended consequences. Earlier marriages, children, food, vice, misery—Godwin, Malthus will have reasoned, did not foresee the abject poverty to which his high-minded egalitarianism must inevitably lead.

7.5.2 Signs and Symbols

For the workers, it is a door that remains permanently closed: 'They merely vegetate' (EQ 164–5). For their bosses, it is no less a veil of tears. The 'sensuality and indulgence' (EQ 164) of the 'licentious prodigal' (EQ 216) ruin a man's health and destroy his peace of mind. It is a net loss without a redeeming gain. The marginal utility from food and drink rises, peaks and then falls. The marginal utility from signs and symbols is a mirage that perpetually recedes. Beyond the flat of the curve, common sense instructs us to sit still and 'enjoy the benefits which we have' (EQ

249). Moderation is the rational choice. The times are out of joint. Rationality itself is no longer the rational choice.

Sweatshop casuals in rat-infested tenements have not gone away. Malthus's positive checks are a fact of life in the Northern factories and the Hogarthian slums. Even so, the standard of life of some if not all in the lower deciles has gone up. Some if not all are enjoying social subsistence sufficient to cover not just physical survival but 'some superfluities and luxuries' (EQ 175) as well. It is not necessarily a positive development. Consumption classes 1, 2 and 3 are good consumption. Consumption class 4, however, is contra-economic. It is money down the drain.

The upper classes have already demonstrated what happens when the income-utility relationship goes into the red. Their outlays are more and more being diverted into 'gaudy plumage' (EQ 180), into the pampering of 'debauched appetites' (EQ 180), into the 'frigid' profusion that 'debases the men that practice it' (EQ 181). It is Galbraith's affluent society in which signs and symbols 'of great frivolity' are being consumed in a mock market where the 'marginal utility of present aggregate output…is zero' (Galbraith, 1958 [1973]: 140, 154). Godwin like Galbraith had warned that enough in economics was a finite finish and not an ever-receding mirage. Malthus, in contrast, wrote like Burke surrounded by assassins. He accused Godwin of exaggerating the importance of frigid and debasing 'plumage' in a dismal world where even the growing demand for grain could not be met.

Godwin believed that marginal consumption beyond its utility peak would add little or nothing to gross national happiness. In excess of a simple and moderate basketful of commodities, any further increment in household spending would be wasteful ostentation, morally and economically bad: 'It is desirable that there should be, in any rank of society, as little as may be of that luxury, the object of which is to contribute to the spurious gratifications of vanity' (EQ 176).

Vanity puts all the clocks on Kensington time. Socrates believed that 'correct belief and knowledge' (Plato, 1982: para. 38a) would be sufficient to curb the soul-destroying hunger for competitive consumption. Godwin, however reluctantly, took the second-best position that mind by itself would not be able to stem the widespread obsession with 'coming out on top, winning and gaining recognition' (Plato, 2012: para. 581b). Godwin knew that the gradual elimination of corrosive and divisive status signifiers would require more than a right-thinker's act of will. Matter as well as mind would have to be on board. Non-satiety cannot be delegated to the psychoanalysts and the preachers. Any levelling in the superstructure presupposes an antecedent levelling in the basis. It presupposes the renunciation of a stratified social structure in which self-advertisement through signs and symbols has been made a way of life.

Wild Peter had no external Other forcing him to catch up, keep up and overtake. He could practise contemplation and withdrawal because there were no Joneses in his path. It is other people who queer the pitch: 'Few are the wants of a human being. It is by our wants that we are held down, and linked in a thousand ways, to human society. They render the man who is devoted to them, the slave of every creature that breathes' (EQ 248).

Consumers are in each other's power. Even a virtuous man, 'if he be inordinately sensible' (EQ 249), will be exposed at all times to the ranking scheme of ambient opinion. Such a man, whatever his stock of wealth, is 'truly a slave' to the 'least sagacious of the bystanders' (EQ 249, 251). The social climber sacrifices his energy and his leisure because 'he burns to be somebody. He cannot endure to be confounded in the crowd' (EQ 154). What one can do, all cannot. It is a cancel culture. The stomach ulcers and the sleepless nights are all in vain. We cancel each other out.

A coward is 'wedded to particular indulgences and a certain mode of life' (EQ 248). He announces his role and position through his designer labels and his trophy car. A man of 'true courage' dispenses with 'luxury and inordinate indulgence' because he is strong-willed enough to resist the 'trivial accessories' and 'innumerable gratifications' (EQ 248, 250) that he rightly sees for the false friends that they are: 'He that desires to be virtuous, and to remain so, must learn to be content with a little' (EQ 250).

He must *learn* to be content. It is a blackboard jungle where his peer group as a whole is learning nothing but invidious comparison. Society is more than other people. It is other people *layered into* horizontal strata. There are the 'rich' and the 'poor'. There are the asset-owners and the labourers. There is privilege, inheritance and ascription. There is social mobility and achieved status. In the blackboard jungle, it is unthinking matter and not flexible mind alone that is teaching the lessons.

The Joneses are more than the Joneses. They are the Lord Joneses juxtaposed to the fetch-and-carry joneses. Not only are there relativities and comparisons out there, they are situated in a time-specific matrix of structured relationships. The deprived have learned the lesson. There cannot be a philosophy of poverty that fails to incorporate the economics of poverty as well: 'Poverty is an enormous evil. By poverty I understand the state of a man possessing no permanent property, in a country where wealth and luxury have already gained a secure establishment' (EQ 162).

A virtuous man will be content with a little. Not so a virtuous man who knows he has been wronged. The fixation, the compulsion to stand out from the pack is not something that can be schooled down to size. Croesus has the precious and Jack Cade does not. The resentment that is caused by inequitable inequality will not disappear until disposable incomes and outlets for display are brought tolerably close to the median. Godwin is not saying there ought to be arithmetical equality in earning, owning and spending. All he is saying is that an approach to a citizenship standard would be likely to make one nation out of the mistrustful tribes.

The need for a change is clear. The intermediate steps are not. Private property is unlikely to be trimmed, taxed or nationalised by a bourgeois state that is the mouthpiece for the bourgeois class. Private property cannot in the short run be pooled: collective ownership 'deserves our fixed disapprobation' (EQ 168). What is left is the property-owning democracy. What is mine is mine. We share our consensus. We do not share our land. Good fences make good neighbours. Failing that, it will have to be the protective state.

7.5.3 Residuum and Relief

The poor-in-work will struggle to make ends meet. The rock-bottom *residuum* will struggle to survive. Living in 'uncommon distress' (EQ 195), the no-hopers turn to charity from the independent for essential food and shelter. A 'poor, half-naked, shivering creature' appeals to 'another creature, with all the exterior of ease and comfort' (EQ 186) for life-saving relief, however 'partial and temporary' (EQ 173).

The situation of the absolutely deprived is 'unfortunate' (EQ 186). It is 'worthy of interference and pity' (EQ 186). Whether the 'cries of humanity' (EQ 200) should actually be answered with a stranger gift is not axiomatic. Life is hard. The deprived should 'depend upon their own exertions' (EQ 189). Like Paley and Malthus, Godwin did not see a safety net as a natural right. Assistance, always discretionary, should be confined to the temporarily unemployed and the permanently unemployable. For the poor who are able to work, Godwin's counsel is that they should find a job.

Godwin is aware of imposters who make a living long-term out of the soft-hearted. Believing as he does in the moral value of sincerity and disclosure, he has little time for able-bodied paupers who cynically counterfeit adversity that they could themselves easily reverse. The decent should not be taken for a ride. Scarce alms should not be distributed until the individual's circumstances had been properly investigated. Rehabilitation should be made a condition. The would-be scrounger should be 'made a valuable member of the community' (EQ 194n).

In the last analysis there is always death: 'Men who are worse than an incumbrance upon the face of the earth, it would be well, to speak in the jargon of the vulgar, if God would be pleased to take to himself.…They are the opprobrium of human nature, and the earth would feel itself lightened by their removal' (EQ 193). Neither Godwin nor Malthus says that it would be right to kill off the incorrigible. The inference is nonetheless that the severity of the 1834 workhouse should be ranked above the refusal of the 1940s Fabians to look a gift cherub in the mouth. If the rich should not be idle, neither should the poor.

References

By W. Godwin

Godwin, W. (1783). *An Account of the Seminary at Epsom in Surrey* (abbreviated as Seminary). T. Cadell.

Godwin, W. (1797 [1965]). *The Enquirer* (abbreviated as EQ). Augustus M. Kelley.

Godwin, W. (1798 [1976]). *Enquiry Concerning Political Justice* (abbreviated as PJ). Penguin Books.

Godwin, W. (1805 [1992]). *Fleetwood, or the New Man of Feeling* (abbreviated as Fleetwood), in *Collected Novels and Memoirs of William Godwin* (Vol. 5). William Pickering.

By T.R. Malthus

Malthus, T. R. (1798 [1970]). *Essay on the Principle of Population, as it affects the Future Improvement of Society, with Remarks on the Speculations of Mr. Godwin, M. Condorcet, and Other Writers* (abbreviated as FE). Penguin.

By Other Authors

Galbraith, J. K. (1958 [1973]). *The Affluent Society.* Penguin Books.
Kegan Paul, C. (1876). *William Godwin: His Friends and Contemporaries* (abbreviated as KP) (2 Vols.). Henry S. King.
Plato. (1982). *Philebus* (R. Wakefield, Trans.). Penguin Books.
Plato. (2012). *The Republic* (C. Rowe, Trans.). Penguin Books.
Rousseau, J.-J. (1762 [1972]). *Emile* (B. Foxley, Trans.). Dent.
Smith, A. (1776 [1961]). *The Wealth of Nations* (abbreviated as WN) (2 Vols.). Methuen.
Swift, J. (1726 [1992]). *Gulliver's Travels.* Wordsworth Classics.
Tawney, R. H. (1921 [1961]). *The Acquisitive Society.* Collins.

CHAPTER 8

The *Essay* Fights Back

Godwin's *Enquirer* was published in 1793, and Malthus's first *Essay* in 1798. Malthus said that the idea for the *Essay* arose out of a conversation about the *Enquirer* with a 'friend' (FE 61). The friend was his father, Daniel Malthus.

Daniel Malthus shared Godwin's Enlightenment ethos of peace and felicity through equality and reason. He was especially impressed by the 16 pages on 'Avarice and Profusion'. Thomas Robert Malthus sought in the *Essay* to persuade him that Godwin's *Political Justice* extended by Godwin's *Enquirer* would lead inevitably to poverty, instability and a relapse into 'barbarism' (in KP I 321). The cause would be population. 'Be fruitful and multiply' was the supreme Jacobin. A country clergyman, a bookworm and a bachelor of 32, Malthus knew enough of the real world to know that misery and vice could not have been God's last judgement.

Malthus had read Smith, Hume, Wallace, Price and Howlett. He had been through the evidence collected by Arthur Young, Morton Eden, William Temple and Admiral Ulloa. He had become convinced that there was a causal relationship between levelling and destitution. Godwin had said little about population but a great deal about deprivation. Godwin had underestimated the extent to which irresponsible childbearing was incompatible with tolerable survival.

D. Reisman, *William Godwin and Thomas Robert Malthus*, https://doi.org/10.1007/978-3-031-62113-0_8

8.1 The First *Essay*

Malthus damns with fulsome praise. Godwin's system is 'beautiful and engaging' (FE 132). It is full of 'spirit and energy', 'force and precision' (FE 132). Its author is 'ardent', 'ingenious and able' (FE 132). Godwin is widely recognised for his 'talents', his 'candour', his 'acknowledged ability and penetration' (FE 69), his 'earnestness of manner' (FE 132). His work is a focus for 'delight and admiration' (FE 132). Godwin ranked generous sociability above self-love and greed. Only Machiavelli and Nietzsche would take issue with that. Good intentions are not, however, enough to raise up Godwin's New Jerusalem. 'That moment can never arrive' (FE 133).

8.1.1 Theory and Practice

Godwin's worldview was seriously flawed. His conclusions, 'unwarranted by his premises…will not admit of application' (FE 132). Abstractions and assertions are not enough to produce a good society. Godwin's paradise is a never-never-land. It is 'a beautiful phantom of the imagination' (FE 133). It is not science. It is not truth. It is not the real world.

Malthus criticised Godwin for ranking ideas above events: 'Mr. Godwin considers man too much in the light of a being merely intellectual' (FE 162). Godwin had overestimated the power of reason and underestimated the material integument: 'The body has more effect upon the mind than the mind upon the body' (FE 153). The mind does not exist in vacuo (FE 163). Hunger, sleep and the passion between the sexes are irresistible impulsions that cannot be remodelled on the orders of a misguided Canute. The cravings and the drives are not a voluntary and conscious choice.

Godwin had paid lip-service to the empirical method. It was, Malthus said, just for show: 'The superiority of the pleasures of intellect to those of sense, Mr. Godwin considers as a fundamental truth' (FE 166). Godwin was all too quick to abandon sense perception for high theory when it suited his purpose. Malthus was not: 'My ideas of philosophy are in this respect widely different from Mr. Godwin's' (FE 154). Malthus extrapolated the presumptive future from recent real-world experience. Godwin, he objected, treated his much-vaunted discovery process as a footnote to his unanchored pronouncements.

It was not entirely Descartes versus Locke. Godwin had seen the link between population and subsistence (FE 199). He had recognised the ubiquity of 'misery and vice' (FE 103). He had made a useful comparison between land-hungry Britain and the American frontier (FE 105). Malthus found much in Godwin's narrative that he could share. On balance, however, it was conjecture that bordered on fiction. There *never* was a Caleb Williams. Godwin was weak on the facts. Godwin had not kept faith with Bacon and Hume. One consequence had been that Godwin underestimated the force of natural law.

8.1.2 The Ratios

Godwin, Malthus said, had made the 'great error' of 'attributing almost all the vices and misery that are seen in civil society to human institutions' (FE 133). Godwin had asserted that most injustice proceeds from 'political and social institutions' (FE 169). Man-made, badly designed, he had seen them as impediments to sustained perfectibility. Godwin had treated property and politics as 'the fruitful sources of all evil, the hotbeds of all the crimes that degrade mankind' (FE 133). Anarchy would cause the repression and the deprivation to disappear. Malthus saw that it would not.

Godwin's system, Malthus announced, is 'an impossibility' (FE 146). 'Light and superficial', 'mere feathers that float on the surface', Godwin's unsupported prognostications are no match for 'imperious necessity' (FE 133). The population is increasing in a geometrical ratio. The supply of food is increasing in an arithmetical ratio. Population, if 'unchecked' (FE 73), doubles itself every 25 years. It is a tendency law, based on what 'can be supposed' (FE 74). It is also a projection. The logic of the mathematical series has been supported by hard data from the New England colonies. Scrap the 'myriads': the 'fatal effects' are 'imminent and immediate' (FE 120). Deduction or induction, Malthus is convinced that the earth is becoming 'encumbered' (FE 147). Ivory-tower Godwin had failed to spot the impending apocalypse.

The evidence is there. Misery 'has existed ever since we have had any histories of mankind' (FE 124). The 'mighty law of self-preservation' (FE 138), the survival of the fittest and the 'goadings of want' (FE 139) are as old as animate life itself. 'Violence, oppression, falsehood, misery', 'rapine and murder', all are encoded in 'laws inherent in the nature of man' (FE 138). It is a gross simplification to pretend that all evil is the consequence of imperfect governments, inequitable decrees or barricaded acreage. It is 'a false conception', Malthus says, to take the symptoms for the disease when the real cause of the distemper is 'the fixed and unalterable laws of nature' (FE 169): 'Repeated experience has assured us, that the influence of the most virtuous character will rarely prevail against very strong temptations to evil' (FE 170).

Resources are scarce. People are in natural increase. The demand for food is growing more rapidly than the supply. Godwin had brushed aside the danger from Cantillon's mice in a barn. He had alleged that three-quarters of the world's land lay idle. He had insisted that the quarter under cultivation was itself capable of 'immeasurable improvement' (PJ 689). He had maintained that the danger of a global food shortage was 'remote' (PJ 689). Malthus does not deny that new land has potential or that the 'further improvement' (FE 127) of old land can postpone the reckoning. His point is simply that a limit exists and that the spring must eventually run dry. Godwin had not understood that oscillation and vibration are the cycle. He had not seen that hunger was the trend.

In the long run even the production and productivity of New England will have run their course. Godwin had treated the want of food under the pressure of population 'slightly' (FE 132). While Malthus assumed (without proof) that the sex drive would 'remain nearly in its present state' (FE 70), Godwin had assumed (without proof) that it would experience a secular decline. Propagation would be an afterthought. Medicine would extend the lifespan. Sharing would meet the greying need (PJ 693). Godsend at the margin would be sufficient to feed the stable census. That was Godwin's story. Malthus dismissed it as a myth: 'No decided effect of this kind has yet been observed' (FE 156). Births were a reality. Food was a constraint. There are substitutes for coal in the sense of Jevons. There are no substitutes for food. Poverty is inevitable. The grain is not there. Malthus had grasped it. Godwin had not.

Plenty is the trigger for population. Population is the primrose path to want. Godwin had said that the day of judgement could be postponed for 'myriads of centuries' (PJ 689). Malthus cited figures of 25, 30 or 50 years (FE 105, 138, 144) to show that the pinch-point was that much more 'imminent and immediate'. They focus the mind: 'Man cannot live in the midst of plenty. All cannot share alike the bounties of nature' (FE 134). Where survival itself is becoming a game of musical chairs, it is to be expected that the Good Samaritan will be the collateral damage of *homo homini lupus*. Hunger makes desperate people selfish. Adam Smith's China is just round the corner.

It will be Hobbes, 'vicious' and 'corrupt' (FE 135), brutish and nasty. The 'inevitable laws of our nature' (FE 176) will take their toll. The struggle for existence will 'depress in want and misery the whole human race' (FE 178). The frenzied competition for fixed availabilities will crowd out Godwin's anarchic egalitarianism in order to crowd in the protective state.

8.1.3 Checks and Correctives

Godwin's utopia, Malthus says, 'would, indeed, be a happy state' (FE 134) if the race between the births and the farmers could somehow be brought to an end. In the world as we know it, the truth is that Godwin's Eden must remain 'merely an imaginary picture', out of touch with 'the real state of man on earth' (FE 134). The real state of scarcity rules out any practicable anarchy: 'The hateful passions that had vanished reappear' (FE 138).

Potluck will not see off the niggardliness of nature: 'The surplus of the rich man might be sufficient for three, but four will be desirous to obtain it' (FE 178). Pressing wants and inadequate food will set in motion the 'black train of distresses' (FE 140). Sooner or later, and even if holdings are made more equal, some participants 'in the great lottery of life' will find that they 'have drawn a blank' (FE 143).

Sharing is counterproductive. It reallocates the deckchairs but does not meet the growing need. Godwin had predicted that, class antagonisms gradually phased out, men will be educated by the real and the impartial spectator to conduct themselves in the best interests of their fellows. Malthus saw clearly that unmanageable numbers had a tendency to stop Godwin's betterment in its tracks.

It is a tendency. It is not an end state. How well a tendency law actually performs in the field is forever dependent on the strength of its ceteris paribus Malthus draws attention to two sets of checks that modify the expectation that history-to-come will crash and burn. The first set is 'positive'. Acting through epidemics, wars and famines, they raise the death rate and thin out the overhang (FE 89). The second set is 'preventive'. Making earlier or later marriage their built-in turning point, they influence the number of childbearing years and with it the number of births.

Full employment, real wage and cheap grain are an incentive in the lower classes to marry young. The more affluent are sensitive not just to their basic necessities but to their social standing. A 'man of liberal education', not wanting to mix with 'moderate farmers and the lower class of tradesmen', will take into account the 'difficulties attending the rearing of a family' (FE 89, 90). He will live in fear that unaffordable dependents will imperil his status and his symbols. Provided that the lower classes can learn to share in his anxieties, 'the vices and moral weakness of mankind, taken in the mass, are not invincible' (FE 170). Improvement is possible. The family can be sized down. It is in the first *Essay*.

8.1.4 Ethics and Economics

Economic growth presupposes a sustained rise in consumer spending. Godwin, Malthus objected, had underestimated the contribution that emulation and profit can make to employment and well-being. Malthus, making himself the spokesman for the working class, objected that Godwin had no right to condemn the 'mischief of profusion' (FE 175) without assessing the burden that slow growth or no growth would put upon the new entrants that the population mechanism was introducing into the labour force. Godwin had failed to see that moderation was a luxury that a growing nation could ill afford.

Godwin, Malthus said, had treated 'the whole system of barter and exchange' as 'a vile and iniquitous traffic' (FE 177). He had failed to see that Adam Smith's system of natural liberty could contribute much more to national happiness than Godwin's good fellowship that could never be more than the icing on the cake: 'The proper office of benevolence is to soften the partial evils arising from self-love, but it can never be substituted in its place' (FE 179).

Malthus advised that benevolence by itself would never be enough to outface the ugly side of imperfect nature. Godwin had come down in favour of a secular morality that relied upon social pressures to protect responsible self-regulators from the fissiparous spin of gain-snatching self-love. Malthus warned that the butcher, the brewer and the baker would simply refuse to serve us on those terms. Christians, Malthus implied, believe that God had favoured the market mechanism in order to ensure that his congregation had enough to eat. Malthus reproached Godwin for having underestimated the force of the quid pro quo.

Godwin had 'rejected the light of revelation' (FE 157). Godwin had situated himself among the 'enemies of religion' (FE 158). Godwin, a humanist and an agnostic, had used sociology when he ought to have used economics. Malthus, a Christian, saw that the unintended outcome of Godwin's benevolence would be misery and vice that free and fair exchange would have gone some way to alleviate. If God is dead, then what remains is not the wealth but the poverty of nations.

Markets and morals, Malthus said, are hand in glove. Circumventing subservience and dependence, supply and demand make the trading partners into friends who reliably meet each other's needs: 'I possess what he wants, he possesses what I want. We make an amicable exchange' (FE 179). An economy built to Godwin's design is, Malthus says, 'absolutely impracticable' (FE 176). Godwin's anarchy is intended to be caring and sharing. Instead, Malthus predicted, it would inevitably 'degenerate into a class of proprietors and a class of labourers' (FE 176). It would be business as usual.

Godwin, congenitally out of touch, had not understood that matter and not mind was the more immediate cause of the individual and the collective good. Progress results from assiduity, exertion, frugality and accumulation: 'Evil exists in the world, not to create despair, but activity' (FE 217). Money makes the world go round. Without an effective incentive, there would be nothing but indolence, lethargy and inertia. The Fall of Man is a burden that we today are obliged to bear. Godwin expects that his anarchy will be a return to the Garden. Malthus knows that there is no going back.

Godwin had seen activity as a fundamental human need. Malthus replied that there was no evidence of such a drive. What was more likely was that beneficent providence had created scarcity in order to protect weak-willed mankind from a Hell on earth. Malthus contended that it was the bodily wants and not an innate instinct of workmanship, undocumented and unobserved, that was keeping man's hand on the plough. Poverty, the will of God (FE 227), gives the hungry and the cold a reason to labour. Necessity is the mother of excellence. Malthus cannot have thought much of Godwin's proposal to minimise the number of hours devoted to manual labour. There would be no one in the fields to grow the grain that feeds us all.

Even the best Samaritan must live in the real world. 'It is to the established administration of property and the apparently narrow principle of self-love that we are indebted for all the noblest exertions of human genius, all the finer and more delicate emotions of the soul, for everything, indeed, that distinguishes the civilized from the savage state' (FE 176–7). It would be a step backward for a civilised man to 'throw down the ladder by which he has risen to this eminence' (FE 177). Godwin had not fully understood the law of evolution. Malthus criticises him for insisting on unattainable perfection when history shows that self-love, fully buttressed by internalised norms, would be the more dependable way to relieve 'the pressure of want' (FE 176).

Godwin's post-acquisitive economics is the high road to the positive checks. An uncompromising reliance on public opinion, Malthus states, will 'depress in want and misery the whole human race' (FE 178). The poor will make a loss and not a gain. Morality is happiness. The deprived will enjoy less happiness in Godwin's unattainable utopia than they would in Adam Smith's pragmatic mix.

Malthus feigns surprise that Godwin's ethics is not absolute but contingent: 'What is morality, individual or political, according to Mr. Godwin's own definition of it, but a calculation of consequences?' (SE I 328). Worse still, it had been the wrong set of consequences. Godwin had associated happiness with the social and political objectives of liberty, equality and fraternity. He made no mention of wealth. His theory of happiness was biased towards perception and away from food. Malthus finds it flat and one-sided. The consequences that Godwin takes into consideration, Malthus says, are only a subset of the runes that he ought to have read.

Malthus expresses his surprise that Godwin appealed to good outcomes rather than to good intentions. Surprised or not, Malthus himself is more than capable of constructing his moral code in the whirlwind of consequence. Man is sluggish. Scarcity forces him to labour. God is a yes-but utilitarian. God understands the means and the ends of this-worldly economics. Malthus, like God, like Godwin, knows that he has to be pragmatic if limited resources are to maximise the happiness of human beings on earth.

8.1.5 The Protective State

Godwin was an anarchist. Malthus was a statist. In the long run the politics would go their own way. In the short run the agenda would gravitate towards the broad middle ground. Both authors acknowledged the need for a protective state. Both recognised that top-down authority had to be bound by a constitution. The frogs had to be defended against their stork.

Malthus in the first *Essay* argues that matter had come to the aid of mind. Civil liberty, he says, owes much to 'the introduction of manufactures' (FE 179). Malthus confesses that he is not 'a very determined friend to them' (FE 179). Godwin most assuredly was not. Be that as it may, both authors accepted that industry and trade had been the necessary evil that saw off the even greater evil of despotic feudalism. Historically speaking, 'liberty came in their train' (FE 179). Without modern capitalism, the modern state would not be able to protect the individual freedom that is the basis for economic improvement.

The devolved economy and the watchdog polity lend each other their full support: 'The superior degree of civil liberty which prevailed in America contributed...to promote the industry, happiness, and population' (FE 197). The future will be less sunny. Constitutional government can postpone but not prevent the day of reckoning: 'Even civil liberty...will not create new land' (FE 197). China now, New England later, Hobbes is just round the corner. It is the law of nature.

Malthus, like Godwin, was afraid of radical dislocation: 'The bursting of the bonds of society is such a separation of parts as cannot take place without giving the most acute pain to thousands' (FE 172). Revolution would unleash civil war and 'constant anxiety' (FE 134). Weak on inbuilt correctives, society would collapse into 'a loose, deformed, disjointed mass, without union, symmetry, or harmony' (FE 171). No one who had studied 1789 would want that. Godwin did not: 'Discussion, reading, enquiry, perpetual communication, those are my favourite methods for the improvement of mankind....Employ no violence....Await the progress of truth' (in Brown, 1926: 262). Neither Malthus nor Godwin was in favour of sudden dislocation. Lasting change is gradual. It is not brought about at the point of a gun.

Living in the here and now, both Malthus and Godwin believed that the state should not venture too far beyond its protective function. Economy and society should on balance be left free to discover their own equilibrium. Misguided intervention would make a bad imbalance worse. It was, Malthus stated, already happening to the most in need: 'The poor laws of England tend to depress the general condition of the poor' (FE 97).

Relief tends to increase the population. Compassion tends to augment the effective demand without also expanding the supply of subsistence that alone can alleviate the distress. The cost of workhouses for the able-bodied and outdoor handouts, less eligible, for deserving widows and orphans tends to divert capital into consumption that could have otherwise been invested in new jobs and additional sustenance. Relief, carefully considered, is profoundly anti-poor. Subsidies tend to 'create the poor which they maintain' (FE 97). They make the number of the needy not less but more.

Adam Smith had made never-ending growth the decisive buttress against absolute destitution. In stationary China where output had peaked 'the poverty of the lower ranks of people...far surpasses that of the most beggarly nations in Europe' (WN I 80–1). Smith compared growth to a factory that is forever creating paid employment for the out-of-work (WN I 362). Malthus criticises Godwin for underestimating the extent to which profit-seeking reinvestment would keep the fringe independent and self-supporting. Greed is good.

Godwin did not see the link between abstention ploughed back for profit and job creation that would draw the poor into the mainstream. Malthus was closer to Smith, but there was a proviso. A saver can be a hoarder who 'locks up his wealth in a chest and sets in motion no labour of any kind' (FE 176). Where the magpie fails to recycle his stash, would-be workers gain nothing from his self-denial: 'The funds for the maintenance of labour do not necessarily increase with the increase of wealth, and very rarely increase in *proportion* to it' (SE II 77, italics in original).

Even, moreover, if the saver does plunge his capital into new hires, still the long-term position of the working class will not be improved. Higher wages lead to earlier marriage and larger families. In less than two decades, children will compete with their parents. They increase in the reserve army will Dutch-auction the workers back to basic subsistence. Godwin did not share with Malthus an interest in fluctuations around the trend. Nor, in expressing his reservations about flat-of-the-curve consumption, did he see that paid employment was only possible because of aggregate demand. If money is not going out, money will not be coming in. Malthus knew it. Godwin, he believed, did not.

Malthus was not confident about the future of the working class. It was, he said, unlikely 'that the lower classes of people in any country, should *ever be sufficiently free* from want and labour, to attain any high degree of intellectual improvement' (FE 149, emphasis added). Deprivation and overwork would ensure that, not *ever sufficiently free*, they remained underinformed and indifferent. Godwin for his own part has no answer to the power asymmetry in present-day economic conditions. In the long run at least the marked disparity between the enlightened and the ignorant will have evolved itself into oblivion. Anarchy is coming in. The protective state is being left behind.

8.2 The Second *Essay*

There was life beyond Godwin. Neither the first *Essay* in 1798 nor the second *Essay* in 1803 focused exclusively on Godwin's misguided dystopia. It was nonetheless the case that Godwin's folly was carried forward from 1798 to 1803 and refuted anew. Book III Chapter 2 of the new edition revisited the earlier Chap. 2 on Godwin's deplorable inconsistencies. Added was a new Chap. 3. It was Malthus's reply to Godwin's attack on the 1798 edition in his *Thoughts on Dr. Parr's Spital Sermon* in 1801.

8.2.1 Absolute Deprivation

Nothing had changed. Godwin had still not absorbed the vital lesson that stratification and class could never and should never be levelled away: 'A state, in which an inequality of conditions offers the natural rewards of good conduct, and inspires widely and generally the hopes of rising up the ladder and the fears of falling in society, is unquestionably the best calculated to develop the energies and faculties of man' (SE I 335). 'Energies' and 'faculties' are a function of 'hopes' and 'rising'. Godwin had turned a deaf ear to the historical record: 'Every case of equality that has yet occurred, has uniformly borne witness to the depressing and deadening effects which arise from the want of this stimulus' (SE I 335). Want of stimulus would be want of food. It would be the positive checks that decimate the poor. It would be Gracchus Babeuf all the way to an early grave: 'Mr. Godwin's system…would very greatly increase the quantity of vice and misery in society' (SE I 328).

Godwin denied that population had ever outstripped subsistence (SE I 328). Malthus countered that the tide, 'silent' but 'gradual', was already lapping at the door: 'Many countries are *now* suffering all the evils that can ever be expected to flow from this principle' (SE I 329, emphasis added). Malthus in places uses weasel words which seem to build in their own 'but'. Circuit breakers like 'many countries' (SE I 329), 'under different circumstances', 'very different', 'infer', 'natural tendency' (SE II 240) and 'inclination' (SE II 245) seem to demote his principle from hard fact to loose conjecture. Critics like Godwin objected that Malthus had blurred the distinction between a tendency law and a natural law. Malthus responded that their facile point-scoring was nothing other than 'a total misconception of the argument' (SE I 329). Critics like Godwin had not understood the message. They had not understood that the word *now* means precisely what it says.

The evils are upon us *now*. The increase in primary produce is even *now* not rapid enough to protect the lower classes from absolute deprivation. Malthus is not saying that, in Europe, as they are in China, the masses are dying of starvation on the street: 'Poverty, and not absolute famine, is the specific effect of the principle of population' (SE I 329). The final limit, although no reason is given, is 'a point which we shall certainly never reach' (SE I 329). It is Zeno's arrow. It is vice and misery all the same.

The tendency law is even *now* making itself felt. Absolute famine is not 'urgent' (SE I 330). Perceived poverty nonetheless is all around. Jack makes do with dingy accommodation situated next door to the dump. Jill eats offal because she cannot pay for fruit and steak. Census data shows that the population in England and Wales is doubling every 48 years. In Ireland it is 40 years. On the Continent it is 36 years (1827: 327). The arithmetical ratio is not keeping pace. 'Striking evidences' (SE II 242) prove 'incontrovertibly' (SE II 243) that the threat is real. They lend credence to the inference that checks must have been 'constantly in action' (SE I 329).

8.2.2 Moral Restraint

As in the first *Essay*, there are in the 1803 edition both positive and preventive checks. Both sets of checks 'arise unavoidably from the laws of nature' (SE I 19).

Positive checks continue to inform the superfluous and the unwanted that 'at nature's mighty feast there is no vacant cover for him. She tells him to be gone' (SE II 127). Three years later, in the 1806 edition, these words themselves were gone. Their meaning was not. Malthus could be hard-hearted. So, of course, could Godwin who in 1797 had noted that God could usefully 'take to himself' the unneeded 'opprobrium' (EQ 193) that had outlasted its economic function. To Malthus it was a positive check. To Godwin it was simply a spring clean. Either way, the non-productive and the unnecessary die.

Preventive checks remain preponderantly the postponement of marriage. The proviso is that there should be no irregular and counterproductive gratifications (SE I 18) such as extra-marital copulation with notoriously unreliable condoms or recourse to prostitutes (classified as vice) who might become pregnant. Even in 1803 there were alternatives. Malthus knew that births could be artificially controlled. He made the value judgement that actions and reactions should be left to lie where they fall.

Abortion was ‘unnatural’ (SE I 18). Contraception was ‘improper’ (SE I 18). Apart from being banned by both Church and state, man-made modes of family planning had a ‘tendency to remove a necessary stimulus to industry’ (SE II 235). Less food would be produced. More people would go hungry. Morality is happiness. Francis Place, John Thelwall, John Horne Tooke and their fellow radicals should have recognised that the feedback worked to the detriment of the poorest of the poor.

The price of grain regulates the supply of celibacy and the demand for weddings. There is, however, another variable which impacts the child-bearing years. It is the target standard of living.

As early as the first *Essay* Malthus had observed that a social actor will rationally delay marriage lest he ‘lower his rank in life’ (FE 76). Adam Smith had said that linen shirts and leather shoes are not luxuries but necessaries where ‘the custom of the country renders it indecent for creditable people, even of the lowest order, to be without’ (WN II 399). Malthus as early as the first *Essay* had followed Smith in employing the logic of social subsistence (MS 56, 127) and not just physical survival: ‘The labourers of the South of England are so accustomed to eat fine wheaten bread that they will suffer themselves to be half starved before they will submit to live like the Scotch peasants’ (FE 116). It is the subculture and not just the nutrients that sets the threshold. We are social animals, sensitive to the pecking order. Even the poor do not want to look shabby.

Conspicuous comparison even in the first *Essay* makes spending and marrying a mutable feast. There were exceptions even in the first *Essay* to Malthus's *ever be sufficiently free*. In the second *Essay* the exceptions have grown in number. Malthus in the second *Essay* draws attention to the power of ‘moral restraint’ (SE I 18). Moral restraint is a prudent investment in social standing. It is, Malthus says, even now ‘the most powerful of the checks which in modern Europe keep down the population to the level of the means of subsistence’ (SE I 305). Costumes and props *keep down* the population. To that extent, Waterman says, they are ‘potentially subversive of Malthus's negative polemic’ (Waterman, 1991: 55). Other things do not remain equal. Other things are blocking Malthus's tendency law at source.

Moral restraint, Malthus observed in 1803, already ‘operates with considerable force throughout all the classes of the community’ (SE I 252). It prevails ‘more, than in past times’ (SE I 252). It is more common in richer than in poorer countries and more prevalent in the higher than in the lower reference groups. In earlier times it 'operated very feebly indeed' (SE I 147). Nowadays it is becoming more common. We can no longer afford the geometrical ratio. What would the neighbours think?

Economic growth through knock-on *embourgeoisement* is declaring war on the population multiplier. Earnings are going up. A more equal start through education and training, a more open road for ambition and achievement, the new dynamic increasingly 'affords opportunities for the inferior orders to rise by personal merit and exertion' (OCL 101). Exhausted metics condemned to 'unwholesome trades and manufactories' (FE 135) lack a toehold in deferred gratification. A better capitalised economy creates new openings—'fewer blanks and more prizes' (SE II 195)—for workers able to exploit the swing towards 'skill and machinery' (PPE I 422).

The 'more intelligent among the working classes' would be 'raised into overseers of works, clerks of various kinds, and retail dealers' (PPE I 482). Better jobs with better incomes would 'infuse fresh life into all classes of the state' (OCL 101). Mounting the ladder, all classes would be gaining an *entrée* into a new world of signs and symbols on which they would only be able to capitalise if they limited the size of their household. Commodities are eating up children. A refocusing of happiness is taking place.

All classes are being exposed to the option demand. Not all are equally prone to take up the challenge. Malthus reports that in his experience the bottom half of the people are the least likely to see the causal link between severe deprivation and self-inflicted pregnancy. Their myopia will not last. Matter is in motion. Mind will not forever lag behind.

Rural Ireland just after the rebellion in the 1790s and the Union with England in 1801 well illustrates the potential. Malthus in 1808, describing the excess population and the low standard of living, reported that the Irish peasant was living in a cottage 'hardly superior to an English pigstye' (Malthus, 1808 [1963]: 39). Low per capita output meant low per capita income. Even in village Ireland, however, there was an emerging perception of a better life than whisky, cheap potatoes and large families. Malthus looked at the backward and underdeveloped bogs. What he saw was modern Singapore. Cheap-and-nasty as Ireland then was, Malthus predicted 'such an elevation in the character and condition of the lower classes of society as will make them look forwards to other comforts' (Malthus, 1808 [1963]: 50).

Rising living standards in rural Ireland would be the cause and effect of dignity and pride. They would be conducive to moral restraint. Arithmetical subsistence would be less at risk from a geometric population (Malthus, 1808 [1963]: 39, 45, 51). Catholic emancipation would add to the momentum. A Churchman but also a liberal, Malthus knew that tolerance is good economics. Self-respect leads to self-control. It keeps the size of the family down.

As the competition for positional standing becomes more democratic and more intense, the blue-blooded themselves will be diversifying the areas in which they seek distinction. Even landowners and aristocrats will be trying their hand in 'the useful arts' that 'are in the highest degree beneficial' (OCL 102). Growth feeds growth where old money and new money converge. A large family is an impediment if status is constantly being won and lost.

Godwin expects his altruistic anarchists, 'noble and disinterested spirits' (SE I 331), to do what is in the general interest because of an internalised sense of duty. Malthus says that 'advantage' and 'prudence' will be more than enough to counteract the 'low satisfactions' that drive men to marry young: 'We can have no rational hopes of success, without this coarse application to individual interest which Mr. Godwin rejects' (SE I 331). 'Romantic gallantry' (SE I 332) belongs to the age of chivalry. We today live in the age of economics. Malthus advises Godwin to move with the times.

Other-regarding self-sacrifice, however noble in itself, can, Malthus says, never be more than a 'weak substitute' (SE I 332) for the stimulus 'excited in man by the desire of providing for himself, and of bettering his condition in life' (SV 245). The equalisation of purchasing power would undam the flood that is more reliably contained by productivity and pay, 'providing' and 'bettering'. Godwin, Malthus comments, failed to see that levelling down would inevitably 'remove the only counteracting weight to the passion of love' (SE I 331). Earlier marriages and mice-in-the-barn offspring would return the poor to the starting line. Personal advancement through moral restraint would have delivered longer-lasting improvement.

Social survival is the new tendency law. *Natura*, however, *non facit saltum*. Sudden change is not to be expected. The Irish peasants, like the English manuals, are slow to adapt. 'No one', Malthus admits, 'can be less sanguine than I am' (in OP 514) about the time it will take for cultural upgrading to filter down (SE I 304). In 1821, reflecting on the economic history of moral restraint, Malthus states that 'its operation has not hitherto been very prompt': 'There is scarcely a country', at least in Europe, where prevention has had 'a very direct effect in diminishing the number' (ER 139).

The effect will be felt but the uplift will be slow. It is the reason why, in Hollander's estimation, Malthus is unlikely to have put much faith in moral restraint (Hollander, 1986: 188). There was also Godwin. To have played up the importance of moral restraint would have been to 'concede much to Godwin and this Malthus did not do' (Hollander, 1986: 210). In the long run even the poor will be travelling up. In the short run the nation will have to accustom itself to the ratios, the subsistence wage, the horizontal supply curve and the iron law. It will be vice and misery. It will be absolute poverty and sometimes even absolute destitution. The result will be a cry for help.

8.2.3 *The State and the Poor*

Gradually, marginally, the invisible hand is likely to be on the side of a more manageable population. Yet things can go wrong. Where they do, the state will be under pressure to relieve the distress that most of our people are too soft-hearted to delegate to the invisible hand of God.

The state would do well to refuse the poisoned chalice. Public money squandered on income maintenance for the able-bodied is incompatible with self-reliance and the work ethic. 'Dependent poverty', dead-end and minus-sum ought to be 'held disgraceful' (FE 98). Handouts to all who self-define to be in need should be phased out in favour of dynamic empowerment aimed at 'raising their condition' (SE II 153). The needy should be reconditioned into 'habits of prudence and foresight' (SE II 153). The poor should learn the meaning of 'sobriety, industry, independence' (SE II 154).

The history of the war on exclusion documents a growing reliance on welfare services such as public housing, slum clearance, affordable transportation, occupational health and curative medicine. Like Adam Smith, Malthus focuses on the primary enabler of state schooling. Rank has its Eton and its Winchester. Most of us go straight to the mine or mill: 'It is surely a great national disgrace, that the education of the lower classes of people in England, should be left merely to a few Sunday schools' (SE II 153).

Education, Smith had said, not only passes on marketable skills but also reinforces the moral mainstream (WN II 309). Malthus was attracted both by the vocational component that positions the poor on the moving staircase up and by the training in good citizenship that immunises the impressionable young against the heresies of 'interested and ambitious demagogues' (SE II 154). Godwin was one of those subversives. In both the *Enquiry* and the *Enquirer* he had warned of the likelihood that state schools would become the Trojan Horse for brainwashing and propaganda. He had expressed serious reservations about the social engineering that had been such a great selling point for Smith and Malthus.

Because of both mind and matter, the attitudes and the skills, Malthus anticipated that schooling would have a positive effect on the geometric ratio. Know-how and prudence in the lower classes would raise them nearer to the 'middle classes of society, whose habits are…certainly superior' (SE II 155). Moral restraint and later marriage would be the unintended consequence of social intervention. It would be state guidance in the sense of Smith. It would not be spontaneity trending towards anarchy in the sense of Godwin.

Malthus as a man of the cloth knew that he could not write off the primitive communism of Christ and his disciples. He cites with guarded approbation the example of the Moravian sect where property in common had not led to destruction of industry or universal want (SE I 336). Outlier observations like this leave open the possibility, not definite but 'plausible' (SE I 336), that the future might be different from the status quo. Once man has been raised up from the 'indolence and apathy of the savage' to the 'activity and intelligence of civilized life' (SE I 336), a new centre ground is bound to emerge. Malthus anticipated that it would be individual self-regulation loosely stage-managed by the state. It would be Smith. It could, of course, be the Moravian sect. It could even be Godwin.

Malthus in the 1803 *Essay* reiterates that Godwin had mistaken the cause for the effect. Godwin's 'great error' had been to hold human institutions responsible for 'all, or most of, the evils which afflict society' (SE II 327). The truth is the opposite, that it had been people and not structures that had been responsible for widespread poverty. The principle of population has been 'confirmed by experience, in every age and in every part of the world' (SE I 336). 'Salutary checks' (SE I 328) on man's intemperate short-termism are a part of that tendency law. We are marrying later. We are targeting a limited household budget on a smaller number of quality children. We are intending that the next generation should tap burgeoning upward mobility to the full.

We are evolving into a middle-class culture of comfort and aspiration. Later marriage is building a breakwater against Malthusian excess. It can be a mixed blessing. Malthus does not consider the possibility that the pendulum might swing from a population glut to a population famine. Even two children can be one child too many. The well-being of the family can impose a negative externality on the wealth and defence of the nation. It might have to be reversed by contra-Malthusian social policies that make the state tax-and-spend to a pro-natalist, pro-immigrant extent that neither Godwin nor Malthus had ever envisaged.

8.3 The Fifth *Essay*

The changes made to the third edition in 1806 and the fourth edition in 1807 did not significantly alter the narrative. In the fifth edition in 1817, Malthus, however, indicated that he was moving on. Six chapters were rewritten, five were new, and there was a new Appendix. In the editions of 1803, 1806 and 1807, Malthus had responded in his Book III Chapter 3 to Godwin's *Reply to Parr*. In 1817 his reply to the *Reply* was dropped. A critique of Robert Owen's new-style egalitarianism took its place. Owen was sunrise. Godwin was sunset. In the sixth and final edition of the *Essay*, Malthus in 1826 added a short note of only 13 lines acknowledging (without mentioning the title) the appearance of Godwin's *Of Population* in 1820. Malthus did not waste words. The statistics had shot Godwin's fox.

A more pressing target had become Owen's *New View of Society*, just published in 1816. Robert Owen was 'a man of real benevolence', an author and an activist for whom 'I have a very sincere respect' (SE I 334). Owen was a caring paternalist. He had set up schools in his factory. He had capped child labour at no more than 12 hours a day. Owen was moving towards common property, producer cooperatives, benchmark equality of income and even communities of no more than 300 families. It was all words. Like More's Utopia, Malthus said, Owenite communitarianism would be yet another invitation to lethargy, inactivity, early marriage, inadequate sustenance and excessive numbers. New Lanark, New Harmony, it would end in tears.

Malthus is correct, Owen had argued, 'when he says that the population of the world is ever adapting itself to the quantity of food raised for its support' (Owen, 1816: 174). Malthus is, however, exaggerating the peril when he plays down the fertility of the land: 'He has not told us how much more food an intelligent and industrious people will create from the same soil, than will be produced by one ignorant and ill-governed' (Owen, 1816: 174). Needs must where the devil drives. Improving farmers will ensure that supply keeps pace with demand. Godwin's 'myriads' will give them the time they require. Smith's China scenario is not on the horizon.

Malthus felt that Owen had not grasped the severity of the problem. The ratios and not just random misfortune mean that, however much an 'intelligent and industrious people' might endeavour to coax blood from a stone, still deprivation is a part of the system. The Bible confirms it: 'You always have the poor with you' (*New Testament*, *Matthew:* 26, xi). Owen had committed the same error as Godwin. He had looked to mind to reverse a law of nature that no one but God is in a position to repeal.

Writing to Samuel Whitbread in 1807, Malthus reminded him that even a Member of Parliament is powerless to calibrate the fertility in the soil to the fertility in the body: 'To banish poverty…is clearly beyond the power of legislature' (LW 4). Privation can be reduced. It can never be eliminated. In appealing to the positive and preventive checks, Malthus was not demonstrating 'hardness of heart' (LW 10) so much as revealing himself to be, in Alfred Marshall's words, a 'kind-hearted clergyman' (Marshall, 1881: 30). Malthus was a friend of the poor. That is why he was an opponent not just of reckless procreation but of the Poor Laws.

The Poor Laws abridge the personal freedom of the lower classes. Unearned benefits such as cash transfers and subsidised cottages were an evil that would 'ultimately check itself as most evils evidently do' (LW 21). Favourable to earlier marriage and additional births, they raise the price of necessities such as food and housing. They lower the real and even the money wage of the poor. They destroy jobs through the increased burden on local taxation. In one way after another, they strike directly at the happiness of the deprived.

8.4 A Moving Staircase

A better way to help the poor would be for the Poor Laws to be abolished (SE I 374). Writing in 1800, Malthus conceded that in the unpredictable ups and downs of wartime disruption they had been 'advantageous to the country' (HPP 13). Speenhamland discretion had rescued many deserving paupers from temporary hardship (HPP 9). In spite of that, state welfare stands 'heartily condemned' (HPP 13). Private philanthropy is no better.

'The humanity and generosity of the higher and middle classes of society' (HPP 13), implanted by Providence as the other-regarding sentiments always are (LW 7), feeds through into increasing numbers, diminishing returns and thence into positive checks.

Well-meaning charity is not always 'beneficial in its effects' (SE II 163). Sometimes it is seriously 'prejudicial' (SE II 163). Poor Laws and Good Samaritans erode the spirit of independence (SE I 359, SE II 236). They extend the false promise of additional grain despite the 'absolute impossibility of executing it' (SE I 368). They leave the poor even more deprived afterwards than they had been before (SE I 358).

Owen had not been much more favourable than Malthus to cash benefits that allow free riders to economise on their duty: 'Can that system be right, which compels the industrious, temperate, and comparatively virtuous, to support the ignorant, the idle, and the comparatively vicious?' (Owen, 1816: 142). Owen, like Malthus, had little time for laziness and dissipation. His solution was not, however, the same. Owen, like Godwin, believed that community in goods and land, the restoration of the 'natural inheritance' to the poor and the termination for all time of the 'injustice and oppression' (SE I 334) of the parasitical rich would successfully integrate the able-bodied into the common enterprise. Refusing donations so long as they were able to work, the poor would recognise it as their debt to their fellows to earn life for themselves and their families. It is all in Hume's waterlogged meadow. We own it in common. We drain it in common. No decent member of our community would ever 'lay the whole burden on others' (Hume, 1739–40 [1969]: 590).

That was Owen's answer to the gradual disappearance of the parasitical poor. Malthus dispensed with the philosophical underpinnings of Hume's meadow in favour of the basic instincts. Malthus felt that the common man, 'ignorant', liable 'to be deceived' (SE I 334), would never grasp the link between uncontracted obligation and the well-informed spectator. Enter liberal economics. Not abundance but scarcity 'can alone overcome the natural indolence of man' (SE I 335). Not good times but bad can alone 'prompt him to the proper cultivation of the earth' and to manufacturing industry, 'necessary to his happiness' (SE I 335). Relief leads to sloth. The more generous the unilateralism, the less the work, the less the food.

Malthus reproached Godwin for failing to see the pivotal role of relief in ramping up the population and ramping down the subsistence. All forms of egalitarianism, Malthus said, are doomed to fail so long as the great law of self-interest remains in force: 'Pre-eminently clear in theory', 'uniformly confirmed by experience', 'no tolerably plausible answer can be given to it' (SE I 336).

Moral restraint itself is at risk should private property become the public commons: 'The encouragement and motive to moral restraint are at once destroyed in a system of equality and community of goods' (SE I 337). Precisely because we are all equal, we all have an equal incentive to rely on our neighbours for small families and bountiful harvests. What one can do, all cannot. Godwin, Owen or the Stakhanovite Moravians, all roads lead to the war of all against each. The best attainable outcome will be a protective state, however 'unnatural, immoral or cruel' (SE I 339).

Egalitarians do not see the harm that their well-intentioned sharing and caring will do: 'The whole nation would shortly become a nation of paupers with a community of goods' (SE II 176). There is no incentive to do one's best if the workshy will receive an identical reward. Levelling destroys the happiness that was intended and multiplies the number of paupers (SE II 177). The future is poor and nasty. Leviathan takes over the decision-making function: 'Any great interference with the affairs of other people is a species of tyranny' (SE I 360). Egalitarians like Owen and Godwin are the enemies both of freedom and of food. They should rely on the quid pro quo of simple market economics instead.

The answer is the moving staircase. The lower classes should experience a 'general and permanent improvement in their condition' (LW 11). 'General and permanent' elevation is the proper route to self-respect. Dependency is not. Nor is an impermanent high.

Malthus, giving evidence in 1827 to the Select Committee on Emigration, agreed that emigration might in the short run reduce the 'prodigious quantity of misery' that is evocatively captured by the numbers actually 'dying of want and disease' (1827: 312). It would, however, not be a solution 'of long duration' (SE II 237) but merely a sticking plaster. It would be a temporary palliative that would in time be cancelled out by an accommodating rise in births. New tastes, skills and 'habits of prudence' would confer a more lasting benefit on the left out. A recrudescence of the Black Plague would postpone the misery but would not prevent it. Economically and culturally, there is no alternative. Some of the poor will always be with us. Some, encouragingly, will escape the trap. Where they are able to do so, some will make every effort to move up.

Irish peasants, dwelling in 'miserable hovels' (1827: 313), do not know that there is a better way: 'They are inclined to be satisfied with the very lowest degree in comfort' (1827: 319). The Marxian bottom tier is deprivation conscious of its deprivation. The Malthusian residuum is not even that. The Irish peasant is stuck in a rut. There is no automatic mechanism that would push him to better his condition. The vicious circle is all the comfort he knows.

Wanted is a new sense of self. Rising wages and full employment empower the manual masses both to respect themselves and to win the respect of others (1827: 326). Aspiring to a higher standard of comfort, they are more likely to practise moral restraint in order to break the link between pay and family size. 'Civil and political liberty' (1827: 319), a 'strict and equal administration of justice', 'perfect security of property' (1827: 326) and religious tolerance, all empower them to move in the direction of the median and the representative.

Education and *integrated* education play a vital role in positioning even the lower grades on the moving staircase of a citizenship in common: 'To give respectability to the schools, it would be very desirable that those who are a little above the class of labourers, should send their children to them' (LW 36). Schools and *comprehensive* schools are the architects of a common culture. Like Owen and Godwin, Malthus looks forward to life-style approximation and equality of respect. The inferiors and the superiors come to see themselves more nearly as one nation. The population imbalance will in consequence correct itself.

Fewer births countervail the eternal fixity of arable land. Poverty shrinks to the deserving old and infirm alone. Purified of the ratios and of the free riders, necessary and generous welfare comes its own: 'I should be the first to propose that those who were actually in want should be most liberally rewarded, and that they should receive it as a right, and not a bounty' (LW 12–3). It will be a right to welfare and still more a philosophical absolute: 'I consider the labouring classes as forming the largest part of the nation, and therefore that their general condition is the most important of all' (1827: 317). The happiness of the masses is 'the most important of all considerations, the one to which all others should give way' (1827: 318). Smith, Paley, Godwin, Malthus or Owen, it is the principle of utility that in the last analysis should be the guiding light.

References

By W. Godwin

Godwin, W. (1797 [1965]). *The Enquirer* (abbreviated as EQ). Augustus M. Kelley.

Godwin, W. (1798 [1976]). *Enquiry Concerning Political Justice* (abbreviated as PJ). Penguin Books.

Godwin, W. (1820 [1964]). *Of Population: An Enquiry Concerning the Power of Increase in the Numbers of Mankind, Being An Answer to Mr. Malthus's Essay on That Subject* (abbreviated as OP). Augustus M. Kelley.

By T.R. Malthus

Malthus, T. R. (1798 [1970]). *Essay on the Principle of Population, as it affects the Future Improvement of Society, with Remarks on the Speculations of Mr. Godwin, M. Condorcet, and Other Writers* (abbreviated as FE). Penguin.

Malthus, T. R. (1800 [1986]). *An Investigation of the Cause of the present High Price of Provisions* (abbreviated as HPP), reprinted in *The Works of Thomas Robert Malthus* (Vol. 7, pp. 5–18). Pickering and Chatto.

Malthus, T. R. (1803 et seq. [1989]). *An Essay on the Principle of Population: or A View of its past and present Effects on Human Happiness, with an Inquiry into our Prospects respecting the Removal of the Evils which it occasions* (2nd ed., 1803; further editions in 1806, 1807, 1817, 1826) (abbreviated as SE I and SE II) (2 Vols.). Cambridge University Press.

Malthus, T. R. (1807). *A Letter to Samuel Whitbread* (abbreviated as LW). Johnson.

Malthus, T. R. (1808 [1963). Review of Thomas Newenham's. *A Statistical and Historical Inquiry into the Progress and Magnitude of the Population of Ireland, Edinburgh Review*, 24, reprinted in Occasional Papers of T.R. Malthus, ed. by B. Semmel (pp. 33–52). Bert Franklin.

Malthus, T. R. (1814 [1986]). *Observations on the Effects of the Corn Laws, and of a Rise or Fall in the Price of Corn on the Agriculture and General Wealth of the Country* (abbreviated as OCL), reprinted in *The Works of Thomas Robert Malthus* (Vol. 7, pp. 87–109). Pickering and Chatto.

Malthus, T. R. (1827). Evidence to the Select Committee on Emigration (Third Report). In *Parliamentary Papers* (Vol. 5, pp. 311–327). House of Commons.

Malthus, T. R. (1830). *A Summary View of the Principle of Population* (abbreviated as SV), in FE, supra (pp. 219–272).

By Other Authors

Brown, F. K. (1926). *The Life of William Godwin*. J.M. Dent and Sons.

Hollander, S. H. (1986). On Malthus's population principle and social reform. *History of Political Economy, 18*, 187–235.

Hume, D. (1739–40 [1969]). *A Treatise of Human Nature*. Penguin Books.

Marshall, A. (1881). *The Economics of Industry* (2nd ed.). Macmillan.

Owen, R. (1816). *A New View of Society*. Longman, Hurst, Rees, Orme, and Brown.

Smith, A. (1759 [1966]). *The Theory of Moral Sentiments* (abbreviated as MS). Augustus M. Kelley.

Smith, A. (1776 [1961]). *The Wealth of Nations* (abbreviated as WN) (2 Vols.). Methuen.

Waterman, A. M. C. (1991). *Revolution, Economics and Religion: Christian Political Economy, 1798–1833*. Cambridge University Press.

CHAPTER 9

The *Reply to Parr*

Godwin replied to Malthus in 1801 in his *Thoughts Occasioned by the Perusal of Dr. Parr's Spital Sermon*. It began with an attack on Mackintosh's *Discourse on the Study of the Law of Nature and of Nations* (1799). It moved on to Parr's Spital Sermon (1800). Then there was Anon of 1798 and his *Essay*.

9.1 Mackintosh

James Mackintosh in 1791, like Mary Wollstonecraft and Tom Paine, had sought to defend the French Revolution against reactionaries and conservatives such as the frightened Burke. In his *Vindicae Galliciae* Mackintosh had argued that in Britain the revolution of 1688 had accelerated the 'progress of light', reconciled *political* with *civil* liberty, and rescued the nation from late-feudal despotism (Mackintosh, 1791 [2008]: 154, 155). The British had shown the French what it means to overthrow a bad government. In spite of that, the nation of 1688 was still not free.

Publications were censored. Dissidents were transported. Assembly was restricted. The commercial and the talented were being held down by inherited wealth. The great body of citizens had no voice in government. The House of Commons had become a synonym for 'corruption' and 'venality' (Mackintosh, 1791 [2008]: 159). Revolution is always inferior to reform. Even so, 'imprisoned grievances' must 'at length have vent': 'Is France to be imitated? Yes!' (Mackintosh, 1791 [2008]: 163).

D. Reisman, *William Godwin and Thomas Robert Malthus*,
https://doi.org/10.1007/978-3-031-62113-0_9

Mackintosh's answer in 1791 had been 'Yes!'. Attending three of the 39 lectures that became the *Discourse* in 1799, Godwin was horrified to find that his erstwhile friend had changed his mind. The French Revolution had been 'prolific of mischief to mankind' (Mackintosh, 1799: 78). The 'excesses' and the 'miseries' could not be written off as 'partial and incidental evil' (Mackintosh, 1799: 79). Street fighting could not be justified as the price of the greater good. The mob had sown panic. Liberty had become chaos. Burke, 'a writer admired by all mankind', had seen that without a protective state there would be no law and less order (Mackintosh, 1799: 44, 57). A civilised life in common is built upon 'the two great institutions of property and marriage' (Mackintosh, 1799: 39). Radicals were going too far. They were pulling to pieces the delicate balance.

Mackintosh was to hold high office in India, to be knighted, to be a professor of law (with Malthus) at the East India College. In 1815 he approached Lord Byron to fund Godwin's work. In 1821 he wrote to Godwin about *Of Population* that 'your reasonings...have changed my opinions' (in KP II 274). In 1823 he reassured Godwin ('Be of good heart') that his new publications would refresh his reputation (in KP II 288). Despite the efforts to rekindle their friendship, Godwin always felt, although he was not mentioned by name in the *Discourse* (RP 16), that Mackintosh in 1799, grown 'lofty, overbearing and scornful', had treated his one-time associate 'like a highwayman or an assassin' (RP 22, 15).

In 1799, writing to Mackintosh, Godwin quoted phrases like 'shallow metaphysicians' and asked pointedly if the 'invective was designed to light upon myself' (Letters II, 67). He clearly felt that Mackintosh, 'the closest, the most dispassionate and candid' (Letters II, 68) of his friends, had betrayed his trust. Mackintosh denied that it was so: 'No particular writer was present to my mind' (in KP I 328). Godwin refused to believe him.

Mackintosh, he complained in the *Reply*, had been 'dissecting and mangling my sentiments and reasonings' (RP 18). Mackintosh had been among the 'Savage Desulators' (in KP I 328) who had been turning public opinion against the true faith that alone would inspire virtue. The 'shop and the hamlet' had to be led: 'The people cannot be profound' (RP 59). The truth which 'cannot be read by the people' must be disseminated through 'circuitous channels' (RP 59) in which the enlightened must take the lead. Mackintosh, Godwin declared, had been a Judas. He had discredited not only his friends but the cause.

9.2 Parr

Samuel Parr was a clergyman and a Cambridge Doctor of Civil Law. Like Mackintosh, he had been an early admirer of Godwin on the freedom of conscience. Godwin had been a visitor to his home to discuss ideas that in some quarters would have been termed seditious.

Parr preached the annual Spital Sermon before the Lord Mayor and other notables at Christ Church, Spitalfields, on 15 April 1800. He took his text from St. Paul's exhortation 'Let us do good unto all men' (*New Testament*, *Galatians* 6: x). Parr's Sermon was published in 1801 in a volume which boasts 22 pages of text and 135 pages of notes. Many of his sources are in Latin, Greek and Hebrew. There are references to Smith, Hume, Bentham, Burke and, importantly, to Godwin's *Political Justice* (Parr, 1801: 66). By 1801 the book had acquired a certain notoriety. Parr made clear that he did not like it very much.

Both Parr and Godwin were high-minded idealists imbued with a missionary zeal to improve the world around them (KP II 74). Both by temperament were recognisably English. Their values in common included liberty, tolerance, tradition, evidence and common sense. Both put frugality before dissipation, the individual before the state, discussion before revolution. Neither played down the importance of human happiness on earth. In the Spital Sermon, Parr nonetheless took issue with Godwin, his personality and his philosophical system.

9.2.1 Universal Benevolence

In an ideal world we should all be benevolent and caring. In the real world, it will always be a mistake to promise more than we can deliver: 'The moral obligations of men cannot be stretched beyond their physical powers' (Parr, 1801: 14). 'The public good is impaired rather than encreased', Parr warned, when 'a succession of airy projects' begets 'eager hopes' that, despite 'tumultuous efforts', ultimately end in 'galling disappointments' (Parr, 1801: 7, 8). The good of all is too important a quest to be lost to galling disappointments. Charity is good. Charity, however, begins at home.

Theorists of 'universal benevolence' do great harm when they interpret the 'generous and salutary dictates of nature' to mean an 'unbounded love' for the whole of the species (Parr, 1801: 10). The truth, less general, is that it is the 'particular affections' of family, kindred, neighbourhood, religion and country (Parr, 1801: 10) that will most reliably evoke finely tuned fellow-feeling. The victims of a foreign earthquake are situated behind a veil. Our children and our workmates are here-and-now.

Parr as a Christian knew that Jesus had nothing but praise for the altruism of the Good Samaritan. Yet Parr had also been exposed to Adam Smith's concentric circles of affection and attachment that lose their intensity the further outward they radiate from the nucleus of familiar faces and 'habitual sympathy' (MS 177). Richard Price had conceived of society as the receding shocks from a quake when he spoke at Old Jewry on a recent revolution in a neighbouring state (Price, 1790: 9–10). Parr, like Price, had not been insensitive to sparks and forest fires. That, however, had been 1789. By 1800 Parr knew that the tables had been turned.

Parr knew about unintended excrescences. Unfocused philanthropy, laudable in theory, was, he said, likely in practice to be 'productive of less good than it promises' (Parr, 1801: 2). Scarce seeds flung at random into the winds will all too frequently set in motion 'a train of evils' (Parr, 1801: 2) that are not anticipated by short-sighted do-gooders when they leap before they look: 'Their opinions are at variance with facts' (Parr, 1801: 8). Today is unknown. Tomorrow is unknowable. God alone has the information needed to act with ineffable ardour in the service of a stranger he has never met. The rest of us will do well to reserve our benevolence for recognisable beneficiaries situated closer to home.

Parr has no patience with the 'wily insinuations' and 'declamatory harangues', the 'artificial and often ostentatious sentiments', the 'trifling, irksome and debasing mummeries' of 'pharisaical' and insidious 'panegyrists' who love to 'delude and inflame' (Parr, 1801: 2, 10, 11). Parr does not name the 'sophists' who, in his opinion, are behind the misguided philosophy of universal benevolence (Parr, 1801: 7). Godwin, oversensitive to fancied slights, was in no doubt that he was Parr's primary target.

Godwin praises Parr for 'the generosity of his sentiments and the warmth of his temper' (RP 20). After that he repeats his message, that big-thinking must not be sacrificed to the little-thinking that crept in after the reign of Terror in 1793 and 1794 had discredited what Godwin himself calls the 'hoarse and severe cry of Jacobinism' (RP 37). A new cry was coming in. Parr 'has condescended to join a cry, after it has already become loud and numerous' (RP 22). Ribaldry and scurrility were in the air. There was 'public odium' (RP 12). Parr had added little to the debate on the causes of vice and the status of original sin. The unspoken accusation was that he had not been sincere.

Godwin criticised Parr for his 'intolerance and contempt' (RP 22). The Spital Sermon had been a Spite-all Sermon. The doctrine of 'universal philanthropy' (RP 46), propounded by Christ himself, had not been refuted. Godwin conceded that his *Enquiry* in 1793 had been 'the child of the French revolution' (RP 2). Since he had always been an 'enemy to revolutions' (RP 5), the false promise of the Bastille and the barricades had never been more than tangential to his narrative. What he believed to be of lasting value was, he reiterated, the high theme of social justice and right conduct. Perfectibility remained hard core. The universal benevolence of the Good Samaritan would reassert itself once anarchy had succeeded to the veil of tears.

9.2.2 General and Particular

Parr had nonetheless touched a sensitive nerve. Godwin had put 'universal philanthropy' (RP 46) above the love of a single, named face in the crowd. The wellbeing of the whole had been made the supreme maximand. The life of the thinker Fénélon was worth more than the life of his valet (PJ 103). A man is *not* a man for a' that.

It is all in the calculus of advantage. Rights and wrongs are costs and benefits: 'Morality...consists entirely in an estimate of consequences' (PJ 175). Man is 'a rational being' (PJ 75). Man is 'a reasonable creature, capable of perceiving what is eligible and right' (PJ 69). Man is a problem-solving creature, employing 'the most eligible means' (PJ 166) to attain a clearly specified end. Man is a thinker and a doer. He is a utilitarian and a maximiser. He is a natural economist. Man is not an impulse buyer, forever going on gut: 'Man is not a vegetable to be governed by sensations of heat and cold, dryness and moisture' (PJ 69). Romeo made a second-best choice. Romeo should return to the crossroads and contract anew.

God is love and not shopping. Parr in his Spital Sermon paid tribute to the emotive dimension in human life that positive science had relegated to the footnotes. Godwin feared that Parr had had Godwin's own Enlightenment rationality in mind. Godwin knew that he was widely seen as cerebral, detached, austere, distant, humourless, 'cold', 'uninviting' and 'unconciliatory' (in KP I 359). He was aware that the party of sentiment was regarding him as pure thought unsullied by any impulse or intuition that would 'unlock the heart' (Letters I, 44). As late as 1824 he was still defending himself against an unseen enemy: 'I have no desire to be regarded as having no sentiments or emotions....I wish to be considered as feeling as well as thinking' (HCE, vii). Godwin in 1801 in his *Reply to Parr* took the opportunity to set the record straight. Parr had misunderstood his message. It was never a binary either/or.

Godwin in the *Enquiry* had made his position clear: 'Passion is so far from being incompatible with reason that it is inseparable from it' (PJ 70). Godwin near the beginning of his long book had stated openly that 'sensible causes' make reason 'abortive' (PJ 54). Disembodied reason may well provide the superior roadmap to the paradise of perfectibility. Yet human nature is what it is. A passage from an unpublished manuscript entitled *First Principles of Morals* and dated 1797 says it all: 'Reason...has not the smallest degree of power to put any one limb or articulation of our bodies into motion' (in KP I 294). A year later he was writing strongly in support of 'the empire of feeling': 'The voluntary actions of men are under the direction of their feelings' (in KP I 294). Three years after that, in his *Reply to Parr*, Godwin repeated what he had already said. Motivation is a mix.

A man is not a stone. Smith, Price and Parr had explained the diminishing strength of subjective sensation with reference to the concentric circles and the amplitude of the ripples. Godwin could see the logic. Emotion falls close to the tree: 'As every man will know more of his kindred and intimates than strangers, so he will inevitably think of them oftener, feel for them more acutely, and be more anxious about their welfare....The benefits we can confer on the world are few....The benefits we can confer upon those with whom we are closely connected are of great magnitude.... It is impossible that we should be continually thinking of the whole world' (in Woodcock, 1946: 149). Close contact and a life in common put a face to a number. It is the logic of political devolution. Intense sympathy makes the moral sentiments that much more intimate.

We rush to succour those kent comrades who share our heart and our hearth. Should I choose to save the life of my aged father in preference to wise Fénélon who is pushing back the frontiers, 'every man will respect my choice' (RP 40). 'Every man' will empathise with my decision to put personal utility before the common good. It is not a rational assessment of the economic payoff. It imposes a cost on the whole for the narrow benefit of the part. Godwin was clearly not 'a consistent utilitarian' (Munro, 1953: 21) to the extent that he allowed emotion to interfere with his impartial estimation of the greater good. It is for all that the choice that 'every man' would make when his nation as a whole turns to 'common deliberation' (PJ 166) and not the cold rate of discount to lay down its priorities for organ transplants and end-of-life care.

The self, the family, the street, the community, the village—the nearer the buck, the greater the bang: 'The benefits we can confer upon the world are few....The benefits we can confer upon those with whom we are closely connected are of great magnitude, or continual occurrence' (in KP I 294). There are the fine-turned outcomes. There is at the same time the affectual release: 'Without feeling we cannot act at all; and without passion we cannot act greatly' (RP 29). Godwin in the *Reply to Parr* stood Parr's interpretation of his character on its head. Even in the age of reason, Godwin declared, the human mind is 'much *more* the creature of sentiment and of emotion, than of the understanding' (RP 31, emphasis added). Especially is this likely to be the case where the sentiment and emotion are experienced close at hand.

Happiness in the small is the epicentre and the core. Happiness in the large is the unintended outcome of the waves and the knock-ons that boost the wellbeing even of anonymous strangers. Domestic gift-giving, Godwin says, can without question be 'an important and paramount public good' (RP 32, 33). It yields 'successive utilities' (RP 41) even to generations as yet unborn and to 'men whom I know not' (RP 39). Society is not a surrogate family. Yet the benevolence shown to a family member might ultimately produce a greater 'mass of human happiness' (RP 41) than the initial act of kindliness shown to one Fénélon once.

The small becomes the large. What begins at home does not end at home. Upbringing is an intergenerational snowball: 'I must be attentive to the welfare of my child, because he is one in the great congregation of the family of the whole earth' (RP 34). The private, as Godwin says in *St. Leon*, is also the public: 'I apprehend domestic and private affections inseparable from the nature of man, and from what may be styled the culture of the heart, and am fully persuaded that they are not incompatible with a refined and active sense of justice' (*St. Leon*, 11). Godwin's novel was published in 1799, the year of Mary Wollstonecraft's premature death. Marguerite in *St. Leon*, like Henrietta in *Mandeville* and Mary Macneil in *Fleetwood*, demonstrates all the qualities of compassion, patience, care and common sense which Godwin associated with the *ewig weibliche* in the person of Mary Wollstonecraft.

A man and a woman *could* marry. They *could* live together. Godwin in 1798 had moved on from the Godwin of 1793. Opposites attract: 'Man marries because he desires a lovely and soothing companion for his vacant hours: woman marries, because she feels the want of a protector, a guardian, a guide and an oracle' (Fleetwood, 167). The man has courage and consistency. The woman has softness and delicacy. The weaker sex looks up to the stronger. It is not known how Wollstonecraft, the first British feminist, made her peace with an intellectual position such as that. Presumably she told her caveman what he wanted to hear and then made all the big decisions on her own.

Godwin speaks of the family unit. It is also the wider society. My child is *our* child. In preparing him for a good life, I am also investing in the good society that has yet to evolve. To save one is to save all. It is a literal interpretation of Christ's 'love thy *neighbour*' which is not generically different from Godwin's universal benevolence. The proximate motivation is different. The endstates, Christian or anarchist, may well converge.

Parr was right. Godwin was rational. Yet Parr, Godwin believed, was also wrong. Parr had failed to recognise that sentiment too was a part of the mix. Godwin valued his friendships and his social circles: his work 'was a product of a critical intellectual *community*' (Philp, 1986: 216, emphasis in original). He valued married life with Mary Wollstonecraft. He valued virtue and virtue is a feeling. It is 'a sentiment of the heart' (Letters I, 49). It is more than the business economist's bottom line: 'A conduct adopted from the hope of reward and the fear of punishment is not virtue' (Letters I, 49). We do good to feel good. The subtitle of *Fleetwood—The New Man of Feeling*—makes clear the need for a mix. P.H. Marshall calls Godwin 'a rational Romantic' (Marshall, 1984: 396). Godwin saw that there was more to the human psyche than the balance sheet alone.

9.3 Malthus

Three years had passed since the first *Essay*. Godwin continued to respect Malthus's anonymity. They had in fact exchanged letters and met face to face.

Godwin was full of praise for 'the author of so valuable a treatise' (RP 56). He applauds his 'simplicity of manner' and the 'liberality of his mind' (RP 55, 56). Of the book and its author, he says, 'I can never speak but with an unfeigned respect' (RP 10). As for the theory of population, he declares that Malthus had indeed broken new ground: 'He appears to me to have made as unquestionable an addition to the theory of political economy, as any writer for a century past' (RP 56).

The propositions are 'valuable', 'conclusive and certain' (RP 56). The core tenets are unimpeachable: 'I admit the ratios of the author in their full extent' (RP 61). The inferences are 'unassailable' (RP 76): 'The principle of multiplication in the human species is without limits' (RP 61). Godwin states that he cannot directly refute any one of the deductions. It is a strange concession in the light of his earlier and his later work. He boasts that he himself, in *Political Justice,* had sketched out the very relationship between population and subsistence 'that had given occasion to Mr. Malthus's Essay' (OP v).

Godwin was the pioneer. Malthus had been to his school. Godwin confesses modestly he can 'take some pride' (RP 56) in figuring so prominently and constructively in Malthus's work without himself being the primary target: 'The main attack of the Essay on Population is not directed against the principles of my book' (RP 10n). At the end of the day, however, Godwin sees that he can never be a Malthusian: 'My understanding confines itself to the task of repelling his conclusions' (RP 61). They are not 'powerfully connected with his premises' (RP 76). They are not true.

The theory is robust. The facts let it down. Inspecting the real world, Godwin reassures the Hobbesians that human life is not teetering on the edge: 'The evil is not so urgent, nor the limitation so narrow, as a terrified imagination might lead us to conceive' (RP 70). The theory predicts that the growth in population will outstrip the growth in subsistence. The evidence is that the differential 'has never in any past instance, in any quarter or age of the world, produced those great and astonishing effects' (RP 70). Mathematically, it is irrefutable. Statistically, it does not stand up.

Circumspice: Long after Adam and Eve had discredited the two-child family, the planet is still not fully booked. Malthus without proof had exaggerated the imminence of the apocalypse. The cruse will never reach the brim. Nor should it. Godwin wrote to Malthus in 1798 that people are a blessing and not a curse: 'If human beings are of any value, it is certainly desirable, *ceteris paribus*, that every country should contain its greatest practicable number of inhabitants' (Letters II, 54). People are labour in the sense of Smith and utility in the sense of Paley. It is the mercantilists Misselden and Malynes in the sense of Chap. 6. Population is a plus. Malthus in his reply reiterated that the real world had clearly not read Godwin's book. Population was growing rapidly. It would continue to grow until it hit its absolute buffer (Letters II, 55).

Godwin does not deny that the positive checks are there. Evidence from past and present confirms that disease and malnutrition do indeed thin out the surplus. Some societies, reinforced by the authority of Aristotle (Aristotle, 1981: para. 1335b), have even resorted to the infanticide of the uneconomic. However 'painful and repulsive to the imagination' (RP 64) the abandonment of a child must be, planned life-taking has been, Godwin states, a necessary evil: 'I had rather such a child should perish in the first hour of its existence, than that a man should spend seventy years of life in a state of misery and vice' (RP 65). Moderate euthanasia would increase happiness overall. Do-not-resuscitate is one policy-option. There are others. Godwin presents himself as a fence-sitter who does not see an urgent need to decide.

Positive checks regulate the totals. Concealed within the *how many*, there will also be the *who* and the *which*. It is a doctor's dilemma which, later evolving into eugenics, is acknowledged by Godwin when he explores the trade-off between Socratic Fénélon and his riff-raff valet. 'Corrupt', 'besotted', 'prepared for degradation and vice', revealing 'scarcely any vestiges…of their higher destination' (RP 64–5), the 'low-minded' will occasionally appeal to our compassion and good will but never to our cost-benefit calculation of entitlement and priority.

Godwin knew that the gold versus the dross of life was a topic on which a philosopher had to have an opinion. Malthus says that nature at her 'mighty feast' instructs the supernumerary 'to be gone' (SE II 127). Godwin, disaggregating the unwanted, establishes that is the 'opprobrium' that is fated for the chop (EQ 193). 'You always have the poor with you'? Perhaps not if it is the residuum and not Fénélon who is first in the queue for a positive check.

Malthus focuses on the positive checks. He would have done well, Godwin says, to have amplified his discussion of the preventive checks that eliminate the overhang before nature bids it to be gone. Godwin, unlike Malthus, never reveals why he is not a follower of Francis Place in respect of contraception, abortion or sterilisation. He does not mention the rhythm method or treat it as nature's way. Prevention to both Godwin and Malthus effectively meant later marriage as a rational choice.

Foresight and forethought, 'virtue, prudence and pride' (RP 72), restrict the number of children pressing on the resource constraint. It is all a matter of affordability: 'I am persuaded it very rarely happens in England that a marriage takes place, without the question having first undergone a repeated examination' (RP 72–3). The message is in the words. *Very rarely. Repeated examination*. It is what Malthus in 1803 was to call moral restraint. Godwin believed that it put paid for all time to the possibility of overpopulation.

Yet there is a class bias. Moral restraint as an investment in itself is either weak or non-existent in 'the lower classes of life....They have no character of prudence or reflection....They have nothing of the pride, arising from what is called the decent and respectable appearance a man makes among his neighbours' (RP 73). Malthus in his 1798 *Essay* had given the example of the 'man of liberal education' (FE 90) who postpones marriage in order to protect his social position. Godwin in his 1801 *Reply* embellished the check that Malthus was to make his own in the 1803 *Essay*. The 'man of liberal education' plans ahead. The 'lower classes of life' live for today. Moral restraint is still a minority taste.

Today's minority dwells in a house of glass. Rational people, sensitive to the courtroom in the street, voluntarily contain family size lest it exhaust their stores on necessaries that they would prefer to invest in symbols. Today's majority will follow their leader. They will convert income into capital in order to enlist social sanctions on the side of personal advancement. Material wants are not unlimited: 'Where a man possesses any reasonable means of pleasure and happiness, he will not bring himself to destroy his own tranquility or that of others by thoughtless excess' (RP 74). No social actor will race headlong into devil-may-care excess. By the same token he will not hesitate to spend what he must on perceived social rank. The future is the moving staircase of affluence, rationality and relative standing. The minority becomes the majority. Mindsets progress. Feckless overbreeding is bid away by the power of public opinion.

Private utility is enhanced. So is the utility of the whole when each noble Athenian grasps the essence of the structural imperative: 'Every man will understand the interests of the community' (RP 74). From the thought follows the deed. Every club member will 'be much influenced in his conduct by the interests of the general' (RP 75). He will subordinate the individual to the collective purpose. It is not a loss but a gain: 'He will love his brethren. He will conceive of the whole society as one extensive household. He will feel his own happiness so entirely dependent on the institutions which prevail, as will remove from him all temptation to touch the ark with a sacrilegious hand. He will not be able to live without character and the respect of his neighbours' (RP 75).

He will know that his own wellbeing is bound up with the wellbeing of time and place. The real spectator in alliance with the invisible spectator will draw him into self-restraint and preventive checks. The positive checks will pale into insignificance compared with the 'prospect of extraordinary improvement in society' (RP 76). It can only get better. Extrapolating into the future, Godwin anticipates that rising living standards, a shorter working week, less ignorance, greater equality, will all be on the side of decency, sobriety and propriety. They will be on the side of moral restraint.

There is also the law. In the short run, recalling the problem-solving statism of Montesquieu, Steuart and Price, Godwin pronounces it 'the first duty of princes to watch for the multiplication of their subjects' (RP 62). Legislation could limit the number of children per family in order to eke out the nation's iron reserves (RP 67). Compulsion is freedom where without deterrence late Malthusians might overburden the public good of subsistence. Free riders indifferent to adding up might reason that 'if any children cannot subsist at my expense, let them subsist at the expense of my neighbour' (RP 74). In the short run a ceiling is a viable alternative to the positive checks. In the long run it will not be needed. Automaticity and consensus will provide.

Godwin rests his case. History-to-come will be favourable to 'the most obvious rules of prudence' (RP 76) and 'the best interests of mankind' (RP 59). It will be favourable to later marriages and smaller families. Malthus in 1798 was right about the lower classes but not about the future. The moving staircase is moving all of us up. It is the law of nature. Moral restraint will trickle down. Malthus is today. Godwin is tomorrow. The 'existing habits of the people' (SE II 38) are not the Ten Commandments. Anarchy grows into itself. It will be safe from the law of population that multiplies like mice in a barn.

References

By William Godwin

Godwin, W. (1797 [1965]). *The Enquirer* (abbreviated as EQ). Augustus M. Kelley.

Godwin, W. (1798 [1976]). *Enquiry Concerning Political Justice* (abbreviated as PJ). Penguin Books.

Godwin, W. (1799 [1992]). *St. Leon: A Tale of the Sixteenth Century* (abbreviated as St. Leon), in *Collected Novels and Memoirs of William Godwin* (Vol. 4). William Pickering.

Godwin, W. (1801 [1968]). *Thoughts Occasioned by the Perusal of Dr. Parr's Spital Sermon* (abbreviated as RP). C.G. and J. Robinson, reprinted *in William*

Godwin Uncollected Writings 1783–1822 (pp. 281–374), J. W. Marken & B. R. Pollin (Eds.). Scholars Facsimiles and Reprints.

Godwin, W. (1820 [1964]). *Of Population: An Enquiry Concerning the Power of Increase in the Numbers of Mankind, Being An Answer to Mr. Malthus's Essay on That Subject* (1820 [1964]) (abbreviated as OP). Augustus M. Kelley.

Godwin, W. (1824). *History of the Commonwealth of England* (abbreviated as HCE) (Vol. I). Henry Colburn.

Godwin, W. (2014). In P. Clemit (Ed.), *The Letters of William Goodwin* (abbreviated as Letters) (Vol. II). Oxford University Press.

By T.R. Malthus

Malthus, T. R. (1798 [1970]). *Essay on the Principle of Population, as it affects the Future Improvement of Society, with Remarks on the Speculations of Mr. Godwin, M. Condorcet, and Other Writers* (abbreviated as FE). Penguin.

Malthus, T. R. (1803 et seq. [1989]). *An Essay on the Principle of Population: Or A View of its past and present Effects on Human Happiness, with an Inquiry into our Prospects respecting the Removal of the Evils which it occasions* (2nd ed., 1803; further editions in 1806, 1807, 1817, 1826) (abbreviated as SE I and SE II) (2 Vols.). Cambridge University Press.

By Other Authors

Aristotle. (1981). *The Politics* (T. A. Sinclair, Trans.). Penguin Books.

Kegan Paul, C. (1876). *William Godwin: His Friends and Contemporaries* (abbreviated as KP) (2 Vols.). Henry S. King.

Mackintosh J. (1791 [2008]). *Vindiciae Gallicae: Defence of the French Revolution.* Palgrave Macmillan.

Mackintosh, J. (1799). *Discourse on the Study of the Law of Nature and of Nations.* T. Caddell.

Marshall, P. H. (1984). *William Godwin.* Yale University Press.

Munro, D. H. (1953). *Godwin's Moral Philosophy: An Interpretation of William Godwin.* Oxford University Press.

Parr, S. (1801). *A Spital Sermon.* J. Mawman.

Philp, M. (1986). *Godwin's Political Justice.* Duckworth.

Price, R. (1790). *Discourse on the Love of our Country.* London: Cadell.

Woodcock, G. (1946). *William Godwin: A Biographical Study.* The Porcupine Press.

CHAPTER 10

Of Population

Godwin began work on *Of Population* in 1818. By 1819 he was saying that 'I never was so deep in anything as I am now in Malthus' (in KP II 259). Published in 1820, *Of Population* was almost as long as *Political Justice*. Its message was that population was a non-issue. Malthus and his *Essay* had 'gotten possession of the public mind' (OP viii). They were diverting attention from continuing injustice that remained as great an evil in 1820 as it had been in 1789.

10.1 A 'Herculean Task'

The Battle of Waterloo in 1815 ushered in a century-long Pax Britannica. It began badly with 'Peterloo' in 1819, the New Poor Law in 1834 and the cholera of 1851. Yet there were also green shoots that marked the inclusion of the deprived. The suffrage was widened after 1832. The unions were given basic rights after 1824. There was the Education Act in 1870 and the National Insurance Act in 1911. Parliamentary socialism was emerging as the democratic alternative to the Sedition Acts on the Right, Marxian expropriation on the Left. The red flag was becoming the Webbs, Keir Hardie and Ramsay Macdonald. The black flag of Bakunin, Kropotkin and Sorel was being discredited by the direct action and the nihilism. *Of Population* in 1820 is a landmark in the transition to social

D. Reisman, *William Godwin and Thomas Robert Malthus*,
https://doi.org/10.1007/978-3-031-62113-0_10

balance. It was a manifesto and a declaration. It was a public affirmation that radicals, levellers and evolutionary anarchists still had something to say.

Calling Malthus 'the foe', Godwin saw his own unexpected reentry into the debate on population as a much-delayed onslaught that would at long last win the war: 'If I am right the system of Malthus can never rise again, and the world is delivered for ever from this accursed apology in favour of vice and misery, of hard-heartedness and oppression' (in KP II 260). Two decades had gone by since the *Reply to Parr*. In that long interregnum the foe had consolidated his head start. It had all happened effortlessly and without real scrutiny: 'It is not a little extraordinary, that Mr. Malthus's book should have been twenty years before the public, without any one, as far as I know, having attempted a refutation of his main principle' (OP vii). *Of Population* was the book that would knock him off his perch. It would be a 'Herculean task' (in KP II 271). It would be worth the effort that it cost.

On Population would prove, once and for all, that Malthus had parked both theory and policy in a blind alley. Malthusianism was built upon 'a contempt for human nature' (OP 512) and an erroneous interpretation of the facts: 'An inherent, rapid and incessant power in the human species to multiply its numbers...is impossible' (OP 403). It is 'a fable' (OP 509). It is 'a way into the clouds' (OP 480). It is science fiction without any practical use.

The *Essay* is 'waste paper' (OP 141). The *Essay* 'has done nothing and worse than nothing' (OP 142). The *Essay* is 'the most extraordinary work ever presented to the world' (OP 516). The *Essay*, with its hateful message of 'monstrous proliferation' (OP 369), differs from 'the views of every philosopher that ever existed' (OP 516). *Of Population* would set the record straight: 'I have resolved not merely to attack Malthus in his remedies, his vice and his misery; but to show that there is no need of any remedies, that the numbers of mankind never did and never can increase in the preposterous way he lays down' (in KP II 271). Owen had eclipsed Godwin in the 1817 *Essay*. Malthus had written Godwin out of the plot. The time had come for the counterrevolution.

Malthus, despite the 'revolting nature of the conclusions he draws from his principle' (OP vii), had won over the open-minded. They would have been better served by the far more persuasive arguments of the *Enquiry* and the *Enquirer*. Godwin never explains why Malthus had been so successful when he, Godwin, had the real purchase on the thrust of history.

Godwin had lived in silence with his obsession for 20 years for reasons which he does not reveal. At last, in *Of Population*, he declares himself ready both to 'dislodge the usurper' whose system proves nothing and to 'build up a Pharos' (OP ix) that would be the next wonder of the world. In the event Godwin's Pharos was not much noticed. A French edition in 1821 was eclipsed on the Continent by post-1789 liberals and economists such as Say. The neglect was only a blip and an aberration. Malthus did not deserve the popularity. Godwin knew that his time would come.

The Godwin of *Political Justice* was widely mistrusted even in the calmer environment of the 1820s. Godwin in *Of Population* took care to reassure his readers they would not be seduced into sin: 'My bitterest enemy will hardly be able to find in this volume the author of the Essay concerning Political Justice' (OP 8). Godwin says that republicanism and redistribution are 'foreign to the subject which is now before me' (OP 8). He makes clear that his new book is not about anarchy. It is about Malthus.

It is therefore a waste: 'I have written a book about nothing' (OP 626). Malthus had 'undertaken no less a task than to argue us out of our senses' (OP 606). Someone had to deflate his balloon. There would have been no need for a book on population if self-deluded Malthus, wrong on every count, had not taken it upon himself to sow 'confusion' (OP 625) and to stretch 'credulity' (OP 4). Godwin was the white knight whose mission it was 'to assail his theory at the foundations' (OP 589) while also showing that his evidence was inadequate: 'The numbers of mankind appear not to have increased' (OP 625). Malthus was making wild assertions about the emperor's new clothes. Worst of all, the Malthusian canon was morally repugnant to any person of common decency. It had to go.

10.2 The Malthusian Heresy

Malthus is not a bad man: 'His honourable character, and his unblemished manners' (OP xii) mean that he cannot be written off as a pedantic manipulator who twists his truisms to favour a propertied elite. In spite of his good intentions, the final product lets the reader down. Marred by 'monstrous errors' (OP 6), it is an 'unreal and fairy edifice' (OP 323). It puts up an 'Egyptian darkness' (OP 315). It calls that darkness the truth.

The Malthusian theory is a 'house of cards' (OP 357). It is built upon 'wild conjectures' spun out from 'gratuitous and arbitrary assumptions' (OP 188), 'false and groundless' nostrums (OP 7) and 'dogmatical maxims' (OP 304). 'Visionary chimeras' (OP 502) congealed into 'loathsome theories' (OP 452) are seasoned with 'odiousness' (OP 51). 'Wholly unproved assumptions' (OP 509) manufactured not from 'pure reason' (OP 317) but from pure 'rottenness' (OP 27) are employed to generate recommendations that are little short of 'gross and degrading' (OP 317).

The Malthusian system commits the 'grossest mistake that was ever made' (OP 317). It relies upon quasi-mathematical logic and self-referential definitions to deduce its propositions from initial postulates that a head-in-the-clouds reactionary had effectively plucked out of the air. Malthus examines what would happen *if*. Godwin believes it would be better to examine 'what does actually happen' (OP 133). The truth lies in 'the affairs of real existence' (OP 136). Statesmen and ordinary people cannot afford to rely on unsupported contentions.

Strong on ambiguity, 'cabbalistical', 'impious' and 'oracular' (OP 313) in his exaggerated self-confidence, Malthus relies upon a contra-Baconian methodology to impute imaginary causes to imaginary effects. Godwin in the *Reply to Parr* had, prematurely and carelessly, accepted the validity of the ratios (RP 61). In *Of Population* he expresses his regret that he had somehow fallen into a trap. In 1820, reversing the position that he had endorsed in 1801, he insists that not one but both of the ratios were 'shadowy and inadequate' (OP 341). It is all a 'fallacy' (OP 27): 'The two pillars of his system are wholly a delusion' (OP 358). They are *wholly* a delusion.

Deduction from axioms is a false friend. It throws up propositions that, '*wholly* a delusion', are unreliable to the point of being 'occult and mystical' (OP 5). Spare logic is not the real world. Malthus, 'summary and dictatorial' (OP 161), 'requires us to believe it, simply because (as he says) it must be so' (OP 342). His approach is a 'vague and unsatisfactory style of generalisation' (OP 354) that precludes any 'severe examination' (OP 314). His 'specious' and 'dazzling simplicity' (OP xvi, 162), 'slight and unsatisfactory' (OP 144), is 'evidently founded on nothing' (OP 1) but the ad hoc and the ad hominem. It is difficult for 'human imagination or…for human credulity to follow' (OP 4). It sheds little light on the real world. It is a 'blunder' (OP 142). Number, weight or measure would have been the better tool.

10.3 Induction from Experience

The datasets that would flesh out the generalisations are imperfect. Malthus accuses Godwin of proceeding from mind to matter without making any serious attempt to quantify the time series and the spot (FE 133, 154, 162). Godwin accuses Malthus of imposing his flights of fantasy on 'real human societies' (OP 198) without devoting more than a 'supercilious and lasting glance at the bare numbers' (OP 321). Malthus accuses. Godwin accuses. Both believed that pontification ex cathedra will never be a trustworthy *est demonstrandum* so long as it does not enter into dialogue with the facts. Both were men of the Enlightenment in the tradition, spelled out in Chap. 3, of Locke and Hume. Simultaneously, both were fully aware that the facts were thin on the ground. God's filing cabinet is closed to visitors. Often an informed guess is all that stands between the social scientist and total unknowledge.

Godwin knew that there were gaps in his dataset. He was prepared nonetheless to hazard an informed guess that was far superior to Malthus's random stab in the dark: 'We have not the smallest reason to believe, that the population of the earth has increased, or that the human race is in any way more numerous now, than it was three thousand years ago' (OP 161). We have not the smallest reason to believe that the numbers on the planet have gone up or that they have put an increasing strain on scarce subsistence: 'There is nothing, in the history of the earth, to authorise this opinion' (OP 234). There is nothing to fear from the Malthusian bogeyman: 'In most countries population is at a stand' (OP 43) or 'nearly so' (OP 354).

Population has typically been at a stand. If anything, it has gone down: 'The further we go back, the more numerous was the population of the globe' (OP 58). Godwin, aware that his sources were weak, believed that such evidence as he could muster pointed to a stationary stock. Two children would succeed to two parents. Malthus, Godwin complained, was catastrophising from the unsupported perspective of assassins already within the citadel and poised to strike. The possibility is remote, Godwin stated, that the world will ever outgrow itself. Such evidence as can be found speaks with a single voice in support of a stable and not an exploding population.

Sweden proves the point. It keeps reliable records. They give little comfort to alarmists like Malthus. The data suggests that the Swedish population had doubled in the last 100 years. Malthus's geometrical ratio predicts a doubling in 25 years. In the last 100 years, the Swedish population ought to have increased by more than 400 per cent. It had not. Tracing the numbers backward through time, Godwin concluded that Sweden was not more populous in his own times than it had been 500 or even 1000 years earlier (OP 502n).

In England and Wales, the first Census in 1801 and the second Census in 1811 had confirmed the Malthusian conjecture that the population was going up. Godwin's response was that the numbers may have been going up but that the population was not. A Census is a step up from the anecdotes and sample surveys of Price and Howlett upon which the first *Essay* had had to draw. Common sense, however, discloses that the results were so far-fetched that they must have been wrong. The Census was transparently 'so much labour thrown away' (OP 231). The population is 'at a stand'. Everyone knows that. Unreliable boffins who cannot tell a hawk from a handsaw should not bite off more than they can chew.

The Census does not mean what it says. The statisticians in 1801 and 1811 had failed to disaggregate by age and gender. Even if today's summing up is what the number-crunchers say it is, tomorrow's total will be system-dependent on the number of women in the childbearing years between 20 and 45 (OP 146, 166). The death of a woman in that age-range has a causative impact on the growth in population. The death of a man does not.

Statistics are at best a *what was*. They do not include an account of the *why*. Subjectivity is underrepresented. Wedlock facilitates but does not maximise. Couples do not inevitably procreate to the limits of what is physically possible. The correlation is weak: 'Early marriages do not greatly tend to increase population' (OP 191). In Persia childbearing has effectively ceased by age 30 (OP 191). There is nothing to fear. The law of nature is not the law of population. Nature is taking better care of her people than Malthus had ever imagined.

In America, the Census in 1790 and again in 1810 had shown that the population had been doubling every 25 years. Godwin was not taken in. The measure was a fluke. The sample was representative of nothing but itself. Malthus had been too quick to build his mighty synthesis on a freak outlier: 'If America had never been discovered, the geometrical ratio, as applied to the multiplication of mankind, would never have been known' (OP 139–40). America was an uninhabited territory with near-infinite access to uncultivated land. Its population had grown because of immigration as well as natural increase. Generalisation from Adam Smith's narrowly self-sustaining China would have produced a different result.

The ratios are simplifying fictions. They assume away the multifaceted complexity of the ceteris paribus. Godwin, Rosen says, denied that they 'follow any laws of nature' at all: 'Godwin insisted on the inclusion of additional factors in the explanation of population increase and decline' (Rosen, 1970: 47). Additional variables would have driven a coach and horses through Malthus's overconfident *what must and will be*.

Besides that, the statistical *what was* is a historical been-and-gone. Different times and different places make each a posteriori only as true as itself. Malthus's data, in Rosen's view, was to Godwin at best a single-use: 'Hence, he argued, Malthus's principles operated only within a particular political and economic system, not in all societies and not permanently in the same society' (Rosen, 1970: 47).

Distortions and deficiencies increase the likelihood of noise on the line. While representative observations might permit a reasonable inference, one-off factoids are the shifting sands of spurious correlation. Malthusian demographics are for that reason a waste. Malthus based his theory on the exception rather than the rule. Beyond the confines of North America in the atypical present day, 'mankind do not increase' (OP 21, 296, 358). Even the fish and the animals do not increase.

The 'earliest records' confirm it (OP 95). Four is two. Allowing for infant and maternal mortality, for epidemics, diseases, wars and other exogeneities, four births per woman would be necessary to ensure two surviving offspring (OP 206). Allowing for celibacy, barrenness and emigration, the number jumps to eight. Eight confinements per couple would sum up to two new inhabitants in the territory. It would be the self-sustaining stationary state. The Malthusian ratios, were they correct, would long since have overpopulated not just Sweden but the globe. It has not happened. The geometrical ratio does not 'tally with the facts' (OP 305). Most of the earth's surface is still not under cultivation. The unused capacity proves the point: 'The power of increase in the numbers of the human species is extremely small' (OP 4).

The population is 'at a stand'. A stand per se is not an optimum. Just as the numbers can be excessive, so, as triangulated by the imperatives of defence, production and felt wellbeing, they might be inadequate: 'The inference from all history is that those countries, other things being equal, have been happiest, where the increase of mankind has been the most encouraged' (OP 304). A moderate increase is not a Malthusian explosion. An arithmetical expansion can be in the national interest even if a geometrical series would be ruinously unsustainable. No one wants

England to be like Old Sarum or Death Valley where Malthusian overpopulation is not much discussed in the pubs and the saloons.

Godwin tabled arguments to show that numbers were not a serious hazard. He extended his discussion from quantity to quality. We can be 'better' even if, 'at a stand', we are not about to be 'more'.

The revocation of the Edict of Nantes, like the French Revolution a century later, shows how better people can contribute to the whole. It drove out of France and into neighbouring countries 'multitudes of her most useful and industrious citizens' (OP 388). The 'spirit of enterprise' and 'general love of adventure' (OP 384) of incomers 'in the flower of their life' (OP 404) can contribute to the moral fibre and economic growth of the immigrants' new fatherland. It can do so, Godwin reports, without putting an intolerable strain on the supply of food. 'A simple and tranquil form of social existence is not hostile to population' (OP 236).

Overheated Malthusians would be well-advised to take a step back from their 'absurd and extravagant' anxieties (OP 144). The danger is as real as Don Quixote's windmills: 'There is absolutely no tendency in the human species to increase' (OP 504). An increase if it did occur might add a new tranche to output and wellbeing. Godwin, primarily a moral philosopher, was only secondarily an empirical social scientist. He believed nonetheless that he had been able to prove that the facts and figures were not on the side of the ratios. The Malthusian theory 'has no existence but in Mr. Malthus's book' (OP 51).

10.4 Moral Restraint

It was a non-issue. Godwin never thought that population would stand in the way of peaceable anarchy. As people learn 'how to moderate, if not wholly to exterminate "the passion between the sexes"', what is bound to emerge, Waterman says, is 'stationary (steady) state equilibrium with stable population and real income' (Waterman, 1991: 55–6). Passion has a low income elasticity. Mind is becoming the active ingredient. The body, satiated with its necessaries and moderate comforts, is less frequently putting in importunate claims for destabilising superfluities.

Statics is equilibrium. Economics, however, is restless change. Malthus saw that disturbance was the order of the day. Even if the physical needs could be satisfied, the social needs would still be multiplying without limit. An unintended consequence is a reduction in the pressure on limited subsistence. Forward-facing couples are practising moral restraint. They are investing in societal location through later marriage and fewer children. They are opting out of the geometrical ratio. Godwin did not warm to rat-race emulation and the divisiveness of conspicuous consumption. He saw, however, that Malthus in leveraging on moral restraint was defusing the threat from his own theory of overpopulation.

There would have been no need for *Of Population* if Godwin had been convinced that the Malthus of 1803 had genuinely evolved beyond the Malthus of 1798 whose theme had been that 'all is despair' (OP 620). Godwin was not certain that Malthus had seen the error of his ways. Malthus, Godwin pointed out, repeatedly qualifies his new check with escape clauses that make it all but a tautology (OP 512–514). Malthus continues to express reservations about the great mass of the people (OP 515). He is forever shifting the cutting edge of moral restraint into a pie-in-the-sky future that is a world away from the misery and vice of the present day.

Yet the discipline of all over each is undeniably there. Moral restraint, Godwin believed, marked an evolution in Malthus's social philosophy from things to people. Malthus was moving from the individualists' factoring down to the organicists' scaling up. Not just animal instinct but other people were becoming more prominent in Malthus's account of the demographic trend. It was a step upwards from the liberals' I to Godwin's own We. It was reducing the distance between the two perspectives.

Godwin looked in the first instance not to economic growth or political democracy but to 'the empire of opinion' for the 'salutary restraint' (OP 571) that would commit Wild Peter to the social good. The justifiable approbation or 'indignation of the vicinity' has a feedback effect on patterns of conduct that extend even to marriage and children: 'There is no man that cannot read the smiles of his fellow-citizens; and there is a tongue in their silent aversion, that speaks with a voice louder than a trumpet' (OP 571). Social sanctions—'the sober judgment of his neighbours' (OP 570)—impress on the social actor the force of the moral law: 'Affairs would go but ill, were it not for its mighty control' (OP 569).

Communities have consequences. Other people to Godwin have a greater influence on human conduct than do non-reflective constraints such as Malthus's sexual passion, Marx's surplus value or Darwin's natural selection: 'Do men go to war because they want the means of subsistence? Far otherwise, war in civilised countries is the offspring of pride' (OP 299). The pecuniary motive separated from invidious comparison affords no more than a weak and intermittent incentive. Malthus, in moving towards moral restraint, was showing a greater appreciation of seeing-and-being-seen as a variable in a socially sensitive couple's contingent costing of marriage and family.

The arithmetical ratio is no more robust than its geometrical counterpart. The evidence shows that every human being is capable of 'producing a much greater quantity…than is necessary for his individual subsistence' (OP 300).

The earth has the potential to sustain a population of nine thousand million (OP 449). Improving landowners had demonstrated that farm produce in England and Wales could be doubled or 'much more than doubled' (OP 494) through an agricultural revolution. Because of science 'the soil of this island would maintain its present population ten times told' (OP 351). Food is not a problem. Population is not a problem.

Traditions and routines should be shaken out of their complacency. Title should be redistributed towards the more efficient. The sea, which occupies two-thirds of the surface of the globe, should be harvested for its fish. The earth is 'inexhaustible' (OP 498). Subsistence is subject to 'no assignable limits' (OP 508). It is man and not nature that is responsible for the bottleneck that Malthus alleges to be the cause of hardship. Godwin refuses to blame the land. If there is a shortage of food, then it is social inequity that is at fault.

10.5 Property and Population

To read Malthus is to meet murder on the way. Yet people were reading Malthus, and the reason was that he satisfied a need. Malthus is likely to have written the *Essay* 'as a piece of pleasantry' to while away the time: 'To his great surprise the world received his communications as a very serious affair' (OP 511). Like Martin Luther at the end of the Roman Catholic imperium, Malthus's *Essay* filled an ideological niche: 'No wonder that his book is always to be found in the country-seats of the court of aldermen; and in the palaces of the great' (OP 564).

The *Essay* in the country-seats and the palaces was read not so much as an account of population as a legitimation of property. Absolution had an economic value. The rich obtained from their pocket philosopher the reassurance that vice and misery were the ineluctable consequence of uncontrollable impulses and lifestyle indolence. Poverty had no known link with man-made artificialities such as the unequal and stratified distribution of income and wealth. The soup kitchens and the rough sleepers will always be with us. It is life and not injustice. There is no way to reverse a tendency that is a law of nature and a gift of God.

Godwin objected that Malthus was de facto reinforcing the conventional wisdom of the ruling class. Malthus 'flattered the vices and corruption of the rich and great' (OP v). The landed and the powerful became his disciples. The deprived and the excluded did not. Vice and misery had not 'done so much for the well being of mankind as Mr. Malthus imagines' (OP 103).

Godwin viewed Malthus's *Essay* with 'inexpressible abhorrence' (OP xii). He termed it an 'offense against God and man' (OP 548). Malthus, he objected, had rewritten history to make it more palatable to the swells and the dandies that had the most to lose. The posh were living well because of the 'inequality of mankind, and the accumulation of property, landed property especially, in few hands' (OP 485). The truth would not have been to their liking.

Property was held in common in pre-Conquest Peru. The outcome had been abundance: 'At no time was there any deficiency of provisions' (OP 63). More people meant more production: 'As the whole wealth of the state consisted in the fruits of the earth, it follows that every additional labour given to the community was so much added to the general stock' (OP 63). A growing population was consuming more because it was producing more. The land was able easily to accommodate the increase. A stationary or a contracting population would have been a 'waste of human life' (OP 64). Only a Malthusian can convince himself that such underperformance is good.

Labour in pre-Conquest Peru, supported by 'fine climate' and 'fertile soil' (OP 67), was 'light' and community oriented while at the same time remaining intensive enough to ensure a moderate level of target prosperity (OP 66). Communal property, at least in Peru, brought out the best in the people. The pre-Conquest Peruvians were distinguished by their 'mildness of character', 'cheerfulness' (OP 61), 'innocence' (OP 66) and truthfulness. There was nothing to be gained from dishonesty or deceit.

There was a 'sublime harmony' (OP 110) between the individual and the collectivity. The service ethic was strong. There was no evidence of the Hobbesian bad seed: 'Let not the system of the universe be calumniated' (OP 110). The Peruvians were noble Houyhnhnms and not odious Yahoos. They were Mrs. Ostrom and not Mr. Olson. Nice guys finish last. They were no match for the Spaniards and the guns.

Liberty and equality sank into 'imbecility and helpless dependence', depopulation and famine (OP 60). Once the Spaniards had privatised the commons, Peru became a civilised country on the European model where enclosures had destroyed lives and uprooted communities. The record speaks for itself: 'Immense wealth has a natural tendency to spread a comparative desert around it' (OP 236). Backwardness is made and not born: 'It is not the Law of Nature. It is the Law of very artificial life' (OP 20).

The noble Peruvians in their state of nature had been benevolent and kind: 'They did not tear each other to pieces, to see who should obtain possession of the means of subsistence' (OP 66). It was only when civilisation redefined the parameters that the selfish side of human nature came to the fore: 'Man delights in control and to inforce submission upon his fellow-man; human creatures desire to exercise leadership and to display authority' (OP 614). The mark of Cain, however latent, however regressive, is not about to go away: 'Brutes we are, and brutes for ever we shall remain' (OP 598).

Nature is a constant that takes its 'for ever' neat. Nurture, however, is a positive force which domesticates the wild beast. First-strike is crowded out by perceived interdependence. Even 'for ever' is 'for ever' on the move. It will take its course but also take its time: 'Nothing is more slow than the progress of nations' (OP 57). Life in the here-and-now has some distance to go before radical reinstitutionalisation can be contemplated.

The future holds its own pot of gold. For now, Godwin counsels, it would be a mistake to jump the gun. The unwarranted communalisation of land and capital would unleash the *bellum* and the depredation that would turn back the clock on rules without rulers. Private property 'has been the source of much improvement and much admirable activity in mankind' (OP 614). Irrespective of what might in the fullness of time unfold, both the 'liberation of mankind' and the 'wealth of nations' (OP 595) presuppose the survival of private ownership under the protection of the state.

Strict constructionists regard partitioned entitlements as *non est disputandum*. Godwin saw them as provisional inns and stopping places on the road to a higher stage in social development. There is no reason to treat title as absolute and incontestable: 'The rich man…has no right to withhold his assistance from his brother-man in distress' (OP 545). The injunction, carried forward from the *Political Justice*, is employed in *Of Population* as the last word on the claimed-up present day. Godwin sees it and Malthus does not. If subsistence is short, the fault is more likely to lie with inequality and stinginess than it is with idleness and short-sighted procreation.

The rich man is a steward and not a principal. He is obliged to do his duty 'to the utmost of his power' (OP 546). He has no autonomous right to employ his discretionary surplus without regard to 'the genuine needs of natural man' (OP 470). The earth is not his or yours but ours. Even private property is collective property. It is held on license from the wider We: 'Whenever I meet a man, I meet a brother. I recognise in him the image of the all-perfect' (OP 505).

Individual wellbeing is situated in a web of externalities and affects. Sympathy is the imaginative exchange of circumstance and condition. It sensitises the property-owner to the legitimate needs of his fellows. If he perceives a locus of distress, he instinctively rushes forward to share what he can: 'Man is an animal that, whatever Mr. Malthus may say to the matter, requires to be tenderly treated' (OP 467). You cannot buck empathy. Compassion is a part of what we are.

Malthus, inclined to individualism, 'calls out to everyone to stay aloof' (OP 578). Godwin, a refugee from strict Calvinism, is more receptive to 'disinterested benevolence' (PJ 313) and the duty to share (OP 560). People do not always live up to their own high ideals: 'It is impossible that we should be continually thinking of the whole world' (in KP I 294). Backsliding is the human condition: 'The spring of action will certainly not be a sentiment of general utility' (in KP I 295). Yet mind is in motion and sympathy is arguing ever more persuasively for gifts. There is reason to expect that the propertied will increasingly want to share their good fortune with the whole.

Approbation and self-approbation are the incentive: 'Society is the source of innumerable pleasures; without society we can scarcely be said to exist' (OP 614). Collectivisation by consent is the result. The haves, responding to the real and the impartial spectator, conform to the general will. They abridge the personal happiness that accrues to the bounded use of private property in order to garner the higher happiness that is the reward for a duty well done. Poor relief, affirmative action, property owners volunteer a part of their endowment because integration is its own reward.

A generalised gift can have a generalised return. It is separate from the feel-good of praise. A contribution to a charity school is an investment in skills, efficiency, growth, upward mobility, moral restraint, smaller families, reduced pressure on marginal land. Malthus did not explore the long-term externalities that can be the unexpected consequence of property opened up to the whole. Godwin, on the other hand, was in no doubt about the spillovers from equalisation. We put in. We take out. Nationhood is a powerful disincentive to act the free rider on the generosity of the public spirited.

We give. We take. We do so behind a Rawlsian veil so thick that we cannot situate our own future costs and benefits in the sequence of surprise: 'No one who lives by the sweat of his brow, can be sure that he shall always be able, without assistance, to support a family' (OP 655–6). 'Time and chance' (OP 581) spare no one the 'ups-and-downs' (OP 583) of unpredictable history-to-come: 'In the chequered scene of our frail existence, "no man knoweth" what calamities await him' (OP 581). Even a great landowner will have a 'constant foreboding in his mind, that he should die in a workhouse' (OP 581).

Life is a lottery. Lacking a crystal ball, it is rational minimax to share and share alike. Offering alms to the disabled and the left behind, the property-owner will know that there but for the grace of God goes every high-flyer on the cusp of a fall. Unknowledge is the closest we can come to the shape-shifting flux: 'Everything under the sun is uncertain. No provision can be a sufficient security against adverse and unexpected fortune' (in KP II 331).

References

By W. Godwin

Godwin, W. (1798 [1976]). *Enquiry Concerning Political Justice* (abbreviated as PJ). Penguin Books.

Godwin, W. (1801 [1968]). *Thoughts Occasioned by the Perusal of Dr. Parr's Spital Sermon* (abbreviated as RP), reprinted in *William Godwin Uncollected Writings 1783–1822* (pp. 281–374), J. W. Marken & B. R. Pollin (Eds.). Scholars Facsimiles and Reprints.

Godwin, W. (1820 [1964]). *Of Population: An Enquiry Concerning the Power of Increase in the Numbers of Mankind, Being An Answer to Mr. Malthus's Essay on That Subject* (abbreviated as OP). Augustus M. Kelley.

By T.R. Malthus

Malthus, T. R. (1798 [1970]). *Essay on the Principle of Population, as it affects the Future Improvement of Society, with Remarks on the Speculations of Mr. Godwin, M. Condorcet, and Other Writers* (abbreviated as FE). Penguin.

Malthus, T. R. (1808 [1963]). Review of Thomas Newenham's *A Statistical and Historical Inquiry into the Progress and Magnitude of the Population of Ireland, Edinburgh Review*, 24, reprinted in B. Semmel (Ed.), *Occasional Papers of T.R. Malthus* (pp. 33–52), Bert Franklin.

Malthus, T. R. (1821 [1963]). Review of W. Godwin's *Of Population, Edinburgh Review*, (abbreviated as ER), reprinted in B. Semmel (Ed.), *Occasional Papers of T.R. Malthus* (pp. 127–142). Bert Franklin.

By Other Authors

Kegan Paul, C. (1876). *William Godwin: His Friends and Contemporaries* (abbreviated as KP) (2 Vols.). Henry S. King.

Rosen, F. (1970). The Principle of Population as Political Theory. *Journal of the History of Ideas, 31*, 33–48.

Waterman, A. M. C. (1991). *Revolution, Economics and Religion: Christian Political Economy, 1798–1833.* Cambridge University Press.

CHAPTER 11

The End of the Debate

Godwin's *Of Population* and Malthus's *Principles of Political Economy* were both published in 1820. It was not quite the end. Still to come were 1821, 1822 and 1826. It could just as well have been the end. Malthus was famous: 'His work is placed on our shelves, by the side of those of Plato and Aristotle' (OP 509). Godwin, sometimes as Edward Baldwin, sometimes as Theophilus Marcliff, was churning out potboiler fiction to feed his family. Poverty, population, justice or economics, the former literary lion was in danger of becoming just another of intellectual history's numerous also-rans.

Of Population had demonstrated to its author's entire satisfaction that Malthus's *Essay on Population* was not fit for purpose. The wider public had inexplicably made it their trustworthy go-to. The *Essay* had won. *Political Justice* had lost. Malthus, until the appearance of Ricardo's *Principles* in 1817, was the leading British political economist of his generation. Ricardo and the classical school made the population multiplier and the theory of diminishing returns two of the fundamental tenets of their mainstream economics. Malthus in 1817 had deleted most of the sections on Godwin from his *Essay*. Godwin was The Juvenile Press. Godwin was yesterday's hack.

D. Reisman, *William Godwin and Thomas Robert Malthus*,
https://doi.org/10.1007/978-3-031-62113-0_11

11.1 The *Edinburgh Review*

The Ricardians saw that Godwin's *On Population* had got the wrong end of the stick. James Mill pronounced it 'beneath contempt': 'He seems not to know the point in dispute'. J.R. McCulloch said of it that 'I do not think I ever knew a more miserable performance'. Hutches Trower found it 'intemperate and abusive', 'rambling' and 'disjointed', a '*pretence* of systematick investigation', 'perfectly impotent'. Ricardo replied to Trower that 'your view of Godwin's book exactly agrees with mine': 'The principle of population is strong enough for human happiness, and it neither wants poor laws nor any other laws to encourage it' (in Ricardo, 1952: 292, 326, 311 emphasis in original, 361). Malthus himself was astonished that Godwin had even dared to put such a catalogue of ignorance and malice in the public domain.

Malthus had long been ostracised by the free-trade *Edinburgh Review* because of his support for the Corn Laws. In 1820 he was invited to write, anonymously, an extended review of Godwin's *Of Population*. He decided that it was not worth very much. Nor was its author. Godwin in his book had set out to sheer. He had returned home shorn. Malthus in his review described *Of Population* as 'the poorest and most old-womanish performance that has fallen from the pen of any author of name' (ER 127). In a letter to Sismondi in 1821 he complained that 'I have lately been attacked, after a delay of twenty years, by my old antagonist Mr. Godwin; but it is a very poor and feeble performance, and the only resemblance of an argument in it is founded on a miscalculation' (in Ricardo, 1952: 376).

Malthus tongue-in-cheeked that perhaps Godwin's reputation 'has been as much too low of late years, as it was too high soon after he wrote his *Political Justice*' (ER 127). *Of Population* would do nothing to restore his standing. *Of Population* was full of the same 'gross errors', 'quite wide of the mark' (ER 130), that had for decades been discrediting misguided Godwin's attempts to demolish the Malthusian ratios. If anything, it had been able to 'establish them on firmer foundations than ever' (ER 128). Godwin, demonstrating the 'enfeebled judgment' of an 'old scold', had not been 'well prepared' for the challenge of 'social argument' (ER 128). Instead of a convincing and well-researched monograph, what he had done was to put on display his 'total want of knowledge', 'false reasoning', 'extreme absurdity', 'abuse, repetition, and irrelevant matter', to such an extent, 'utterly disgraceful', as to leave the reader 'profoundly in the dark' about the extent to which the theory of population had really moved on from earlier theorists such as Price (ER 137, 138). Weak on 'general information' (ER 136), weaker still on convincing calculations (largely farmed out to David Booth), *Of Population* in a word was 'nonsense' (ER 140).

Malthus objected to the 'very insufficient estimates', the 'malice', the 'discreditable' lack of coverage (ER 135). Godwin, so it seemed, had gone public on population 'as if he had never opened a book on the subject' (ER 130). Malthus pointed to his own later editions, bristling with statistics, to show that Godwin had piled error on error because he had ignored the facts.

The English population was *not* 'at a stand'. The American population was doubling itself due *not* to incomers but to domestic increase. Misery and vice were *not* the remedy for but the consequence of an excessive population (ER 140). As for the theory, Godwin had exaggerated the importance of the geometrical ratio. Any significant expansion, even if 'strictly regular', would be enough to confirm the universality of the Malthusian law (ER 129n). The famine would be postponed. It would not be prevented. Starvation worldwide is inevitable. A hundred years, a thousand years, Godwin was playing word-games when even 'strictly regular' would be enough to destroy us all.

Godwin had alleged that Malthus was an enemy of the lower classes. Malthus used the platform of the *Edinburgh Review* to make his position clear. Poverty is not inevitable. Moral restraint by limiting the supply of manpower pushes up the real wage. The Poor Laws should be tightened up but definitely not suspended. Godwin had understood nothing. His 'numerous misrepresentations', 'instead of weakening the statements of Mr. Malthus, tend to establish them on firmer foundations than ever' (ER 129). His 'gross mistakes' will only 'establish more firmly the doctrines of the Essay on Population' (ER 140).

A year after the *Review* Godwin was back. Writing as Anon. in *The Examiner*, he said that the evidence had decisively refuted the assertions of misguided Malthus: 'Plenty and good government could never beget children in a geometrical ratio' (PQ 475). Writing as L'Ami des Hommes in the *Morning Chronicle*, he repeated his message: 'The population of the earth is actually at a stand' (POP 481). If misguided statisticians say it is going up, then it is the estimates themselves that are misguided.

Malthus 1821 had been his reply to Godwin 1820. Godwin 1822 had been his reply to Malthus 1821. Malthus 1826 was his last word on Godwin. Malthus in the 1826 *Essay* inserted a short note indicating that it would be 'unedifying' to the reader and 'disagreeable' to the author to 'return abusive declamation in kind' (SE II 252). Every 'candid and competent inquirer' will know that misguided rant 'does not require a reply' (SE II 252). Malthus no longer regarded Godwin as a serious adversary. There was in any case no need for him to reply through the *Essay*. The two editions of his *Principles of Political Economy* in 1820 and (posthumously) 1836, overlapping the final revisions of the *Essay*, gave Malthus an opportunity to say what remained to be said. It was not much. There is in the *Principles* no mention of Godwin.

11.2 Malthus's *Principles*

The prophets of Paris had gone too far. Condorcet had gone too far: 'Nature has set no term to the perfection of human faculties….The perfectibility of man is truly indefinite' (Condorcet, 1795 [2012]: 2). Godwin had gone too far: 'The human mind in every enlightened age is progressive' (PJ 3). Betterment is in the air. Ten steps to paradise, 'it will never be reversed' (Condorcet, 1795 [2012]: 2).

Malthus knew a mirage when he saw one. Pangloss, Godwin and Condorcet were speaking too soon when they predicted an end of history where 'the sun will shine only on free men who know no other master but their reason' (Condorcet, 1795 [2012]: 130). Mind, Malthus warned, can be conned into cumulative deviation that spirals away from truth and virtue into a new barbarism of vice and misery. Matter can be deformed by falsehood and tyranny because, as Godwin himself admits, free will is never extinguished by mutable necessity: 'Man is to a considerable degree the artificer of his own fortune' (OP 615).

Malthus, careful not to confuse seasonal fluctuation with an unstoppable trend, knew that Eden would not last. He saw that humankind can end up in thrall to Hayek's uninhibited search or Gosplan's Gulag rather than to Godwin's anarchy that makes every train run to an inspirational message.

Malthus was a man of caution. While he did not believe in a trend-free cycle of rise and fall, he was quick to warn that light at the end of the tunnel was not guaranteed. It would not in any case be Godwin's light so much as a sensibly modified mix of market and state that did not depart too radically from the status quo. Desiring improvement in mind and matter, Malthus contributed what he could to progress through his books and papers, the East India College, the Political Economy Club and the British Association for the Advancement of Science. He feared that food, population and aggregate demand, like Bunyan's 'lusts, pleasures, and profits of this world', would stand in the way of Bunyan's pilgrim as he seeks to escape the 'miry Slough' that blocks his path to salvation (Bunyan, 1678 [2008]: 18, 38). Betterment would be an uphill struggle. Like Godwin, Malthus concluded that nature could be niggardly but that man had it in his power to approach the celestial city at journey's end.

11.2.1 The Arithmetical Ratio

More than two decades separated the *Principles* from the first *Essay*. The law of nature had not been repealed. The ratios, arithmetical and geometrical, were still piping the tune. The land could not be pushed beyond its extensive and intensive limit.

Man cannot live without food. The price of grain tracks the increasing difficulty of growing staples on 'the worst land in cultivation' (PPE I 100). Malthus, in the same year as Ricardo's *Essay on Profits*, stated in 1815 in his *Nature and Progress of Rent* that rents and money wages have a secular tendency to rise as the margin moves ever further in the direction of the barren hilltops and the cropped-out dustbowls (INQUIRY 130). Real wages are not affected. De facto index-linked, they remain the same.

It is all a function of diminishing physical returns. More means worse. New plots are less fertile or less accessible. Existing plots do not yield proportionately more to further doses of fertiliser, drainage, rotation and mechanisation. Output expands to feed an expanding population (PPE I 101). It does so at a rising real cost. Productivity per acre grows at a slower rate than the increase in demand: 'No improvements in agriculture which we have ever seen or heard of equal in any degree the power of population to increase up to the additional means of subsistence' (PPE I 550).

Subsistence is doing what it can. Improvements are allowing the farmer, even on 'waste lands', to grow and sell at 'a much less expense' (PPE I 264). If state-of-the-art know-how and best-practice equipment were universally adopted, the English population could safely reach twice its present size without having to go hungry. If all land were squeezed up to its physical limit, the earth could support fully 15 times its current census. But that is all. At that point the grain possibilities curve will have hit a wall. The nation will be able to consume more and better manufactures. As for primary produce, however, all that stands between life and death will be Smith's 'carcase of a dead dog or cat...though half putrid and stinking' (WN I 81).

Improvements make possible a greater supply at a lower price. Diminishing returns along a single curve do not preclude an outward displacement in the graph. An increase in productivity will not permanently match growing supply to growing demand. Perceived progress will only be of 'short duration'. 'Short' can be 'a hundred years together' (PPE I 277). 'Duration' can be several centuries or more (PPE I 332). Calendar time is of no interest to the patient Reaper. The arithmetical ratio does not go by the clock. All that is certain is that time is not eternally rubber. At some point, the diners and the dinners will not mesh. The population, gone into the red, will be demanding more of essential nutrition than the earth can physically supply (PPE I 164). The land will be holding the people back.

There are brakes: consider 'the temper and customs of nations' (GROUNDS 162). There are frictions: 'The transfer will be slow and difficult' (GROUNDS 161). They are not the equal of the headcount that, 'short duration' or 'myriads' of generations, ultimately 'overtakes the additional produce' (PPE I 207). Sooner or later, there will not be enough of the basic necessities to go round.

Grain is the most necessary of the necessities. Relying on survey data tabulated in Morton Eden's *State of the Poor* in 1797 and *Estimate of the Number of Inhabitants* in 1800, Malthus reports that as much as 40 per cent of the median worker's income is spent on bread (OCL 89). It is an extreme case of Engel's Law. For that reason, a fall in the supply of grain, traded in a highly competitive marketplace ruled over by the law of one price, will feed through into a 'nearly proportionate' (PPE I 265) rise in money wages. It has to do so. 'The wages of the labourer cannot sink below a certain point' (PPE I 572).

The subsistence wage cannot sink below the cost of the core calories essential for survival and for effective labour. It is more than the bodily minimum. Needed for social as well as physical subsistence, the lowest feasible wage must be in line with 'the actual habits of the country' (PPE I 307). The floor must allow for 'the necessaries and *accustomed* conveniences' (SE II 46, emphasis in original) on which no well-integrated social actor can be expected to economise.

Smith said it. Marx said it. Ricardo said it: 'The natural price of labour, estimated even in food and necessaries…essentially depends on the habits and customs of the people' (Ricardo, 1821 [1951]: 96–7). Alfred Marshall said it: 'In dress conventional wants overshadow those which are natural' (Marshall, 1920 [1949]: 74). Malthus was hardly alone when he observed that the money wage could not sink below a known minimum. Pay must compensate for the cost of grain (PPE I 162). It must also empower the socially aware to purchase the essential signs and symbols of their rank.

11.2.2 The Geometrical Ratio

The *Principles* picks up the narrative that Malthus had initiated in 1798. Population has a tendency to double every 25 years. Reaching the anxious present day, by now 'four should stand in every square yard' (PPE I 228). Even the planets and the stars would have been enlisted to accommodate the overspill. It has clearly not happened.

A 'benevolent Creator' (PPE I 228) had been wise enough not to cap the endowments of air and water but to make the supply of basic food-stuffs scarce. Hardship had enlisted the work ethic on the side of production, the positive and preventive checks on the side of demand. The geometrical ratio is arrested not just by the cull of the unwanted but also by rational choice. Mind augmenting matter is not prepared to let unplanned parenthood do its worst. The 'man of liberal education' has shown how far population can be contained by 'those habits which are the most favourable to regular exertions as well as to general rectitude of character' (PPE I 346). Increasingly it is the turn of the lower classes, drawing upon the latent 'prudence of the poor' (PPE I 305), to evolve upwards into 'beings "who look before and after"' (PPE I 51).

Social subsistence is a serious hurdle. Relative and not just absolute deprivation lies behind the voluntary conversion to moral restraint. Looking up at the class above them but also down at the lower depths below, the newly included 'cannot acquiesce in the thought of depriving themselves and their children of the means of being respectable, virtuous and happy' (PPE I 251). New habits and canons are being formed. Upscaled self-definition is challenging the tendency to overcopulate like mice in a barn.

Economic growth, creating plural and countervailing nodes of influence, has a tendency to 'check at once the power of the crown and the violence of the people' (PPE I 434). Capitalism is the cause and effect of the new-style premium on meritocracy, ambition, accomplishment and achievement. The lower classes learn to respect themselves. The upper classes learn to respect them (PPE I 251). The open road is in turn the cause and effect of moral restraint. No one who has successfully earned his higher status will risk becoming *déclassé* through an irrational rebarbarisation into the geometrical ratio.

Economic growth is plus-sum. Cheapened consumables raise real wages: 'There is no apparent limit to the quantity of manufactures' (SE I 400). The cost of 'objects of convenience and comfort' (INQUIRY 139) typically falls with scale. Living standards, 'most decidedly improved' (INQUIRY 139), compensate the worker for the rising cost of grain. A rising population makes it all happen. More people are more labour and more happiness (PPE I 162). Malthus denied that his 'ultimate objective' (SE II 210) had been to freeze the expansion. Population Malthus is *More Population* Malthus. More people are good.

More people are more supply and more demand: 'There is no reason to say that they might not go on increasing in riches and population for hundreds, nay, almost thousands of years' (PPE II 43). The nation can 'continue increasing for ages' (SE II 110), for 'ten, twenty, or even fifty years' (PPE I 308), nay, for 'hundreds of years' (PPE I 311), until, 'in the course of some centuries', it 'contain two or three times its present population' (SE II 111). It can go on increasing until 'every man in the kingdom be much better fed and clothed than he is at present' (SE II 111).

The geometrical ratio is precisely what Old Sarum and Death Valley most need to jump-start their advance. The precondition is food: 'The necessaries of life…create their own demand' (PPE I 165). Not, however, their own supply. Necessaries do not keep pace with births. Checks make themselves felt. History proves it. Looking backward to look forward, it is Malthus all the way from *too few* to *too many.*

In 1820 as he had done in 1798, Malthus confirms that he has singled out 'the causes which practically keep down the population of a country to the level of its actual supplies' (PPE I 345). He says that his 'steady and unshaken confidence' in his theory of growth is confirmed by 'every country with which we are acquainted' (PPE I 11). The experience of 'any country' (PPE I 350) shows it is true. So, however, is the tendency towards vice and misery (SE II 205). It is always there.

11.2.3 Aggregate Demand

The demand for input is derived from the demand for output. The demand for labour is derived from the demand for commodities. *Hoc opus, hic labor est.*

Say's Law states that total supply is the gateway to total demand. Withdrawals matched by injections cannot interrupt the continuity of the circular flow. One deer is bartered for two beaver. One linen shirt is exchanged for one two-pound note. Either way, Adam Smith had insisted, a balance sheet always balances: 'What is annually saved is as regularly consumed as what is annually spent, and nearly in the same time too; but it is consumed by a different set of people' (WN I 359).

Lauderdale in 1804 had been less confident about the dark underside of morally desirable frugality. Should 'due bounds' not be observed, Lauderdale had cautioned, a stagnationary overplus of outlay postponed would be the counterpart of unsold stocks of goods and unemployed reserves of labour: 'Parsimony, when pushed beyond a certain extent…must be fatal to the progress of public wealth' (Lauderdale, 1804: 220, 271).

Ricardo, like Smith, said that imbalance was inconceivable: 'Productions are always bought by productions' (Ricardo, 1821 [1951]: 291). Keynes, like Lauderdale, said that shortfall was forever a threat: 'There has been a chronic tendency throughout human history for the propensity to save to be stronger than the inducement to invest' (Keynes, 1936 [1973]: 347). Then there was Malthus. Malthus knew that some abstention was the precondition for capital-powered growth but that excessive prudence could underspend the economy into demand-deficient oversupply. Like Lauderdale, he knew that he had to find a middle way.

Inadequate consumption leads to underemployment equilibrium. Yet 'extravagance' too is recessionary to the extent that it squanders resources potentially available for reinvestment (PPE I 373). Desired withdrawals and planned injections must be equal and at an 'intermediate point': 'If consumption exceed production, the capital of the country must be diminished….If production be in a great excess above consumption, the motive to accumulate and produce must cease from the want of will to consume' (PPE I 9).

Great production waits upon 'great consumption' (PPE I 481). A dearth of spending leaves a gap in ex post take-up: 'A passion for accumulation must inevitably lead to a supply of commodities beyond what the structure and habits of such a society will permit to be consumed' (PPE I 265). A glut of spending by the same logic converts long-term investment into short-term disposables. Macroeconomics is the science of moderation. It should respect the Greeks' golden mean.

The tendency to extremes is 'the great source of error in political economy' (PPE I 359n). In morals, in politics, in the national income accounts, the optimum will be situated somewhere between *de minimis* and *de maximis* at the point where 'a certain effect is the greatest; while on either side of this point it gradually diminishes' (1814 [1986]: 102). *Too little, too much*, it is all a matter of getting the proportions right (PPE I 9).

Perfectibility in the sense of Godwin can be hijacked both by expenditure and by abstention in the sense of Malthus. Population is not the only worm in the apple. In his approach to total demand, Malthus adopts an intermediate perspective. Neither the discrete individual nor the statistical whole, he disaggregates the significance of the contribution to the level of the productive input. There are three classes in society not so much because of grouped self-presentation or sub-cultural patterning as because there are three factors of production in economics. Their significance in supply is not the same. Nor is their input into aggregate demand.

11.2.3.1 Labour

Godwin said that labour alone, never permissive capital or passive land, had the capacity to create new value. Malthus, breaking with Ricardo, was drawn to a utility-based rather than a total-cost or a labour-embodied theory. Both labour and capital, Malthus argued, experience the toil and trouble that accompanies the birth of a new commodity. Only land is spared the burden of subjective 'real cost' (Marshall, 1920 [1949]: 282). Only land, manna from heaven, a free gift from God, is exempt from an upward-sloping sacrifice curve. At the zero-rent margin even the transfer payment made to the landowner drops out of the farmer's budget. Its absence has no effect on the quantity supplied.

Some value if not *all* value, Malthus saw the factor labour as an input into net supply. Simultaneously, he saw it as an important source of total demand. The working class is on balance a spending class. The economy depends on its working-class consumption. Without its working-class take-up a nation can be 'only partially prosperous' (1827: 317).

Working-class consumption is an important part of our 'national happiness' (SE II 193). Wage-earners are the largest single class of society (PPE I 423, 550). It cannot be the wealth of nations—'Perish such riches!' (PPE I 236)—where the great majority are being excluded from the means of the greatest happiness. In the words of Adam Smith, 'what improves the circumstances of the greater part can never be regarded as an inconveniency to the whole' (WN I 88). Numbers count. Malthus knew it was true: 'The best, and...the most advantageous manufactures in this country, are those which are consumed by the great body of the people' (SE II 193).

It was true in ethics. It was just as true in macroeconomics. Thence the risk. Not only is the subsistence wage too low to facilitate a discretionary spend but the share accruing to labour is less than the aggregate value of the national product. There is 'much more reason to fear that the working classes will consume too little for their own happiness, than that they will consume too much' (PPE I 473). The proletariat is not buying enough. Seen from the perspective of the supplying estate, only a minority of businesses can score a competitive rate of profit from sales to farm labourers and factory operatives alone (PPE I 471, 472). The factor labour is not able to 'create an effective demand for wealth' (PPE I 350).

Living 'from hand to mouth', on rock-bottom pay because of the population mechanism, the hard cases 'seldom think of the future': 'All that they earn beyond their present necessities goes, generally speaking, to the alehouse' (SE I 359). Yet there are gradations even within the working class. The affluent worker already has a noticeable presence in total demand. As incomes rise, ever more of today's rock-bottom manuals will be moving upward from subsistence into a discretionary spend.

The lower classes are benefiting from upskilling and upgrading. Ascending the ladder of net 'health and prosperity' (PPE I 456), they are acquiring 'a decided taste for conveniences and comforts' that will have 'become plentiful compared with food' (SE II 85). 'Necessaries and conveniences' (SE II 28) will be trickling down. Luxury and 'superfluity' (SE II 228n) will be spreading out from the few to the many (SE II 193). A 'great alteration for the better' is even now occurring 'in the food, dress, and houses of the lower classes of society' (PPE I 254). It is only a matter of time before every Ford worker will be able to afford a Ford car.

Yet the way is not the will. *Joie de vivre* is not the only fruit. Most workers are today deficient in 'both the power and the will to save' (SE I 359). What they earn, they spend. Tomorrow it will be different. Travelling upwards along their consumption function, they will be earning for themselves the option to 'save a sum' (SE II 111), to hold 'a part of their wages disposable' (PPE I 425n), to accumulate 'small capitals' (PPE I 427). Moral restraint limits the supply and pushes up the wage. With it comes middle-class morality. The lower classes will have the money. They will not necessarily be quick to part with it.

Rising incomes can be the new Calvinism. The young, telescopically planning for marriage and children, will be tempted to abstain from marginal consumption classes 3 and 4. The ambitious, hungry for a shop or smallholding of their own, will be looking to good pay to 'furnish a large surplus' (PPE II 30). Whatever their reason, the possibility is real that the thrifty will be spending less than they earn. Their frugality loosens the link between Ford cars and Ford workers. It will keep Henry Ford and later President Hoover awake at night. We eat out to help out. If we stay at home, the restaurants shut down.

A simplified Malthusian scenario would be that pay in excess of subsistence would be self-liquidating through earlier marriage, larger families, a backward-bending supply curve and a sub-cultural proclivity towards 'indolence, drunkenness, and waste of labour' (SE II 196). A sophisticated Malthusian scenario, no less Malthusian, would be that high pay stimulates 'exertions' (PPE I 452). It fosters 'habits of industry, economy and prudence' (SE II 235–6). It puts backbone into the 'deferred gratification' (SE II 97) that propels economic growth into Rostow's take-off range (Rostow, 1960 [1964]: 7–9). In the first scenario the workers do not save. In the second scenario they do. They do so at the expense of total demand.

The workers on the moving staircase are likely to put a part of their rising income aside. They are likely to make use of self-help clubs, provident societies and country banks to 'furnish a tolerable security against want' (SE II 182). Small savings become a part of an upgraded way of life: 'The knowledge and prudence of the poor themselves, are absolutely the *only* means by which any general improvement in their condition can be effected. They are really the arbiters of their own fate' (PPE I 306, emphasis in original). The 'prudence of the poor' (PPE I 305) is self-help in spades: 'Nothing could be done in this way, but by the labouring classes themselves' (PPE I 474).

The labouring classes, like the rest of us, are driven by 'the desire of bettering our condition, and the fear of making it worse' (SE I 363). Prudence can be the means through which they convert rising incomes and social mobility into a ratchet that seals in their newly won status. Money in the bank is, however, unseen and unknowable, whereas baubles and trinkets are conspicuous consumption that advertises the change of state.

Public display is the gift that keeps on giving. So is the silent endowment prudentially locked away. Both spending and saving make a unique contribution to economic growth. Malthus, like Lauderdale and Keynes, saw that the two pillars of the arch had to be in balance. Forethought as well as indulgence was a threat to the knife edge. The possibility was always there that demand-led expansion might collapse into demand-deficient stagnation for which the market economy provided no lower turning point.

Godwin could not see the threat. Progress to him was neither more consumption nor more saving but more leisure and more wisdom. Because population was 'at a stand', Malthus's attempt to integrate headcount into the theory of aggregate demand was an answer in search of a question. Malthus was able to parry and defend. Godwin had underestimated the happiness that material improvement could bring. More urgently, Godwin had failed to recognise that macroeconomics and perfectibility would always be at daggers drawn. The working classes might save too little and consume too much. Equally, they might save too much and consume too little. Either way, *classes laborieuses, classes dangereuses* 1789, 1929, it is not the golden mean. Economics goeth before a fall.

11.2.3.2 Capital

The middle class is a saving class. Parsimony leads to investment which leads to growth. The precondition is aggregate demand. Stock will go into landfill and plant will be idle so long as final output is not being sold (PPE I 499). The middle class is, however, a saving class. It does not like to buy what it has sacrificed so much to produce. It is dependent on the other two classes to keep it afloat.

Labour is its market but also its input. The profit-seeker in that way has a stake both in high wages and in low. Godwin, Ricardo and Marx argued that wages are a 'deduction' from profits (PPE I 81). Employers in competition for market share have an incentive to pay no more than the starvation pittance. Malthus was less comfortable with the diagnosis of an intrinsic incompatibility: 'Wages and profits very often rise together' (1827: 317). Where both are 'high at the same time' (PPE I 310, PPE II 227), neither factor will be under any compulsion to squeeze the other in order to survive.

Malthus is a market economist. He knows what every businessman knows, that the 'principle of demand and supply is the paramount regulator of the prices of labour as well as of commodities' (PPE I 241). An increase in the demand for labour is the most reliable way to make the working class better off. The capitalist class is a saving class. It ploughs back rather than distributes. Its profits are 'the most important source of ...accumulation' (PPE I 199n). A larger pool augments the fund that will be reinvested in succeeding time periods in the employment and maintenance of labour (SE I 380). The whole of the working class will be 'simultaneously improved' (LW 35). Malthus does not assume fixed coefficients or a proportionate relationship between wage-capital and hires (PPE I 261, PPE II 203). The direction of travel is nonetheless clear. Reinvestment raises wages. Compassionate employers like it that way. No decent person, even if he is in business, will be comfortable with the bare minimum (1827: 317).

It is not the end of the story. Rising wages encourage childbearing. The supply of labour rises in response to the rise in demand. After a lag of 16–18 years, manpower will go up and wages will go down (PPE I 357). The profits that result are the antidote to physical subsistence. The capital class is a saving class. Reinvestment will automatically grow the demand for labour.

Labour and capital are complements and not rivals. Each contributes to the other's net worth. Pullen is right to see the consequences that are also the causes as a double-sided symbiosis. Not unidimensional but mutually validating (Pullen, 2022: 27–8), it is a circular flow in which spending as well as earning makes a necessary contribution to the smooth functioning of the whole (SE II 247). Capital saves. Labour consumes. The demand-side loop makes possible the supply-side loop. Vauxhall workers buy Vauxhall cars. Luton would become Old Sarum if the two sides to the wage-bargain were bent on class conflict. Grenville and Pitt were wrong. They should have banned Godwin's *Political Justice* when they had a chance.

One hand washes the other. It might not last. Godwin believed in progress. Malthus considered that the future was printing claims on which it would predictably have to default.

Demand and supply have their own logic. A growing population leads to an increase in the price of grain. Rents rise as cultivation expands on to marginal land. Money wages rise to ensure the workers a constant subsistence. The prices of manufactured goods fall due to increasing returns (PPE I 325). Profits, trapped between the moving millwheels, become the shock absorber. Feeling the squeeze, they have a secular tendency to fall (PPE II 197). Falling profits for capital means fewer jobs for labour. Less income means less consumption. Aggregate demand comes under threat. The third class, the landowning class, might be able to fill the gap.

11.2.3.3 Land

Landowners are a spending class. Rent, a costless surplus, renews itself year on year. The share of rent in the gross national expenditure experiences a secular rise. The geometrical and the arithmetical ratios cast a long shadow. Feudalism belongs to the past. It is nonetheless to the landed aristocracy that a nation menaced by a slump will turn for effective demand.

In a boom the take-up will be preponderantly assured by the labouring and profit-seeking classes. In a downswing the nation will have to turn to its unproductive consumers. The military, the bureaucracy, the sterile lords have the attraction in Malthus's macroeconomics that they absorb unsold supply but do not add to the surplus. The way in which they cover a demand-side shortfall looks backward to Petty's pyramid building on Salisbury Plain and forward to Roosevelt's New Deal.

A rising population fed at the low-yield margin will automatically be redistributing the national income towards the factor land. It is a built-in stabiliser that countervails the drift into a savings-induced recession. Whatever reservations Malthus will have had about the wasteful ostentation of prodigals and spendthrifts, the crucial point is that they met a need for reflation that had been overlooked by Smith and Say when they argued in support of unbounded abstention. Total demand can be less than total supply. Where it is, the idle rich will be there to lean against the prevailing winds.

The idle rich have a high profile in politics as well as economics. They are the traditional elite that underwrites 'the propriety of the state' (GROUNDS 167). The pre-industrial way is the precondition for the age of textiles and steel: 'The interest of no other class in the state is so nearly and necessarily connected with its wealth and power, as the interest of the landlord' (PPE I 225). Godwin knew special pleading when he saw it. Malthus on macroeconomics was just another instance where a backward-bending economist 'flattered the vices and corruption of the rich and great' (OP v).

The landowner modulates the ambitions of the upstart commercial class. He cannot expect that his historic function as an escape valve will last forever: 'His relative condition and influence in society will probably rather diminish, owing to the increasing number and wealth of those who live upon a still more important surplus—the profits of stock' (INQUIRY 142). To say that because of capitalism 'the *pernicious* power of the landlords was destroyed' (SE II 84, emphasis added) is not to say that *the whole* of the landlords' influence has shifted across to the capital-owning class.

Diluted and diminished, the landed interest retains a high profile both in aggregate demand and in the state. It continues, where it is needed, to protect the balance between *too little* and *too much*.

11.2.4 *The State*

The state cannot and should not perpetually be up-and-doing in a misguided attempt to save the day (PPE I 259): 'Governments should not interfere in the direction of capital and industry, but leave every person, so long as he obeys the laws of justice, to pursue his own interest in his own way' (PPE I 13).

The bias is towards the liberal absolutes of respect and toleration. The perceived self-interest of the factored-down individual is the most reliable guiding light. The 'officious meddling of governments' (PPE I 14) is the least. It would be 'dangerous', 'impolitic' (SE II 224), 'puerile', 'ineffectual' (SE I 355), 'evil' (PPE I 14), counterproductive and inequitable (PPE I 474) for the state to challenge the 'great laws of supply and demand' that will 'generally direct us into the right course' (PPE I 516). 'Ignorance and rashness' at the core are no match for 'the natural direction of industry and capital' in the periphery (PPE I 20).

The benchmark in economic and social life should be 'the healing power of nature' (SE I 20). Bad laws excite 'public indignation' and bring 'discredit' upon legislation (PPE II 14). Everyone benefits when they are repealed. Taxation, 'a great evil' (PPE I 521), skims away capital that could otherwise have been used to create employment and foster prosperity. Artificial restriction of working hours and child labour only makes family poverty worse (PPE I 474). Navigation Acts and colonial monopolies force scarce capital into unprofitable trades (SE I 396). Licensed combinations, whether of employers or employees, 'ought to be avoided' (1824b: 601): they have a 'pernicious effect' on the 'natural level' of pay (1824b: 601). Nature knows best. It is true in medicine: 'almost all' is 'in itself bad' (SE I 408). It is true in politics as well.

Vadere sicut vult. Laissez-faire. Governments should not interfere—except when they should. The meta-principle to Malthus as it is to Godwin is not the moral primacy of the discrete individual but rather a rational problem-solver's concern with the specific consequences of a specific intervention. Malthus saw himself not as a hard-line libertarian but as an open-minded pragmatist forever in pursuit of the most efficacious means to a clearly specified end (PPE I 518). Hands-off or hands-on, the red lines should not be drawn until it becomes known 'if they are applicable to the case before us' (GROUNDS 158). The evidence comes first. Where it establishes that corrective action 'may be necessary to prevent greater evils' (SE I 409), only then should the state rise to the challenge and become involved.

The evidence is sine qua non. Yet the need for a state corrective must also be 'universally acknowledged' (PPE I 18). Malthus, in common with Godwin, believed that legislation should be broadly in step with the attitudes, norms and conventions of the nation as a whole. The central value system should in general be respected even if full democracy in the sense of one-man-one-vote remains for the foreseeable future too great a risk.

In some cases Wicksellian near-unanimity will not be a problem. Even Godwin accepted that most people in the imperfect present day would probably be in favour of a protective state. In other cases, the people might not at first recognise where their own interest lies. Bounties to encourage grain exports are cited by Malthus as an instance where the masses would do well to let themselves be led.

Bounties have unexpected consequences. The hungry might not at first understand that they will eat more and eat better tomorrow if grain is being sent abroad today. Bounties are in principle bad (1827: 321). Where, however, food at home is being made artificially scarce, the higher prices will be an incentive to domestic farmers to expand their cultivation as a hedge: 'It is impossible always to be secure of having enough if we have not, in general, too much' (SE I 407). Less today, more tomorrow, once the consensus catches up with itself it will see clearly that bounties are in the national interest.

The Corn Laws have a similar effect on tillage. Using a sliding scale to exclude cheap imports from Poland, America and France, they shield the home-grown supply of food (PPE I 217). The domestic price will exceed the international price but at least the quantity will be secure. Contrived misallocation is superior to comparative advantage and global free trade precisely because our own lower classes are less likely to go hungry. Insurance and risk-avoidance make sense. Anarchists like Godwin recognise no borders. Englishmen regard it as a desirable end, a rational means, to fry their own fish first.

Subsidies and statutes aimed specifically at grain deliver a windfall return to the landed interest. Malthus brushes aside the intersectoral redistribution in order to argue that it is the whole and not the part that makes the greater gain. Higher prices are in 'the permanent interest of the consumer, in the character of which is comprehended the whole nation' (SE I 410). Not only does the whole nation enjoy a more reliable supply of an indispensable necessary, it also benefits from a more prosperous class of rent-recipients. Landowners neither sow nor reap. They are for that reason ideally placed to provide effective demand in a slump. Landowners are a national asset. Recognising their function, the state should defend the age-old practices of primogeniture and entailing (PPE I 439). Our aristocrats should not be forced into the free market for land even if the parcelling out of estates would expand the supply and reduce the price of grain.

On the expenditure side, the state should assure the provision of essential public goods like state schooling. Education inculcates bottleneck skills and appropriate attitudes. It teaches respect for property without which long-term investment in agriculture and industry would not take place (PPE II 27). Talking population, it puts children on the road to a middle-class standard of living that is the surest way to contain the geometrical ratio.

The relief of the poor was more controversial. Malthus was not opposed on principle to outdoor relief for large families or the seriously incapacitated. As he said in 1796 in his never-published *The Crisis*: 'It is the duty of society to maintain such of its members as are absolutely unable to maintain themselves' (in James, 1979: 53). In respect of the able-bodied, he believed that the public sector should build workhouses and provide workfare, competitively remunerated. In a recession there should be direct labour.

The state should hire the unemployed on a temporary basis, 'for a short time' (1827: 321), until full employment is restored. Labour should be channelled into public works such as roadbuilding that do not compete with private output, unsold and unsaleable (SE I 365, PPE I 591). Money can be found through the customs duties (PPE I 508) and, 'favourable to wealth' (PPE I 484), the national debt. Public finance is not an insuperable obstacle to doing what is right.

Malthus could have made relief a national rather than a local or parish responsibility. He could have called for the abolition of the Settlement Laws in recognition of the widening modern catchment. He could have proposed a top-up grant for the poor-in-work, often paid by the piece. Malthus does not exhaust the census of policy-tools. Even so, it is striking how far his proposals for the *quid* without the *quo* separate him from pure-blooded liberalism and from Godwin's uncompromising resistance. As

Patricia James says: 'He was at heart a paternal interventionist' (James, 1979: 313).

In 1798 Malthus had recommended the phasing-out of the Poor Law. By the time of the fifth *Essay* in 1817 and the *Principles* in 1820, he had become more receptive to short-run palliatives. Relief would 'soften the harsh corrections' (SE II 411) forced upon the blameless by the 'time and difficulty' (PPE II 573) of a market economy shocked and disrupted by cyclical downturn, wartime blockade and post-war demobilisation. His guarded proposals for state support were an embryonic acknowledgement that relief goes beyond compassion. Where the cause of distress is a social and not just a personal failing, it would be a dereliction of duty for the state to privatise what is de facto a public responsibility.

For all that, the state should know where to stop. Welfare spending run wild would 'terminate in increased poverty and distress among the labouring classes' (PPE II 260). Keynes-type macroeconomic injections would create an unsustainable demand for labour and 'paralyse individual efforts' (PPE II 60). Statesmen, however wise, are powerless to address the big issues of population, cultivation, employment, a general glut or a national emergency (PPE I 511). Governments should not attempt the impossible. The poor will always be an open sore. All that the state can and should do is to provide temporary relief on a short-run basis (SE I 347). It should leave it to households and firms to internalise their spillovers.

In succouring the needy, Malthus, like Godwin, looks to private philanthropy and benevolence to enter with the state into a mixed welfare world. Malthus invites 'landlords and persons of property' to employ the frictionally out-of-work on their estates while waiting for the natural correctives to restabilise a viable balance (PPE I 511). Non-state actors have a role to play. It is a hands-on recognition that the state is not the only counterweight to social and market failure.

11.3 Godwin's *Thoughts on Man*

Already 75 years of age, 38 years after the first *Enquiry*, Godwin in 1831 brought out a collection of 23 essays revealing truths that had 'never by any preceding writer been laid before the public' (TM 260). He said they were 'as youthful and energetic a kind as were ever to be found in…the full vigour of my composition' (in KP II 316). He cannot have expected that they would bring in much money. The world had moved on from 1793. There was less interest in 'intellectual or moral truth' (TM v). Addressing himself to 'plain men', employing 'clear and unambiguous terms' (TM iv), he felt nonetheless that he had a duty to share with others his vision of the world as he saw it.

11.3.1 Approaching the Truth

Godwin's title, *Thoughts on Man*, describes the theme of his book.

It is *thoughts*. Perception is the nearest ignorant humanity can ever approach to the irreducible hard core that can never be fully known. Matter is no more than 'sensations existing in the human mind' (TM 436): 'Of the possibility of matter I know nothing; but with the possibility of mind I am acquainted' (TM 449). Mind constitutes 'the great essence of, and gives value to, our existence' (TM 7). I think, therefore I am.

It is *man* because introspection is the least unreliable way in to the ideas and impressions that govern human action: 'I look into my own breast….I can do little more than that' (TM 261). Sense perception is an exercise in psychological distance: 'If there were no percipient being to receive these sensations, there would be no heat or cold, no taste, no smell, no sound, and no colour' (TM 381). The objective properties of the things themselves are not knowable. They may not exist. All that I can calibrate is what passes through the 'theatre of the mind' (TM 380).

The alpha and the omega is 'know thyself'. 'The wisest man that ever existed' (TM 260) enjoined the Athenians to presume not God to scan: 'Only the temperate man will know himself and will be able to examine what he knows and does not know' (Plato, 1973: para. 167a). Knowledge is subjective, self-ish and idiosyncratic: 'Each human creature is a mystery to his fellows' (TM 373).

Thyself, myself, ourselves, what is probable nonetheless is that to factor down is also to scale up: 'The analysis of the individual may stand in general consideration for the analysis of the species' (TM 261). We are all different. We are not, however, so different as to preclude meaningful generalisations about the real, existing elephant. Each single individual knows a little. No single individual knows a lot. We come together to pool and share.

Aggregation is rough and ready. Potluck is blunt. The wisest man that ever existed said that it might work: 'It would be a great good for men if each of us should perform the things he knows and should hand over what he does not know to those others who do' (Plato, 1973: para. 172d). I am a unique shutter. You are a unique lens. Together we might add up to a workable camera. But communication will always be second best.

Knowledge is the *summum bonum*. The truth will set us free. By definition, however, it will only guide us out of the cave if we know what it is. The limiting case is the self-confident investigator who, in the spirit of Weber's instrumental rationality and Pareto's logico-experimental method, dispassionately 'collects premises and deduces conclusions' (TM 93). Even empiricism backed up by reasoning must ultimately fall short. Passions, impulses and emotions will inevitably blindside the scientist and divert him from the truth. 'No man is always a sage' (TM 68). Pope said that 'the proper study of mankind is man' (Pope, 1732–34 [1891]: Epistle III). Godwin followed Pope, but with an all-too-human reservation. 'Human frailty' will always be man's 'fatal weakness' (TM 68).

Plotting his course, the scientist will make use of 'systems of thinking' and 'systems of action' which are used as a crutch 'from day to day, and from year to year' (TM 93). The observer interprets today's external reality through the heuristic of yesterday's explicatory conventions. The drill is durable, conservative, tried-and-tested. Applied in conformity with precedent, it wins the stuck-in-a-rut the sympathy of the real spectator, the admiration and 'approbation of his fellows' (TM 323).

Simultaneously, it strikes 'a responsive chord' (TM 325) in the psyche of each enlightened and sensitive self: 'The truly virtuous man would do as he ought, though no eye observed him' (TM 322–3). The socialised actor who presses the median button enjoys the unqualified approbation of the impartial spectator, the 'competent jury' (TM 323): 'A virtuous man...is a man who, being in full possession of the freedom of human action, is engaged in doing those things which a sound judgment...pronounces to be good' (TM 236).

The real and the impartial spectator will be in complete agreement that the selective standard can only be the 'general benefit' (TM 236), the 'general good' (TM 233), the 'general advantage' (TM 300). That is just the problem. A time-honoured standard may be handing on a tradition-driven outlook and map. People believe what their fathers believed (TM 245). It is an impediment to a fresh and unprejudiced response. Knowledge is prestreamed. Sense perception is trapped in a web of handed-down expectation.

Memory is a risk: 'Institutions, once deeply rooted in the habits of a people, will operate in their effect through successive revolutions' (TM 91). Never-satisfied entrepreneurs and intrepid adventurers pursue novelty because the kaleidoscope is the essence of the risk-lover's quest. To the mould-breakers, 'to be alive' is 'to change the scene' (TM 97). The majority of their fellow citizens are less willing to depart from fossilised systems which presort discovery into a standard design. Reality moves on. Ideas lag behind.

Today is *what is. What is* is seldom the same as *what was*. The intellectual schemata for all that must have a high degree of intertemporal stability if they are successfully to orientate the perplexed. The collective code of right and wrong keeps all of us on message: 'The laws of morality…are matured within us by experience.…I come to feel the ties which bind men to each other; and the wisdom and necessity of governing my conduct by inexorable rules' (TM 96–7). Godwin does not say that the rules, however 'inexorable', are the best-possible means to a best-possible end. What he says is that they are capable of imposing order where otherwise there would be 'perpetual research' (TM 250). Bounded inquiry may not lift the curtain on the real world. Non-rational religion has long traded in catechisms that Godwin himself had rejected as unfounded. Still it is a point of departure. It can lead to the discovery of something new.

Imitation is everywhere: 'We are all apes, fixing our eyes upon a model' (TM 185). We copy the leader, 'gesture by gesture' (TM 185): 'The same fact under the same circumstances has been performed a thousand times before' (TM 188). The downside of the 'immutability' is 'eternal and wearisome repetition' (TM 189). It is always the same livery or mitre regardless of the unique, named footman or bishop. The king never dies. The upside of the quasi-permanence is the quasi-prediction. In the science of knowledge as in the science of economics, slow change is preferable both to no change and to runaway change: '*Festina lente*, Hasten, but with steps deliberate and cautious' (TM 136).

The approach to the truth is particularly challenging where action and reaction are uncertain precisely because they are the future that is yet to be made. The human mind is uncomfortable with 'we know not what'. Extrapolation, however flawed, is often the best we can do: 'We are unwilling to be disturbed; we have a mental *vis inertiae*' (TM 113). Indeed we do. However comforting it may be, it may nonetheless be blocking the way in to the truth.

History-to-come is a minefield of conjecture: 'We can…by no means be secure that we have attained to a perfect result' (TM 259). Reason betrays. Calculations deceive. Accidents disappoint. Confusion misperceives. Socialisation neutralises the propensity to excess: 'It is the business of education to tame the wild ass, the restive and rebellious principle in our nature' (TM 108). Accumulated knowledge terminates anxious search. Social order is an investment in a quiet mind. It is not, however, the whole truth. Past and future, there is too much truth for a single code to navigate the system out of the woods: 'Of the present there is necessarily no image' (TM 274).

11.3.2 The One and the Many

Man is born free. Yet each discrete atom is a part of an overarching whole. How can I be an I if I must be a We as well?

The one precedes the many. The individual at birth is not a blank sheet of paper. The endowment ab initio is not peas-in-a-pod. Godwin in 1798 made a note to himself that 'there exist differences of the highest importance between human beings from the period of their birth' (in KP I 295). In the *Thoughts* he repeated his assessment that, however much 'folded up and confused' (TM 270) it may be, nonetheless the buried treasure is there: 'There are various peculiarities...which the child brings into the world with him' (TM 31).

Social determinists like Helvétius put all inequalities down to acclimatisation. Godwin's reaction is that 'this is not true' (TM 41). Independent of life experience, antecedent to conditioning, there is a hard core of innate talents and predispositions that, 'Godlike' (TM 9) and lasting, it is a bedrock of nature that cannot be elided into mutable situation (TM 268). Life in common is both the effect and the cause of the 'inexhaustible varieties of man' (TM 25). Each man has a 'true and native field' (TM 36). It is a quasi-sacred circle in which he will 'shine' (TM 37), where he will feel 'at home' (TM 45). A good society is one in which all members are in a position to 'assert themselves' (TM 23) in the 'suitable sphere' (TM 43) where they are 'best fitted to excel' (TM 31). A bad society is one in which each irreducible essence is sliced and diced to match the superordinate requirements of an uncompromising whole.

It would be a 'pitiful miscarriage' (TM 46) for the naked self to be made a square peg in a round hole. Such a waste can be the result of individual ambition or parental pressures. It can also be the consequence of inborn aptitudes 'trampled in the mire' (TM 23) by the straitjacket imperative of an economic role.

The warping due to working is more extensively discussed by Rousseau or Marx than by Godwin. While Godwin does deplore the distortion and discomfort caused by the division of labour, he prefers to focus on post-industrial anarchism where work and alienation will shrink into the margins. In the society of the future, 'know thyself' and 'be thyself' will converge. Each individual will be 'satisfied with himself' (TM 35) irrespective of his output or productive efficiency.

The maximand will shift from economic throughput to personal fulfilment, from time-and-motion to Abraham Maslow. Each individual will be given the opportunity to identify his natural niche and unfold his native capabilities. No genius born 'amidst the chill blasts of poverty' (TM 29) will be denied the equal start and open road that he needs to make the most of his potential.

'Every man has his place' (TM 51). Innate essence pushes and pulls him to that place. So, crucially, do other people. It is the Many as well as the One that gives him his postcode and his reference number. On the one hand there is personal fulfilment. It is the free gift of the physical self. On the other hand there is social obligation. It is inculcated by childhood and adult socialisation. Man is 'most beneficially engaged' (TM 25) where he settles in to that place that best matches both the constants and the variables to which he is exposed.

Narrow self-interest causes the homeless monad to focus his goal-attainment on his personal and private pleasure. Enlightened self-interest expands our perspectives to incorporate 'the pleasure of our neighbours' (TM 307). A holist and a communitarian, Godwin knows where his true loyalty lies: 'In all cases our best judgment should always be at the service of our brethren of mankind' (TM 306). The needs of the whole should always be ranked above the wants of the part. Wild Peter, in the spirit of Tocqueville, will object that he was born to be Wild and not to be pooled. Godwin will reply that no man is an island. Individual liberty is a function of the context in which his unique self makes its home.

Man is a social animal who moves with the herd. In his judgements as in his perceptions, the 'hundreds of faces', the 'hundreds of voices', the 'hundreds of human needs' come together in 'the expression of one common sentiment' (TM 7). Anarchy would be impossible if each person withdrew to tend his own garden. As it is, the 'one common sentiment' is the logic behind equality of respect. Jackdaw sits with jackdaw. It is an unconscious bias and a felt gregariousness that transcends the differences that divide.

A social organism is bigger than one individual doing one thing once. Big Thinking treats all of us as threads in an interdependent weave. Suicide was made a crime because it deprived the nation of a subject. Malnutrition and disease could be outlawed for the same reason. Contagions cannot be allowed to afflict innocent bystanders with unanticipated spillovers. Restless capitalism, characterised by 'commotion', 'hazard' and even 'momentous catastrophe' (PJ 488), itself strikes a familiar chord. Richard Titmuss was sharply critical of the 'modern choleras of change' that make some people 'the social pathologies of other people's progress' (Titmuss, 1968: 133, 157). Adam Smith had prepared the ground when he deplored what had recently occurred in Fashion Street: 'The weavers of Spitalfields were plunged into the most severe distress by the fashion of muslins rather than silks' (WN II 132). The river had shifted its bed. It was not the fault of the weavers that a fickle consumerhood had moved on to something new.

Godwin knew that Smith was right. We as small cells in an embedding collectivity have no right to trample Aristotle, St. Paul, Titmuss and even Adam Smith under foot in our scramble to avoid our responsibility for our own: 'We are all members of one great community, and we shall never sufficiently discharge our duty in that respect, till, like the ancient Spartans, the love of the whole becomes our predominant passion' (TM 305). We belong not to ourselves so much as 'to the entire body of which we are a part' (TM 305).

We are all Huguenot weavers, experiencing severe distress within earshot of the Spital bells. We are all Malthus's able-bodied, put out of work by oversaving and inadequate demand. Buckingham Palace, Professor Titmuss and Lady Muck, we are all exposed to the bombs, the Boche and the Blitz. Archbishop Paley had said that poverty was a learning experience. It was an investment in good character that the nation had no real obligation to relieve (Paley, 1785: II 158–9). Godwin did not agree. Insisting that we belong not to ourselves but to our body politick, he seems to be on the point of treating poverty as yet another market failure. It must not lie where it falls.

11.3.3 The Benevolent Society

Hobbesians are 'angry' (TM 119), 'rapacious', 'revengeful', 'deadly', prone to 'ferocity', capable of 'a thousand deceits' (TM 116). They are given to 'riot and plunder' (TM 112), 'crime' (TM 118), 'contention, uproar and violence' (TM 120). They have 'evil qualities' (TM 116) which make the wolf in wolf's clothing a 'fearful and dangerous foe' (TM 117).

They are, however, *rara avis*: 'The sons of rapine constitute the exception to the general character' (TM 120).

Hobbesians are a minority on the fringe. Not giving his source, Godwin draws upon casual empiricism to conclude that they are only 'a very small part of our race' (TM 117). The majority of our people practice 'courteous assistance' (TM 112). We demonstrate philanthropic 'kindness for a being of our own species' (TM 115). We reveal a preference for tranquillity and not hostility, mutual aid and not competitive depredation. Our social feelings are strong. The majority of our people want to live in peace.

Crimes are being committed. It does not prove that the deviant, any more than their knife or gun, are doing what unfree will had programmed them from birth to do. More powerful than nature and genes, it will have been environment and upbringing that instilled in them antisocial 'impulses over which they have no real control' (TM 242). The victim of 'circumstances which act upon him from infancy' (TM 240), the criminal is constrained by 'shackles' that he has inherited from his youth (TM 245). While pity or compensation would be going too far, still the liability for his failings and 'frailties' (TM 242) cannot be laid solely at the criminal's door.

Breaking the law may not even have been a conscious choice. Criminals grow up criminal. There is an element in their portfolio that 'it is not in our power to change' (TM 249). Prevention is different. A commercial culture is a web of interdependence and exchange: 'It is through the effect of this necessity, that civilised communities become what they are' (TM 122). Needing each other as we do, it would clearly be counterproductive to clip the freedom that supports us. That way lies 'barren and ungratifying mediocrity', 'imbecility and inanity' (TM 124). Respect for each other's dedicated sphere of competence would have been a more effective strategy for raising each other's well-being.

Self-love can be a cause of social integration where the happiness of both parties is enhanced by a commutation of superfluities. Yet it can also be at the root of division and conflict. Income and wealth, as in the *Enquiry* and the *Enquirer*, separate the fellow citizens into the propertied and the poor. Fortunes are unequally distributed (TM 318). Purchasing power is not the same. Opulence and inheritance feed through into social status and thence into envy and felt injustice: 'The division of rank is too much calculated to split society into portions having a certain hostility to each other. In a free state we are all citizens: it is desirable that we should all be friends' (TM 316). We can all be friends so long as the differentiating agency is talent. It is more difficult to be friends where we are separated by the unbalanced ownership of land or capital. Godwin says it. Malthus does not.

The commercial age, Godwin contends, is one nation split into two by money. Consumables on display advertise social location: 'Mankind are but too prone to pay a superior deference to those who wear better clothes, live in larger houses, and command superior accommodations' (TM 314–5). The rich have disproportionate influence on the laws and in the state. They control the means of communication that are the 'essence of liberty' (TM 31). Without the diffusion of information and the chance to debate the truth we will not all be universalised into a citizenship entitlement.

Mind must change matter. There must exist a social consensus in favour of levelling and moderation. Selfish exchange must give way to 'disinterested benevolence' (TM 224). It would raise the overall level of happiness in the nation as it already does in the family (TM 225).

It will be plus-sum anarchy. Malthus says that because of runaway population it will approach Smith's China instead. Godwin makes one last attempt to show that the mathematical deductions and the freestanding ratios have totally discredited Malthus and his system: 'Restiff and uncomplying nature refuses to conform herself to his *dicta*' (TM 395). New York City, Malthus would predict, will grow in a hundred years to the nonsense value of 5,257,493 inhabitants: 'But does any one expect to see this realised?' (TM 395). Let alone 7,888,121? Where would they all live?

The evidence does not lend credence to Malthus's exaggerations and false alarms. What 'repeated experiment' (TM 407) does suggest is that not catastrophe but improvement is in the air. Sensitive social indicators bear it out. Alcohol used to be the opium of the masses. Now, like early marriage, it is going out of fashion.

Pubs are closing down. Whereas in 'rude and barbarous times' Gin Alley was on every High Street, in present-day society 'the rage of drinking is now gone by' (TM 329). Godwin does not quote any proof or spell out his reasons. All that he does is to point to the evolution in public opinion. The drinker will convert from Marshall's beer to Marshall's tea to escape 'shame…for unworthy conduct': 'He will obey the general voice of the community, that he may be at peace with himself' (TM 330).

It is an argument suspended by its own bootstraps. Alfred Marshall said that the causal variable would be economic growth. An upward trend in disposable income means that the deprived residuum would no longer be forced into 'drink, ignoble jests, and noise' to screen out the sadness of tenement housing and the memory of unremitting toil (Marshall, 1873 [1966]: 107). Marshall, like Smith and Marx, believed that material upgrading would bring about a radical transformation in mind. Godwin saw public opinion as the primary cause of improvement. Benevolence is coming in. It is pushing the Hobbesians out.

Yet matter is always there: 'The mind cannot subsist without the body' (TM 8). Even Socrates must eat. The task of the persuaders will be greatly simplified by the levelling up of living standards, the levelling down of agglomerated wealth and the mechanisation of unfulfilling activity. Participation in 'the happiness of the great body of his countrymen' (TM 330) enriches the harvest of ever-greater feel-good: 'The affection we entertain for those towards whom our partiality and kindness are exercised, is the life of our life' (TM 234). Sustained *embourgeoisement* itself narrows the visible distance between rich and poor, 'splendour and luxury', 'delusive honour and consideration' (TM 465). A convergence in the symbols of self-presentation revitalises 'the intercourse of my fellow creatures' (TM 454). It reinforces the perception of 'our common nature' (TM 456).

11.3.4 After Market Economics

Production, consumption, distribution and exchange all contribute something to the onward march of spirit on earth. Godwin had no serious interest in the *minutiae* of *how to* economics: 'I have never been more than an occasional student of what is called Political Economy, that is of calculations of revenue, resources, trade and the means of subsistence' (in Grylls, 1953: 182). What did interest him was 'the connexion of those subjects with my more congenial speculations respecting the morals, the independence and the happiness of man in society' (in Grylls, 1953: 182).

Godwin's economics is an extension of Godwin's ethics. Malthus was keen to perpetuate the hegemony of demand and supply. Godwin believed that the lifespan of the conditioned reaction was nearing its end. Godwin had no need to follow Malthus down the rabbit hole of the margin, the wages fund or aggregate demand. Increasingly, all this would be superseded by a new economic system which, like Marx, he is careful not to describe in detail. Economics will be spontaneity and community. That is all that we today can know about the economics that is yet to come.

Consumer sovereignty is giving way to social-ist convergence. Individual and social needs are taking the place of private and personal wants.

Non-satiety is being replaced by the awareness of a ceiling beyond which the constructive use of leisure will replace directionless growth. Alienation, exploitation and social division caused by the maldistribution of income and wealth are yielding to post-market exchange in which the power to purchase will no longer stamp its name on Smith's, on Malthus's market-clearing price.

The profit motive on the side of supply will fade away at the same time that superfluity and emulation on the side of demand are being superseded by production for the utility of all. Land and capital will no longer be allowed to pay a subsistence wage. They will no longer be able to convert the value added by productive labour into the luxuries of the few.

Malthus can churn out a market-clearing price from the Marshallian cross of demand and supply. Godwin is less willing to parrot the orthodox economists' common book of prayer. His heterodox economics of benevolence, not static but dynamic, looks forward to a new institutional order in which mind will take over from matter the responsibility for designing a new and more rational social game.

Malthus, like Adam Smith, looked to a rising national product to improve household and domestic well-being. Godwin, while not denying the role of economic growth in underdeveloped England, relied primarily on the power of the mind that he regarded as 'infinitely superior' (TM 15). The human imagination and not the momentum inherent in matter is the cause of originality that, validated by public opinion, pushes and pulls the process of improvement. Godwin says that 'the inventions of the human mind are exhaustless' (TM 199). It is true. It is the function of equality and agreement to select the winning option from a plethora of possibilities.

Perception can get things wrong. Liberty in 1789 had destroyed the old regime without creating a new one. Free markets had not provided an antidote to the disharmonies of grab. Misery in the mines and mills was a problem without a turning point from within. Robespierre, Smith or Marx, not every philosopher is in touch with the true imperatives that will survive the winds and currents of experimentation. Yet some philosophers will be. They will glimpse what is necessary. They will take a lead. Mind will bring anarchy into being. Matter will not: 'If I dismiss from my creed the existence of inert matter, I lose nothing' (TM 448). Without the correct ideas, however, man in society will lose any chance of doing lasting good.

References

By W. Godwin

Godwin, W. (1798 [1976]). *Enquiry Concerning Political Justice* (abbreviated as PJ). Penguin Books.

Godwin, W. (1820 [1964]). *Of Population: An Enquiry Concerning the Power of Increase in the Numbers of Mankind, Being An Answer to Mr. Malthus's Essay on That Subject* (abbreviated as OP). Augustus M. Kelley.

Godwin, W. (1822a [1968]). 'The Population Question', *The Examiner*, 6 January (abbreviated as PQ). In J. W. Marken & B. R. Pollin (Eds.), *William Godwin Uncollected Writings 1783–1822* (pp. 474–476). Scholars Facsimiles and Reprints.

Godwin, W. (1822b [1968]). 'Population', *Morning Chronicle*, 11 January (abbreviated as POP). In J. W. Marken & B. R. Pollin (Eds.), *William Godwin Uncollected Writings 1783–1822* (pp. 479–488). Scholars Facsimiles and Reprints.

Godwin, W. (1831 [1969]). *Thoughts on Man: His Nature, Productions and Discoveries* (abbreviated as TM). Augustus M. Kelley

By T.R. Malthus

Malthus, T. R. (1798 [1970]). *Essay on the Principle of Population, as it affects the Future Improvement of Society, with Remarks on the Speculations of Mr. Godwin, M. Condorcet, and Other Writers* (abbreviated as FE). Penguin.

Malthus, T. R. (1803 et seq. [1989]). *An Essay on the Principle of Population: Or A View of its past and present Effects on Human Happiness, with an Inquiry into our Prospects respecting the Removal of the Evils which it occasions* (2nd ed., 1803; further editions in 1806, 1807, 1817, 1826) (abbreviated as SE I and SE II) (2 Vols.). Cambridge University Press.

Malthus, T. R. (1814 [1986]). *Observations on the Effects of the Corn Laws, and of a Rise or Fall in the Price of Corn on the Agriculture and General Wealth of the Country* (abbreviated as OCL), reprinted in *The Works of Thomas Robert Malthus* (Vol. 7, pp. 87–109). Pickering and Chatto.

Malthus, T. R. (1815a [1986]). *The Grounds of an Opinion on the Policy of Restricting the Importation of Foreign Corn* (abbreviated as GROUNDS), reprinted in *The Works of Thomas Robert Malthus* (Vol. 7, pp. 151–174). Pickering and Chatto.

Malthus, T. R. (1815b [1986]). *An Inquiry into the Nature and Progress of Rent, and the Principles by which it is Regulated* (abbreviated as INQUIRY), reprinted in *The Works of Thomas Robert Malthus* (Vol. 7, pp. 115–145). Pickering and Chatto.

Malthus, T. R. (1820, 1836 [1989]). *Principles of Political Economy* (abbreviated as PPE) (2 Vols.). Cambridge University Press.

Malthus, T. R. (1821 [1963]). Review of W. Godwin's *Of Population, Edinburgh Review*, (abbreviated as ER), reprinted in B. Semmel (Ed.), *Occasional Papers of T.R. Malthus* (pp. 127–142). Bert Franklin.

Malthus, T. R. (1824a [1986]). 'On political economy' (abbreviated as PE), reprinted in *The Works of Thomas Robert Malthus* (Vol. 7, pp. 257–297). Pickering and Chatto.

Malthus, T. R. (1824b). Evidence to the Select Committee on Artizans and Machinery (Sixth Report). In *Parliamentary Papers* (Vol. 5, pp. 598–601). House of Commons.

Malthus, T. R. (1827). Evidence to the Select Committee on Emigration (Third Report). In *Parliamentary Papers* (Vol. 5, pp. 311–327). House of Commons.

By Other Authors

Bunyan, J. (1678 [2008]). *Pilgrim's Progress*. Penguin Books.

Condorcet, Marquis de (1795 [2012]). *The Sketch (Esquisse d'un tableau historique des progrès de l'espirit humain)* (J. Barraclough, Trans.), in *Condorcet: Political Writings* (pp. 1–147). Cambridge University Press.

Grylls, R. G. (1953). *William Godwin and his World*. Odhams Press.

James, P. (1979). *Population Malthus: His Life and Times*. Routledge.

Kegan Paul, C. (1876). *William Godwin: His Friends and Contemporaries* (abbreviated as KP) (2 Vols.). Henry S. King.

Keynes, J. M. (1936 [1973]). *The General Theory of Employment, Interest and Money*. Macmillan.

Lauderdale, J. M. (1804). *An Inquiry into the Nature and Origin of Public Wealth*. Arch. Constable.

Marshall, A. (1873 [1966]). The future of the working classes. In A. C. Pigou (Ed.), *Memorials of Alfred Marshall* (pp.101–118). Augustus M. Kelley.

Marshall, A. (1920 [1949]). *Principles of Economics* (8th ed.). Macmillan.

Paley, W. (1785). *Principles of Moral and Political Philosophy* (2 Vols.). Exshaw, White and Others.

Plato. (1973). *Charmides*, in *Laches and Charmides* (R. K. Sprague, Trans., pp. 57–94). Bobbs-Merrill.

Pope, A. (1732–34 [1891]). *An Essay on Man*. Cassell.

Pullen, J. (2022). *The Macroeconomics of Malthus*. Routledge.

Ricardo, D. (1821 [1951]). *Principles of Political Economy and Taxation*, in *The Works and Correspondence of David Ricardo* (Vol. I). Cambridge University Press.

Ricardo, D. (1952). *Letters 1819-June 1821*, in *The Works and Correspondence of David Ricardo* (Vol. VIII). Cambridge University Press.

Rostow, W. W. (1960 [1964]). *The Stages of Economic Growth*. Cambridge University Press.
Smith, A. (1776 [1961]). *The Wealth of Nations* (abbreviated as WN) (2 Vols.). Methuen.
Titmuss, R. M. (1968). *Commitment to Welfare*. George Allen and Unwin.

CHAPTER 12

Conclusion

Justice came first. Godwin and Malthus were near contemporaries in an age of uncertainty that extended from the republicans and revolutionaries of Old Jewry to the widening of the suffrage and the triumph of iron and steel. Blue-blooded traditionalism was losing its monopoly in society and state. Capital and labour were demanding a place in the sun.

It was the age of Rousseau on nature, Smith on self-interest, Locke on property, Hume on evidence, Jefferson on politics, Hartley on psychology, Burke on license. The American revolution, the industrial revolution and the French revolution had shown that both mind and matter were in motion. The year 1789 had been the end and the beginning. Whether in Somers Town or in rural Okewood, history was laying down the gauntlet to a world in transition that could not escape the challenge of right and wrong.

Both Godwin and Malthus had a background in Protestant individualism and Biblical Christianity. Each had a commitment to service which had little or nothing to do with personal advancement. Each had been tempted out of comfortable replication into deism and the natural order. Both were moderate Whigs. Neither had any desire to be flagrantly party-political. Both were deeply invested in the embedded values of discussion, compromise and respect for idiosyncrasy that made England a nation apart. Both were in favour of gradual, automatic and cumulative

D. Reisman, *William Godwin and Thomas Robert Malthus*,
https://doi.org/10.1007/978-3-031-62113-0_12

evolution. Both were strongly opposed to revolutionary Cromwellism that would trample the habits and memories of cultural conservatism underfoot.

Both Godwin and Malthus held a common capital in achievement, rationality, empiricism, sense-perception, liberal quasi-democracy, peer-group discipline, social standing, pragmatic interventionism and the middle ground. Each assigned pride of place to virtue rather than expediency. Each made truth and happiness the benchmark for moral legitimacy. Scaling up as well as factoring down, each addressed his agenda for reform at once to self-perceived well-being and to the health of the collectivity. A doctor saves a patient. A philosopher saves a nation. Both Godwin and Malthus were system-builders and Big Thinkers. Neither would make a high-return contribution to the one-damn-thing-after-another of single-issue problem-solving in the Ministry or the Cabinet.

Godwin was the more radical. He rejected the liberal growthman's worship of material enrichment through supply and demand. He came down in favour of stateless homeostasis and output by consensus in the long run, strictly minimal regulation in the here and now. Since the population is at a stand and the planet is rich, Godwin saw no need to exit a Malthusian bottleneck that did not and would not exist. Although hardly pro-profit, he was closer than Malthus to Spencer's *Man* versus *the State*, further removed than Malthus from Pigou's *Economics of Welfare*.

Malthus was the more moderate. He had no objection to the invisible hand complemented by the protective state so long as the government in respect of land and population did not overstep its bounds. Communal ownership would be subverted by opt-out free riders because selfishness is the law of nature. Poor relief would encourage the workshy to featherbed on the philanthropic because indolence lives by the law of gravity. Malthus was by temperament a Samaritan. He also knew that an excess of compassion would break the bank. Only the very short-sighted would allow the communistic and the improvident to impose a costly externality upon their nation as a whole.

Malthus believed that the institutional integument, allowance made for rising productivity in agriculture and moral restraint in births, would be broadly similar in the long run to the laws and conventions of his own present day. Godwin, pressing forward beyond the veil, was confident that the future would be radically different from the inequities and biases of the class-riven past. Private land and capital, invidious comparison, social stratification, *dirigiste* government, marriage for life, civil war, international conflict would all crumble away under the weight of their own contradictions. In their place there would arise a new and fully liberated mode of human interaction. It would be built around the spontaneous and unorchestrated unfolding of integration, approbation, leisure, near-median outcomes and the citizenship equality of respect.

It would be a future, as Godwin envisaged it, of *enough* but not *too much*. It would be individual autonomy situated within the matrix of non-coercive community. It would not be anything-goes. It would be hard facts in place of wild suppositions. Precisely because it would not be prepared to cut corners on knowledge, it would also be a future in which public intellectuals and informed persuaders would occupy a unique and Plato-like position of influence. The ignorant and the common must be led. The knowledgeable must draw upon their superior grasp to shape the narrative. A new social divide will open up. That way lies progress. Unlike Atlantis, Utopia, Nowhere and even Magnesia, it will be built to last.

History-to-come or sunk cost gone by, one thing is clear. Godwin and Malthus lived a long time ago. We today are confronted with narrow new issues on which the macroscopes of the past never passed an opinion. Anarchy has been eclipsed by the new Hobbesianism of sectarian bigotry and recrudescent neo-imperialism. Population takeoff in rich countries is giving way to stagnation or even contraction as a result of family planning, the two-income family and old-age pensions in place of filial support. Godwin and Malthus were different from each other. They were different from thee and me.

The destinations were different. The mechanism is the same. Both Godwin and Malthus looked to beneficent history to lift the long eighteenth century into the new age of reason that relies on knowledge to settle disputes and get things done. History is rapidly losing patience with the long twenty-first century. Informed debate, however, remains the cutting edge. Some readers find Godwin's *Justice* dull. Others proclaim Malthus's *Principles* turgid. No author can please every reader who opens his book. More important than the *de gustibus* is this. A sincere exchange of opinion is more likely than hate speech, unsupported dogmas, culture wars, bombs and missiles to ensure the survival not just of troubled neighbourhoods but of the world village as a whole.

Index

D. Reisman, *William Godwin and Thomas Robert Malthus*,
https://doi.org/10.1007/978-3-031-62113-0

V

W

Y

GPSR Compliance

The European Union's (EU) General Product Safety Regulation (GPSR) is a set of rules that requires consumer products to be safe and our obligations to ensure this.

If you have any concerns about our products, you can contact us on ProductSafety@springernature.com

In case Publisher is established outside the EU, the EU authorized representative is:

Springer Nature Customer Service Center GmbH
Europaplatz 3
69115 Heidelberg, Germany

The manufacturer's authorised representative in the EU is Springer Nature Customer Service Centre GmbH, Europaplatz 3, 69115 Heidelberg, Germany. If you have any concerns regarding our products, please contact ProductSafety@springernature.com

Printed and bound by CPI Group (UK) Ltd, Croydon, CR0 4YY
01/10/2026
02225967-0008